The Long War Against Piracy: Historical Trends

James A. Wombwell

Occasional Paper 32

Combat Studies Institute Press
US Army Combined Arms Center
Fort Leavenworth, Kansas

Library of Congress Cataloging-in-Publication Data

Wombwell, James A., 1956-
 The long war against piracy : historical trends / James A. Wombwell.
  p. cm. -- (Combat Studies Institute occasional paper ; 32)
 Includes bibliographical references.
 1. Piracy--History. 2. Pirates--History. I. Title.
 G535.W67 2010
 364.16'4--dc22

                                                        2009028633

First printing, May 2010.

Foreword

The Combat Studies Institute is pleased to present Occasional Paper 32, *The Long War Against Piracy: Historical Trends*, by CSI historian James A. Wombwell. This study surveys the experience of the United States, Great Britain, and other seafaring nations in addressing the problem of piracy at sea, then derives insights from that experience that may be relevant to the suppression of the current surge of piratical activity. Wombwell, a retired naval officer, traces the course of several outbreaks of piracy during the past 300 years in a variety of geographical areas. Although each case varies in its details, Wombwell concludes that enough similarities exist to permit several useful generalizations. Among these are the causes of piracy, the factors that permit the behavior to flourish, and the range of countermeasures that have been available to policymakers seeking to eradicate the problem. When conditions are favorable for piracy to develop, and no strong response is made by the forces of law and order, what began as low-level brigandage often grows to outrageous proportions, ultimately requiring significant military resources to suppress or eliminate the threat posed to legitimate commerce.

This Occasional Paper is a timely work because of the dramatic surge of piratical acts in the Gulf of Aden and off the Horn of Africa in recent years. Although piracy has been a problem for several decades in other international sea lanes, the actions of the Somali pirates have focused world attention on the issue. This study is especially pertinent to the US Army because the historical record clearly indicates that piracy seldom, if ever, has been eradicated solely through naval operations alone. As Wombwell makes abundantly clear, only when nations have acted to remove piracy's enabling conditions ashore through military and/or political means has the scourge of piracy truly been eliminated. Moreover, in almost every case, because of the extensive resources needed to combat piracy, the nation taking the lead against the pirates was a dominant military power, either on a world or regional scale. Thus, as the author suggests, the land forces of the United States may at some point be called on to assist in making the waters off the Somali coast safe for international commerce once more. Should that time come, James Wombwell's survey of the historical context of the problem may be instructive to both policymakers and Soldiers. *CSI—The Past Is Prologue!*

William G. Robertson
Director, Combat Studies Institute

Preface

Modern-day piracy is no joke. After thousands of years, pirates remain a serious threat to innocent mariners in many parts of the world. Moreover, their mode of operations has changed little over that time. They are criminals—thieves and murderers—who prey on defenseless sailors at sea and in port.

As a former naval officer, I take pride in the actions of the United States Navy against pirates. But a closer examination of piracy through the ages reveals that piracy cannot be eliminated by sea-based operations alone. In the end, piracy is a land problem and must be solved ashore, whether by force or political means. This Occasional Paper examines the actions taken by nations against pirates in the past and sheds light on how contemporary leaders should approach the current piracy crisis plaguing Africa and Asia.

I am grateful to all those who helped me with this project. I want to acknowledge Dr. William G. Robertson, Director of the Combat Studies Institute, who conceived the project and encouraged me along the way. I also want to thank Mr. Kendall Gott, Chief of the Research and Publications Team, for his advice and support. An old shipmate, Rear Admiral Kendall L. Card, discussed his role in some of the recent events off the coast of Somalia, and his staff pointed me toward some useful sources of information. Mr. Tray Green, an accomplished game designer and budding historian, provided me access to a number of books and other piracy-related sources. My wife, Paula, and daughters Heather and Katherine, kept me motivated and on track. Finally, Mrs. Marilyn Edwards' outstanding editorial work greatly improved the initial draft. This book is much better because of their assistance. As always, any omissions or errors in judgment in this work are mine alone.

Contents

Tables

Figures

Chapter 1

Introduction

They struck at night, quickly scrambling over the side of the ship. Ten pirates, armed with knives and pistols, quickly overcame the unarmed crew. After ransacking the ship, the buccaneers moved the crew to their vessel. The crew was held captive on the pirate ship for 6 days and then set adrift in one of the ship's boats. The pirates sailed away with their prize and later disposed of part of the cargo at one of the many ports that welcome such freebooters.[1]

Although this sounds like a story from the "Golden Age of Piracy," when English and French pirates terrorized the Spanish Main, the incident did not occur 300 years ago, but in the Straits of Malacca in October 2000. The crew was lucky; it was rescued by Thai fishermen after drifting in a boat for 11 days. The pirates managed to dispose of almost half of the *Alondra Rainbow*'s cargo, some $10 million worth of aluminum ingots, before they were captured off the coast of Goa, India. No one knows what happened to the cargo they sold.

Until recently, when Somali pirates made the headlines after a series of seemingly ever more audacious attacks in 2008, most people did not realize that piracy still existed. But it does and it may, in fact, be more prevalent today than during the Golden Age of Piracy in the late 16th and early 17th centuries. This Occasional Paper examines piracy in its historical context and looks at the modern dilemma facing the world's maritime nations. The study considers piracy over both time and space, looking at the practice in the Caribbean Sea, Mediterranean Sea, Asian waters, the Persian Gulf, and the Indian Ocean/Gulf of Aden. It shows how nations, primarily the United States and Great Britain, dealt with piracy in the past and points to ways in which it may be effectively countered in the present.

Merchants have been plagued by pirates for almost as long as their ships have sailed the seas. The Sumerians, Babylonians, Cretans, and Egyptians all mention piracy in their ancient records. According to Sumerian documents, Sumer was raided by pirates from what is now the Persian Gulf more than 4,000 years ago.[2] Hammurabi (1948–1905 BC) included a law against piracy in his famous code. This is the first known written law against piracy.[3] According to Greek writers, Crete, which dominated the Aegean Sea from 2000–1400 BC, was the first nation to develop a navy. The Cretan Navy was, in part, built to suppress pirates in the region.[4] After pirates entered the Nile delta and attacked shipping in the 14th century BC, King Amenhotep III of Egypt established a special maritime police squadron to patrol the delta area and protect shipping.[5]

As maritime trade expanded, pirates found more opportunities for plunder. Most people are familiar with the exploits of Blackbeard, Captain Kidd, and the other famous pirates of the 17th and 18th centuries. However, less well known are the pirate outbreaks of the 19th and 20th centuries. A line from the United States Marine Corps hymn, "to the shores of Tripoli," reminds us that the United States fought the Barbary pirates in the 19th century. Piracy was not just a European or Western phenomena; pirates also plagued China, Southeast Asia, the Persian Gulf, and the Indian Ocean as well. Therefore, piracy has existed for thousands of years over a wide geographic area.

The economics of commercial shipping, whether in the 14th century BC or the 19th century AD, facilitated piracy. Since merchants are most interested in maximizing profit, merchant ships throughout the ages have typically been lightly armed and sparsely manned. Ship designers usually concentrate on increasing cargo space not defensibility. Therefore, heavily armed pirates have almost always been able to overwhelm their victims, whether in port or at sea.[6]

Piracy has also been a cyclical phenomenon that concludes when the priates themselves are countered decisively. Piracy usually begins small scale, with attacks on vulnerable ships in dangerous waters. Initially, pirates are more of a nuisance than a threat, but in the absence of organized resistance, piracy flourishes. As their attacks increase in frequency and intensity, they begin to affect seaborne trade.

Once piracy begins to affect commerce, nations respond. Initially, the response to piracy is limited and disjointed because nations often view pirates differently. For example, the English did not, at first, view the Caribbean pirates negatively since they preyed on Spanish shipping. Once the pirates began to affect English shipping, British commercial leaders lobbied the government to use the Royal Navy to suppress piracy. Conversely, since they were frequently victimized by English pirate attacks, the Spanish considered England a "nation of pirates." They treated all Englishmen harshly, often summarily executing those captured at sea, regardless of the legitimacy of their actions. Moreover, during the early stages of a nation's maritime development, piracy often served as that country's first avenue for trade.[7] That was certainly the case with early English and Dutch piracy, which was used to make inroads into the areas controlled by Spain and Portugal. The profits generated by English and

Dutch pirates encouraged merchants to invest in maritime commercial enterprises, whether legal or illegal. Soon, the Dutch Republic and later England became dominant maritime powers.

Another important historical reason why nations have historically viewed piracy in unique ways was their use of privateers. Essentially, privateers were state-sponsored pirates. They were civilian auxiliaries commissioned by authorized government officials to attack an enemy nation's merchant ships. A letter of marque issued by their government legitimized their piratical activities. But Spain, frequently the victim of privateering attacks, did not recognize the validity of most privateers' letters of marque and usually treated them as pirates.[8] For this study, pirates and privateers are used interchangeably since privateers often slipped over into outright piracy when legitimate targets were difficult to find.

In the final stage of the cycle, the threat from piracy becomes more prominent and nations organize and dispatch antipirate naval forces. Typically, these are unilateral operations conducted by the dominant naval power in the region. Powerful naval squadrons seek out and destroy pirate forces at sea. Equally important, they eliminate pirate support operations ashore by assaulting their strongholds. Despite the best efforts of those naval forces, unless they are successful in eliminating the shore support systems, they cannot completely eradicate piracy. Thus, in many parts of the world, even though piracy has been suppressed from time to time, it has continued at low levels, waiting to reemerge when conditions became more conducive to such activities.

Although piracy can occur anywhere in the world, it begins as a local phenomenon. In other words, it requires specific conditions to flourish, as follows:

- *Favorable maritime geography.* Pirates need easy access to fertile shipping lanes, preferably far from naval or police forces that might oppose their activities. They gravitate toward places where they can easily acquire plunder, which is the primary reason why they became pirates. Consequently, piracy often occurs near chokepoints or established sealanes. Moreover, they rarely attack vessels far out to sea because it is much more difficult to locate victims on the open ocean.

- *Favorable political climate.* Pirates exploit instability and uncertainty, whether the result of war, civil strife, legal ambiguity, jurisdictional conflict, or the failure of governmental functions. Each of those situations produces desirable conditions since they reduce the likelihood of government opposition, often result in weak or inadequate security measures, and open up opportunities to cultivate relationships with corrupt officials who allow them to act without fear of reprisal.

- *Safe havens ashore.* Pirates must have safe, secure ports where they can obtain logistics support, dispose of their stolen goods, recruit replacements, gather intelligence, and hide from law enforcement agencies. Sanctuaries may emerge because piracy is a culturally acceptable practice among the people involved or they might develop under the patronage of corrupt officials and merchants who profit from the pirates' activities.[9]

While most nations have laws against piracy, there is little international agreement on what piracy is and how to combat it. Nations view piracy differently depending on whether they are victims or tacit co-conspirators. For example, many Somalis view the indigenous Somali pirates that emerged in the first decade of the 21st century as heroes. During interviews, Somali pirates often claim that they are merely protecting Somalia's sovereign waters and retaliating for foreign exploitation of Somalia's maritime resources. Most other nations view them as out-and-out thieves.

Frequently, national rivalries prevented successful legal proceedings against pirates. Thus, Great Britain (GB), the dominant naval power by the early 18th century, was disinclined to act against the Barbary pirates because they disproportionately preyed on the shipping of Britain's enemies, France and Spain. Although GB had the naval power to eliminate or suppress the Barbary pirates, British leaders chose to negotiate safe passage for their ships instead of taking direct action against the Barbary corsairs.

Moreover, states have often favored pirates from their country, and those who receive the stolen goods, over other nation's victims. Piracy requires safe havens ashore, where the brigands can rest, refit their ships, and dispose of their ill-gotten goods. For example, American colonists, angered by the Navigation Acts, were only too willing to buy cheap pirate plunder. Many fortunes were made by corrupt colonial merchants and officials who allowed pirated goods to be sold in their local markets.

Since there is no international tribunal to try and punish pirates, prosecution is left to the nation that captures them. In the case of the Somali pirates, the United Kingdom is reluctant to apprehend them because British authorities do not want to prosecute them in British courts, and British officials are reluctant to turn them over to Somalia since the pirates could justifiably claim asylum because of the harshness of Sharia law practiced in Somalia. The United States circumvented that concern by negotiating a bilateral treaty with Kenya that allows the United States to turn over Somali brigands to Kenyan authorities for prosecution.

Thus, piracy is a tough, enduring, problem. Pirates are difficult to find and even more difficult to eliminate. Short of the historic method of punishment—execution—modern pirates have little to fear from the international judicial system. They can operate with impunity at sea, confident that they will extract ransom or steal valuable items from vulnerable merchant ships cruising the world's oceans.

In the modern period, piracy has thrived in different parts of the world at various times. There were two significant periods of piracy in the Caribbean Sea. Pirate attacks against Spanish treasure ships began soon after the Spanish began extracting wealth from their new colonies. The Golden Age of Piracy lasted from the 1670s through 1725. This is the age of piracy with which most people are familiar. It eventually ended when the impact on British commerce forced the British to react with a heavy hand. The Royal Navy, which emerged as the dominant naval power after a series of wars with France and Spain, eliminated piracy in the Caribbean by 1730.

But piracy in this region reemerged in the second decade of the 19th century when Spain's South and Central American colonies began to break away from their mother country. Since the newly emerging nations had limited naval power, they relied on privateers to attack the Spanish. Spain retaliated by issuing letters of marque to privateers who also preyed on neutral shipping. American merchant ships were a favorite target of the Spanish privateers because of their resentment over American support to the South and Central American rebels. The United States and Britain reacted by stationing naval squadrons in the region, and by 1826, those naval forces had, once again, eliminated piracy in the Caribbean.

Piracy in the Mediterranean dates back to the Greeks and even earlier. But one of the greatest pirate empires was based in the Barbary principalities on the north coast of Africa. Although they maintained nominal allegiance to the Ottoman Empire, they were essentially independent states who depended on piracy for their existence. The Barbary corsairs were state-sponsored pirates motivated for both financial and religious reasons—attacking infidels was almost as important as capturing Christian goods and slaves. They remained a threat to commercial shipping in the Mediterranean for more than 300 years. Despite naval operations by the United States and Great Britain, the Barbary pirates were not eliminated until France invaded North Africa in the 1830s. Land operations in this case were crucial to the elimination of the Barbary pirate threat.

Political upheaval caused by the Greek revolt against the Ottoman Empire in the 1820s led to an outbreak of piracy in the eastern Mediterranean. Exploiting the turmoil, Greek pirates preyed on shipping from all nations. Their success eventually forced Britain and France to act. The navies of these two powers settled the question of Greek independence and then acted against the pirates. But the Greek pirates avoided capture or death by abandoning their boats when located and fleeing ashore. This prompted the British naval commander to threaten the fledgling Greek Government with actions ashore if it did not act to eliminate the pirate's safe havens. Once again, land operations proved to be a necessary element in the suppression of piracy.

Piracy has also existed in Asian waters for thousands of years. The narrow straits of Southeast Asia are still home to many pirates. The Straits of Malacca, through which more than 50,000 commercial vessels transit each year, have always been an attractive location for pirates. The restrictive waters cause ships to slow and the many coves and bays make perfect hiding places for pirates. In the 19th century, the Royal Navy eventually suppressed piracy in the area by maintaining an active, year-round presence in the area. When local pirates attacked an American merchant vessel in Qualla Battoo in the 1830s, an American warship was dispatched to retaliate. Fear of reprisal put a damper on further depredations of American ships, although ships of other nations continued to suffer attacks.

Similarly, Chinese corsairs have operated with impunity for thousands of years. In the early 19th century, as the Manchu dynasty weakened, a vast pirate confederation rose up along China's southern coast. This league of pirates challenged the power of the central government and defeated the Chinese Navy in several engagements. Because of the government's weakness, they eventually co-opted the pirates into the government, since they were unable to suppress them with force.

Pirates continued to plague Chinese waters for another 100 years. Both the Royal Navy and United States Navy maintained permanent stations in the region to discourage piracy. British and American sailors conducted a number of operations against Chinese brigands throughout the 19th century and into the 20th century.

It was the increasing number of piratical attacks in the Straits of Malacca that eventually drove home the problem of modern-day piracy.

There was little piracy in the region until the mid to late 1970s. Then, in the early 1980s, the International Chamber of Commerce set up the International Maritime Bureau (IMB) in response to a surge in maritime crime. As concerns about piracy increased, the IMB began tracking pirate attacks and giving advice on how to mitigate the risks of piracy. The United Nations also acted by redefining piracy and the means available to nations to counter the threat. Finally, in the 1990s, the IMB established the Piracy Reporting Centre in Malaysia. All of this attention eventually led to a decrease in attacks in the region although piracy has definitely not been eliminated in the Straits and surrounding waters.

Piracy also flourished in the Persian Gulf for thousands of years. Pirate states emerged along the coast of what is now the United Arab Emirates. When Arab corsairs began affecting British trade, the British Empire acted by sending two expeditions against the Arab pirates. Although they burned ships and razed villages, the British effort was ineffective because it was primarily sea based. A third expedition in the early 1820s, which included a significant land component, was successful in convincing Arab leaders that it was in their best interests to cooperate with the British.

Today's newspapers are flooded with articles about piracy off the coast of Somalia. This piracy follows the traditional cycle. Initially, it consisted of a few events amounting to nothing more than an annoyance. But the lack of response emboldened the Somali pirates to the point where they began attacking cruise ships, expensive yachts, and now a cargo ship carrying tanks and a supertanker. Such highly visible attacks caused a reaction from many of the world's maritime powers. Consequently, in 2009 the US-led Combined Task Force (CTF) 151, an antipirate naval force, began operating off the coast of Somalia. Although it has not had much success capturing pirates, its presence clearly serves as an inhibitor and presages perhaps other actions.

The following chapters examine piracy in the West Indies, the Mediterranean, Asia, and the Middle East. Using the three primary conditions for the growth of piracy as a framework they will demonstrate how those conditions contributed to the expansion of pirate power and how neutralizing or eliminating their effect facilitated the suppression of piracy. As will be seen, in almost every case, more than raw naval power was required to eradicate piracy.

Notes

1. Richard L. Parry, "Indonesian Waters Become Centre of World Piracy Boom," *The Independent*, 25 January 2000, http://www.independent.co.uk/news/world/asia/indonesian-waters-become-centre-of-world-piracy-boom-727302.html (accessed 20 November 2008).

2. Ralph T. Ward, *Pirates in History* (Baltimore: York Press, 1974), 1.

3. Ibid., 2.

4. Ibid., 4–5.

5. Ibid., 7.

6. Peter Earle, *The Pirate Wars* (New York: Thomas Dunne Books, 2005), 17.

7. Ward, 64.

8. Frank Sherry, *Raiders and Rebels: The Golden Age of Piracy* (New York: Hearst Marine Books, 1986), 23.

9. Martin N. Murphy, *Small Boats, Weak States, Dirty Money: Piracy and Maritime Terrorism in the Modern World* (London: Hurst & Co., 2008), 28–45.

Chapter 2

Piracy in the West Indies

Piracy in the West Indies emerged not long after Columbus discovered the Americas. The French privateer Jean Fleury captured three Spanish treasure ships containing gold, jewels, and other Aztec finery in 1523.[1] Up until then, Europeans had little knowledge of the fantastic wealth of the New World. But the news quickly spread, and by the 1530s, pirates based in the Old World regularly preyed on Spanish ships in the Caribbean. Piracy flourished in the region for more than 200 years until British naval power finally suppressed it around 1730. But piracy experienced a resurgence in the second decade of the 19th century, only to be put down once again, this time by American as well as British naval forces. (Figure 1 shows the Caribbean Islands.)

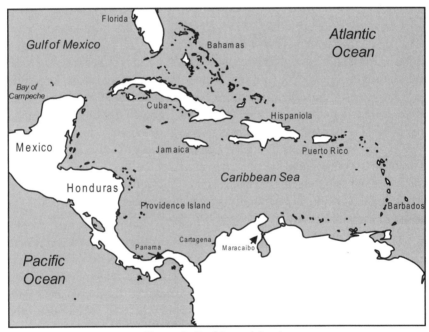

Figure 1. Caribbean Islands.

The three primary conditions necessary for piracy to flourish, favorable maritime geography, favorable political climate, and sanctuaries ashore were clearly present during both phases of West Indies piracy. There were numerous uncharted islands, coves, and inlets near the main Caribbean shipping channels. Pirates used those isolated spots to hide and wait for their prey. Then, when they spotted a victim, the buccaneers swooped down on the unsuspecting merchant ship and quickly took it before the merchant ship's crew could respond. In addition, the many narrow channels of the Caribbean made it easier for the brigands to locate and attack their victims.

The political climate also made piratical activities much easier. The English, French, and Dutch Governments used pirates and privateers to protect their Caribbean possessions and to weaken Spain economically. Throughout most of the 16th and 17th centuries, Spanish authorities viewed the English, French, and Dutch colonies in the West Indies as intrusions into Spain's sphere of influence that needed to be eliminated. There were numerous battles between those colonists and Spain. Since the navies of England, France, and the Dutch Republic were relatively small, they could not station naval forces permanently in the Caribbean to protect their fledgling colonies. Lacking official naval protection, the colonies used pirates and privateers as their first line of defense against the Spanish.[2]

Privateers were essentially legalized pirates. Their commission, or letter of marque, gave them permission to attack the vessels of any nation listed in the document. Although privateers were technically only supposed to be used during time of war, Spain fought an almost continual undeclared war in the Western Hemisphere for more than 200 years. Colonial governors often issued letters of marque during peacetime, despite government directives not to do so. With the cover of such documents, privateers were free to prey on any vessel flying the flag of an enemy nation. The situation was further complicated because privateers often turned into pirates at war's end when many privateers found it difficult to return to peaceful activities. European nations finally outlawed privateering in the mid-19th century.[3]

The main difference between privateers and pirates was their ultimate purpose. Since privateers were state sanctioned, their goal was to protect or strengthen the nation by weakening its enemies' merchant fleets and commercial power. Although privateering provided those involved with the opportunity to obtain wealth, from the perspective of the state, the primary objective was to weaken enemies of the state, not to enrich private citizens. Thus, privateering complemented mercantilist theory since the destruction of enemy merchant ships reduced competition and, therefore, improved the nation's opportunity for garnering wealth. Buccaneers preyed on ships from all states; every nation's shipping was a pirate's enemy. [4]

Of course, piracy was often in the eye of the beholder. What one country deemed as a valid privateering activity was, in many cases, considered piracy by the victim nation. On more than one occasion, Spanish officials executed captured privateers with their letters of marque hanging around their necks.[5] Although Queen Elizabeth I knighted Francis Drake for his exploits, Spanish officials considered him a pirate and protested the honors given him.[6] Such attitudes were not, however, exclusive to the Spanish. It might come as a surprise to American readers to learn that the English writer Charles Johnson included a chapter in the appendix of his *History of Highwaymen and Pirates*, published in 1813, about the "wicked and daring pirate" John Paul Jones, an American naval hero.[7]

The political climate also affected the third element, sanctuaries. Since the English, French, and Dutch settlements needed the pirates to serve as their first line of defense, they welcomed the buccaneers, as well as their stolen goods, into their ports. Pirates needed the ports to refit their ships, buy food and water, and enjoy their ill-gotten gains. In addition to the protection the freebooters provided, colonial merchants welcomed pirate goods because they could be bought cheaply and sold at a profit.

Over time, as political conditions changed, so did the location of sanctuaries. The first pirates were based out of Europe and sailed to the Caribbean looking for prey. By the 1620s, they began to develop bases closer to their targets.[8] Tortuga, located off the northwest coast of Hispaniola, was the first great pirate sanctuary. It maintained its reputation as a pirate haven for almost 100 years. Jamaica was another important pirate stronghold. But the English eventually closed Jamaica to the buccaneers when the political climate in England changed. With Jamaica no longer available, the freebooters shifted their base of operations to the Bahamas and, to a lesser degree, the American colonies. Pirates were often seen in Boston, Newport, Philadelphia, and New York in the 1600s.

The causes of West Indies piracy changed over time as well. Initially, it was a commercial war tacitly sponsored by European nations. Pope Alexander VI had in 1493 issued a papal bull dividing the world between Spain and Portugal. Embracing the economic theory of mercantilism, Spain sought to eliminate all foreign commerce within its sphere of influence. Consequently, Spain only allowed its colonies to trade with the mother country and treated all foreign merchants, even legitimate ones, attempting to trade with its Caribbean possessions as smugglers and pirates.[9] Many nations, England and France in particular, resented the monopoly granted by the Pope and actively ignored it. Consequently, they encouraged, if not assisted, private interests trading with the Spanish colonies. The Spanish colonists, in turn, were willing to trade with foreigners, despite edicts by the King, because Spanish products were either unavailable or too costly.[10] When the Spanish reacted harshly to the traders, an undeclared war broke out between Spain and other nations. There was "no peace beyond the line."[11]

Soon, state-sponsored piracy, using privateers, flourished in the Caribbean. Spain was almost continuously at war with either France, England, or the Dutch Republic from the 16th through the early 18th century. Again, lacking the resources to build and maintain large national fleets, England, France, and the Dutch Republic used privateers to augment their naval forces. With normal trade disrupted by war, shipowners were frequently willing to risk their vessels on privateering cruises.

Finally, by 1670, the damage inflicted by the privateers and buccaneers so weakened Spain that they were no longer needed. England used pardons to entice pirates to give up the trade. When that failed, the English resorted to pirate hunters. Now lacking state sponsorship, pirates began attacking ships of all nations. Thus, piracy became a commercial venture against anyone sailing the ocean.[12]

Piracy has always followed a cyclical model, ebbing and flowing over time.[13] Initially, it was small scale and generally ignored by the Spanish, who were the primary victims of piracy in the West Indies. Over time, as pirate attacks became more brazen, the Spanish responded with force and wiped out the buccaneers' strongholds. But the Spanish did not permanently eliminate the brigands' sanctuaries so, after a short hiatus, the buccaneers returned to their former haunts and began attacking Spanish shipping again.

The first phase of piracy in the West Indies only ended when the dominant naval power, Great Britain, chose to apply its resources to the problem. When the War of Spanish Succession ended in 1713, the Royal Navy reigned supreme on the seas. With peace at hand, British merchants wanted to expand their trading relations throughout the world. Piracy was not conducive to maritime commerce, thus Britain began a concerted effort to end piracy in the West Indies. The British campaign, which involved legal and political reforms as well as naval operations, successfully suppressed piracy in the West Indies for almost 100 years.

A second round of piracy in the West Indies erupted in the late 1810s when Spain's colonial possessions in South and Central America sought independence. Once again, the three primary conditions that facilitate piracy came into play. First, political turmoil made piracy possible. The fledgling South American and Central American nations issued letters of marque to privateers authorizing them to attack Spanish ships. Spain, in turn, unleashed privateers against the shipping of the new nations.

The perpetrators of this second phase of West Indian piracy, primarily Spanish privateers, again used the many uncharted islands and coves in the Caribbean to prey on shipping. Most of the Spanish privateers and pirates operated from bases in Cuba and Puerto Rico. But, as in other periods, the privateers were not always judicious in whom they attacked. Since their sanctuaries were close to the shipping lanes used by American and British merchants, Spanish corsairs began preying on both nations' shipping.

Although the United States was not at war with Spain, Spanish officials and merchants provided sanctuary and support to the brigands. Many Spaniards believed such actions were justified because of American and, to a lesser degree, British support for the rebels. Thus, they were only too willing to buy the pirates' stolen goods; supply them with food, weapons, and naval stores; and provide them with safe havens out of reach of the American and British naval forces.

Eventually, the Spanish buccaneers' depredations sparked a response by the United States and Great Britain. Working together, the American and British Navies eliminated the pirate threat in a few short years. But, given Spanish complicity with the corsairs, it was not an easy task. The pirates were not completely eradicated until the Americans and British gained Spanish permission to pursue the brigands ashore. Only then was piracy finally ended in the Caribbean.

Caribbean Piracy, 1500–1730

The first period of piracy in the Caribbean had two phases. During the first phase, piracy was an extension of warfare against the Spanish Empire. Most of the buccaneers, whether English, French, or Dutch, were nationalists waging war against Spain. Moreover, since those nations had small navies, they used the pirates to augment the defenses of their fledgling island possessions. By the 1670s, the nations sponsoring piracy, particularly England, no longer needed the assistance of the buccaneers to protect their overseas possessions. Additionally, they realized that pirates disrupted trade and endangered relations between nations. Consequently, they tried to entice the buccaneers into abandoning piracy by granting pardons for their crimes. But many of the brigands were uninterested in legitimacy and expanded their scope of targets, including the vessels of their native countries. During this phase of piracy, the pirates were at war with the world, and in turn, their home countries were at war with them.

The activities of the pirates and privateers during the first phase have been described as "piratical imperialism." British and French authorities used pirates and privateers to put pressure on Spain, hoping Spain would eventually recognize the legitimacy of their New World colonies. Moreover, since Spain forbade foreign trade with its colonies, piracy was a way to obtain goods from those markets. Finally, piracy and privateering removed commercial competitors, which according to mercantilist theory, strengthened the economies of the countries sponsoring piracy. Thus, nations used piracy to advance national goals.[14]

Spain's problems began not long after Cortes conquered the Aztecs in 1519. The promise of great wealth induced many Spanish colonists to abandon the islands for the mainland. By the 1560s, perhaps as few as 1,000 Spaniards lived on Hispaniola, half of whom lived in Santo Domingo, 200 on Puerto Rico, 240 on Cuba, and only a handful on Jamaica. Similarly, the Spanish Government increasingly focused on its mainland possessions, to the detriment of the islands. Only Havana, which superseded Santo Domingo as the most important island port, continued to grow after sailors discovered a new route to Spain through the Florida Straits and Old Bahama Channel in 1519. Spain eventually constructed a new fort in Havana to protect the treasure fleet that rendezvoused there before setting out to cross the Atlantic.[15]

Before that happened, disaster struck. In 1523, Jean Fleury, a French privateer operating out of Honfleur, captured two of the three ships transporting Cortes' treasure back to Spain off the Azores. Fleury captured 62,000 ducats of gold, 600 marks of pearls (approximately 140 kilograms), and several tons of sugar.[16] Although this was a legitimate act of war, Spain considered it an act of piracy and executed Fleury when he was captured in 1527.[17] While there were widespread rumors about the great wealth of the New World prior to this, Fleury's capture confirmed the truth of those rumors. At first, French privateers concentrated on Spanish ships in the eastern Atlantic, but by the 1530s, more than 30 French vessels sailed to the Caribbean each year looking for Spanish treasure ships.[18]

The French and Spanish continued to wage war against one another in the Caribbean despite intermittent peace between the two countries throughout the rest of the 16th century. Resentment over the May 1493 decision by Pope Alexander VI to give Spain control of all lands west of a line 100 leagues west of the Azores and Cape Verde Islands fueled the conflict. Neither France nor England accepted the Pope's pronouncement. While the Treaty of Cateau-Cambrésis (1559) established peace in Europe, French and Spanish diplomats decided to ignore all violence west of 46° W. "No peace beyond the line" meant that French corsairs were allowed to take whatever they could, and the Spanish were equally free to punish

French intruders as they saw fit. Whatever happened west of the line would not affect their relations in Europe. This agreement remained in effect until the Treaty of Ratisbon in 1684, when Spain and France agreed to implement the peace accord throughout the world, not just in Europe.[19] England and the Dutch Republic eventually came to similar understandings with Spain as well.

French corsairs were the primary threat to Spanish interests in the Caribbean through the first half of the 16th century, but by mid-century, the lure of Spanish treasure enticed interlopers from other nations. Much of the attraction was due to an increase in silver exports from Spain's New World possessions. The surge in production was caused by the discovery of a new method of extracting silver from previously played-out mines and two new silver strikes in Mexico. The Spaniards needed labor, primarily slaves, to work those mines, which opened up an avenue for trade for non-Spaniards.[20] Thus, the desire for Spanish silver, whether earned through legitimate trade or taken through piracy, enticed more and more English and Dutch sailors and merchants, along with the French, to test their luck in the Caribbean during the second half of the 16th century.

Among those drawn toward the New World were the English seadogs John Hawkins and Francis Drake. Hawkins and Drake exemplify the type of pirate prevalent during the first phase of piracy. While they showed little mercy to their Spanish victims, they were loyal Englishmen who did not prey on English vessels. Their piratical ventures made both men wealthy and famous; each was knighted and held in high regard by Queen Elizabeth I. But their actions also underscored the gray area between privateering and piracy. Even though Hawkins and Drake sailed with Royal approbation, Spanish officials considered them pirates and would have speedily executed them if they could have captured either man.

John Hawkins was an English merchant and slave trader. Hawkins led three slave ships to the Caribbean in 1562, where he made a fortune by selling 300 slaves to the Spanish. Two years later, from October 1664 until September 1665, Hawkins led a second, even larger, trading expedition to the New World. This time, his squadron included one of the queen's ships. Once again, he traded some 400 slaves for Spanish silver and made even greater profits. When the Spanish ambassador protested, Hawkins claimed he was nothing more than a peaceable merchant.[21]

His third cruise, which set out in October 1567, did not go as well. Some Spanish officials wanted to trade with Hawkins. In one case, Hawkins and the governor staged a mock battle to provide the governor with an excuse for trading with the English. In other locations, he used force to make the Spanish buy his slaves. Finally, in September 1568, Hawkins and his flotilla limped into San Juan de Ulúa, the harbor for Vera Cruz, in need of supplies and repairs. Soon thereafter, a Spanish fleet arrived with the new colonial viceroy, trapping Hawkins in the harbor. The situation resulted in a stalemate. Even though Hawkins was outnumbered and outgunned, he controlled the harbor. The Spanish could not remain off the coast indefinitely because they needed supplies and were threatened by bad weather. Consequently, Hawkins negotiated a truce with the viceroy, allowing him to remain in San Juan de Ulúa to refit his ships and enabling the Spanish to enter the port. But the viceroy reneged on the agreement as soon as he realized he was bargaining with men he considered pirates. On the night of 23 September, the Spanish attacked without warning and decimated the English squadron. Hawkins and Drake managed to escape in two ships. Although Drake made it back safely, only 15 of the men in Hawkins' ship survived the trip home to England.[22]

The Battle of San Juan de Ulúa proved to be a watershed event. From that date forward, the English, especially Drake, sought revenge for the Spanish attack. Drake led successful voyages to the West Indies in 1570, 1571, and 1572. Then, from November 1577 until September 1580, Drake circumnavigated the globe, attacking Spanish vessels with impunity and capturing many valuable prizes.[23] Queen Elizabeth I, who was one of his backers, profited immensely from Drake's successful voyage and recognized his feat by knighting Drake soon after he returned home.[24]

Drake's example and the defeat of the Spanish Armada in 1588 opened the door for even more English incursions into Spain's New World domain. From 1588 through 1603, English sailors set out on 100 to 200 piratical voyages each year.[25] The government did little to control those ventures. "Piratical imperialism" encouraged commercial expansion, boosted ship construction, and served as a cheap means of waging war against the Spanish.[26] Moreover, it was profitable. During that same period, English adventurers brought back between £150,000 to £300,000 in Spanish booty each year.[27]

Spain's problems increased when the Dutch revolted in 1568. At first, the Dutch confined themselves to smuggling, trading Dutch products for salt and tobacco. Between March 1599 and December 1605, 768 Dutch ships traded for salt along the coast of Venezuela. But as the Dutchmen waited to load their ships, they began attacking Spanish coastal vessels using armed sloops and pinnaces. By 1606, Dutch freebooters had virtually eliminated all Spanish shipping along the northern coast of South America.[28]

The successes of the English, French, and Dutch marauders hurt Spain financially. Since the Spanish crown borrowed extensively against the wealth extracted from its colonies, it was crucial that the treasure fleet arrive safely. Consequently, starting in 1564, all ships were ordered to sail to Spain in one of two heavily armed convoys. One left in April and the other in August. Treasure ships from Mexico and Central America congregated in Havana in late spring or early summer. Once the convoy was organized, it set out for Spain, escorted by two to eight warships.[29]

But the convoy system was not entirely successful, and by the early 17th century, Spain was bankrupt. Spain's financial problems contributed to the growth of piracy in the Caribbean. Since the crown was only concerned with the safety of the treasure fleet, small ports were left to provide for their own defenses. Few of those harbors could afford to adequately fortify themselves, so most Spanish towns were vulnerable to attack.[30] Moreover, because Spain could not afford to police the entire Caribbean, buccaneers rarely encountered Spanish warships. Free to go wherever they pleased, the corsairs soon terrorized Spaniards throughout the West Indies. To stop illegal trade with foreigners and to better protect those settlers still living on the islands, in 1605, Spanish officials began relocating the remaining colonists into a few population centers where they could be better protected and more closely controlled. Spanish soldiers destroyed crops, burned towns to the ground, and forcibly removed citizens from areas that traded with foreign merchants.[31] They left behind only the pigs and cattle, which thrived in the benign environment.

That decision produced dire consequences for the Spanish. Foreigners soon moved into the void left by the forced relocation of the Spanish colonists. Up until that point, English, French, and Dutch adventurers sailed for the Caribbean from European ports. Now the foreign corsairs began to shift their bases to the Caribbean, where they were closer to their targets. The buccaneers' new ports provided them the three elements they needed to flourish: geographic advantage, political support, and sanctuaries ashore.

Among the first interlopers were French hunters who settled on the island of Hispaniola in the first quarter of the 17th century. They survived by trading with Dutch merchants, who bought hides, tallow, and dried meat from the hunters. The hunters became known as *boucaniers* because they dried their meat over a grate made of green wood called a *boucan*. Given that sailors subsisted almost entirely on salt pork while at sea, the *boucaniers'* dried meat became quite popular and a brisk trade ensued.[32]

Since the Spanish considered the entire Caribbean a closed area, they reacted harshly against all foreigners encroaching on their territory. When French Huguenots established a colony at Fort Caroline near present-day Jacksonville, Florida, in 1564, the Spanish reacted ruthlessly. They attacked the settlement and killed all of the inhabitants in 1565. Then, they established a new colony at St. Augustine to guard against further French incursions and to protect Spanish shipping entering or leaving the Straits of Florida.[33] In 1593, Spanish authorities captured 10 Dutch merchant vessels while trading with Spanish towns. Convicted of smuggling, they executed the ship captains and condemned the crews to servitude as galley slaves.[34] The Venetian ambassador to London reported in 1604 that Spanish authorities tortured the crews of two English ships caught trading with the Spanish. They cut off the hands, ears, noses, and feet of the crewmen, smeared them with honey to attract flies and other insects, and left them to die tied to trees.[35] Such atrocities encouraged retaliation, which furthered the violence in the region.

Spanish soldiers also hunted down and killed both the *boucaniers* and the wild cattle and pigs that the *boucaniers* hunted for their livelihood on Hispaniola. Stripped of their ability to support themselves, many of the *boucaniers* fled to Tortuga, a small island off the northwest coast of Hispaniola, and turned to piracy. The French *boucaniers*, whose name was soon corrupted into buccaneers, became implacable enemies of Spain. Operating close to shore in dugout canoes, they stealthily attacked larger Spanish vessels. In turn, they used those boats to capture bigger ships in which they ranged farther and farther throughout the Caribbean. By 1665, the buccaneers commanded large sailing vessels and operated with impunity throughout the Caribbean. Although the Spanish raided Tortuga from time to time, it remained the stronghold of the French buccaneers from 1630 until about 1710.[36]

Since most of the other Caribbean islands were also left uninhabited by the Spanish, foreigners moved in and filled those voids as well. Pirates, smugglers, and colonists established settlements on many Caribbean islands. Great Britain acquired Barbados (1621), St. Kitts (1623), Montserrat (1632), and Antigua (1632). Then, in 1655, British forces captured its Caribbean crown jewel, Jamaica. Similarly, France obtained Martinique (1635) and Guadeloupe (1635) and the Dutch took Curacao (1634).[37] Although Spain refused to acknowledge their legitimacy, there were permanent English, French, and Dutch colonies in place throughout the Caribbean by mid-century.

Figure 2. Jamaica and Hispaniola.

Two of the most important pirate havens were Tortuga and Port Royal, Jamaica (figure 2). Each island met the three conditions needed for piracy to flourish. They were favorably located near important sealanes. Tortuga dominated two important straits: the Windward Passage between Cuba and Hispaniola and the Mona Passage between Puerto Rico and Hispaniola. Likewise, Jamaica was close to the shipping lanes between Cuba and Central and South America.[38] Thus, both locations provided the buccaneers geographical advantages over their enemies. The political climate also favored piracy. Since neither England nor France had sufficient naval forces to protect their island possessions, the buccaneers served as the first line of defense for both islands. Therefore, local officials were reluctant to take any action against the pirates. Finally, since both islands prospered financially because of the brigands, the freebooters found protection and support on both Tortuga and Jamaica. Despite the presence of a French governor, Tortuga really behaved like an independent pirate kingdom for more than 60 years, generally ignoring the French crown.[39] Similarly, buccaneers operated with impunity out of Jamaica for more than 30 years.[40]

Although the Spanish raided Tortuga on several occasions, they were never able to put it out of business. The first Tortuga-based buccaneer was Pierre le Grand, who captured a large treasure galleon in 1620 with 28 men. Unlike most buccaneers, le Grand supposedly sailed the ship back to France, sold the contents, and lived out the rest of his life in grand style.[41] France laid claim to the island in 1628 although it had to fend off counterclaims by the English between 1631 and 1635.[42] As noted previously, even though Spain did not populate its many Caribbean islands, it was unwilling to allow trespassers to settle on the islands either. Thus, Spain carried out a series of raids in 1631, 1635, and 1638. During the 1635 raid, the Spanish hung all of the men they captured and deported the women and children. Still, the buccaneers always returned to the island once the Spanish left.[43]

Weary of the Spanish attacks, the buccaneers requested aid from the French governor of St. Kitts. In 1642, the governor sent Jean le Vasseur, a French engineer, to help. Le Vasseur built an almost impregnable fort overlooking the harbor and, after cutting ties with St. Kitts, established himself as the ruler of Tortuga. Not long after the fortress was completed, the Spanish attacked again. This time, they were soundly defeated. For the next 12 years, Tortuga was the undisputed center of piracy in the Caribbean. There were brothels, taverns, and gambling halls for the pirates. It was also a thriving commercial center. Dutch and French merchants brought guns, ammunition, powder, cloth, and brandy, which they traded for the buccaneers' plunder.[44]

Tortuga underwent a period of instability from 1654 until 1665. In 1654, the Spanish attacked in force and captured the island. They left a permanent garrison on the island to prevent the buccaneers from returning. Unfortunately for the Spanish, they had to withdraw the troops the next year when an English invasion force arrived off the coast of Hispaniola. Soon thereafter, an Englishman took over although he was deposed by a French adventurer in 1659. By 1665, the island was securely under French rule. Tortuga continued to serve as a safe haven for pirates although it was eventually superseded by Petit Goâve, a more remote port on the west coast of Hispaniola, around 1670.[45]

Jamaica also served the interests of pirates for many years. Oliver Cromwell dispatched a large force under Admiral William Penn and General Robert Venables to the West Indies in December 1654. Their mission was to seize Hispaniola. When they failed to take Santo Domingo, they set their sights on the lightly populated island of Jamaica and captured it instead. Despite several Spanish attempts to retake the island, Jamaica was firmly under English control by 1660.[46]

The Spanish threat led to a decision that soon turned Port Royal, Jamaica, into the "wickedest city in the world."[47] Lacking proper military support and worried about another Spanish attempt to retake the island, in 1657, the governor of Jamaica invited all of the English pirates based on Tortuga to move to Jamaica in an effort to bolster his island's defenses. By 1665, more than 2,000 corsairs operated out of Port Royal.[48]

Jamaica was ideally suited as a pirate haven. It was located near the shipping lanes from Panama, where the Spanish accumulated their South American treasure for further transfer home to Havana. Intermittent warfare between Spain and England made it easy for freebooters to acquire letters of marque, thus giving their activities the veneer of legitimacy. Finally, Port Royal quickly became a secure haven for the buccaneers. English merchants welcomed the brigands' booty and provided the pirates with taverns, gambling houses, and prostitutes, as well as naval stores, weapons, ammunition, and powder. During much of the second half of the 17th century, the island's prosperity depended almost entirely on piracy rather than agriculture and commerce. [49]

Since almost any action taken "beyond the line" was, to some degree, legitimized by the Treaty of Cateau-Cambrésis, it was often difficult to distinguish between legitimate military operations and piracy. The career of Captain Christopher Myngs underscores that difficulty. Myngs, commander of the 44-gun frigate *Marston Moor*,[50] reached Jamaica in January 1656. Soon after he arrived, Myngs participated in a fruitless raid against Santa Marta, Venezuela. In October 1658, as commander of the Jamaican naval squadron, he tried to capture the Spanish treasure fleet. When that venture failed, the British force burned two Spanish towns and captured two ships. The next year, Myngs achieved more success when he sacked the Venezuelan towns of Cumana, Puerto Caballos, and Coro. The total take was £200,000 to £300,000. The Spanish responded to Myngs' attack by declaring him a pirate and condemning him to death.[51]

The Spanish death sentence was not the only problem Myngs soon faced. When he returned to Jamaica, Myngs claimed that Admiralty laws did not apply to his plunder and proceeded to dispose of the goods without handing over a share to the government. The governor of Jamaica arrested Myngs and sent him back to London for trial in 1660. His arrival coincided with the restoration of Charles II, and in the confusion, Myngs avoided punishment for his transgressions. Instead, he was sent back to Jamaica in 1662 in the 34-gun frigate *Centurion* with encouragement from Charles II to continue harassing the Spanish.[52]

Myngs quickly resumed his semipiratical operations. In October 1662, Myngs attacked Santiago, Cuba, and captured six ships as well as a significant amount of treasure. That success encouraged substantial buccaneer support for his final Caribbean endeavor, an assault on the town of San Francisco in the Bay of Campeche. Supported by 1,500 English, French, and Dutch buccaneers in 12 ships, Myngs seized the town in February 1663. He also captured 14 Spanish ships and extorted 150,000 pesos from the town's citizens. But the brutality of the attack triggered vehement Spanish complaints, and Charles II forbade further attacks on Spanish possessions.[53]

One of the most infamous Jamaican buccaneers was Henry Morgan. Morgan was never a pirate according to English law because he always had a commission from the governor of Jamaica, however dubious that authority might have been. Still, Morgan and his men committed numerous piratical acts and atrocities during their engagements with the Spanish.[54] Morgan probably accompanied Myngs during his 1662–1663 operations. In 1663–1664, he accompanied John Morris on a 22-month-long voyage along the coast of Central America, during which they plundered three Spanish cities. By 1668, Morgan was elected admiral of the Jamaican privateers.[55]

Sir Thomas Modyford, the Governor of Jamaica, authorized Morgan to conduct another expedition in early 1668 to thwart a rumored Spanish attack on the island. Even though his commission did not authorize land operations, in January 1668, Morgan led 700 English and French buccaneers in 12 ships against Puerto Principe, Cuba. Unfortunately for Morgan, the Cubans got wind of the operation and fled the city with their treasures. The rovers were only able to extract about 50,000 pesos from the remaining citizens. Disgusted by the lack of success, the French buccaneers abandoned Morgan, leaving him with about 500 men. With those men, he attacked Portobello, the collection point for Spanish treasure on the Isthmus of Panama. This operation was more successful. Morgan and his men captured the city, three forts, and 100,000 pesos. Morgan returned to Jamaica with a vast amount of plunder, which lessened the governor's unease about Morgan exceeding his commission by attacking Cuba.[56]

In April 1669, Morgan led another campaign against Maracaibo and Gibraltar, Venezuela. Although many of the residents fled before he arrived, using torture, Morgan and his men managed to extort 125,000 pesos from those they captured. When Morgan tried to return to Jamaica, he found himself trapped by the Spanish governor, who blocked the exit from Lake Maracaibo with three warships. Even though he was outgunned, Morgan managed to blow up the largest Spanish warship with a fireship and capture the second one in battle; the third went aground and sunk. Morgan returned to Jamaica in May, and once again, the enormous amount of booty he returned with prevented the authorities from looking too closely at his actions.[57]

Morgan's most famous exploit was the sack of Panama in 1671. Although there was peace between England and Spain in 1669, Spanish retaliatory raids on Jamaica gave Governor Modyford the excuse he needed to authorize another expedition. In August 1670, Modyford ordered Morgan to counter any planned attack on Jamaica by attacking the Spanish wherever he wished. When word got out that Morgan was sailing once more, almost every buccaneer in the Caribbean responded to the call. Morgan set sail in December 1670 with more than 2,000 men in 33 ships. After taking Providence Island, the buccaneers captured the Spanish fort San Lorenzo, which protected the mouth of the Chagres River. During that battle, more than 300 Spanish soldiers and 100 rovers were killed. With his remaining force, some 1,500 to 2,000 pirates, Morgan and his men paddled up the Chagres River toward Panama in canoes and sloops. The trek took 2 weeks, much of it on foot through dense jungle. Finally, on 27 January 1671, the half-starved buccaneers reached the Pacific Ocean. The next day, they assaulted the city of Panama and quickly overran its inexperienced defenders. For the next 3 weeks, the pirates ransacked the town and tortured its remaining citizens, forcing them to reveal the location of additional booty. When Morgan left Panama, it took 200 pack mules to carry all the plunder.[58]

Unfortunately for Morgan, the assault took place after the Treaty of Madrid (July 1670) took effect. In one of the more important clauses in the treaty, Spain acknowledged England's New World colonies, and in return, England agreed to enforce the peace settlement throughout the world, not just in Europe. With the repudiation of the doctrine of "no peace beyond the line," which legitimized piracy in the Caribbean, two of the main conditions for piracy, political turmoil and sanctuaries ashore, were undermined. From this point forward, the buccaneers could no longer count on Jamaica as a safe haven. Still, the treaty did not grant England the right to trade with Spanish colonies, so opportunities for conflict remained.[59]

Although Modyford did not learn of the treaty until May 1671, the commission he gave to Morgan clearly exceeded his authority. Responding to Spanish complaints about the attack, Charles II replaced Modyford with Sir Thomas Lynch. Lynch arrested Modyford and sent him back to England where he was imprisoned in the Tower of London for 2 years. Morgan was also arrested and conveyed to England in April 1672, but his good fortune held and he was never imprisoned. Instead, the King knighted Morgan and returned him to Jamaica as the deputy governor of the island when Lynch was ousted from office in 1674. Morgan retained that title until 1682 when Lynch returned to Jamaica and dismissed him.[60]

The English were not the only ones preying on Spanish vessels. Both the Dutch and French were active throughout the 17th century. The Dutch proved particularly troublesome to Spain. They conducted illegal trade with the Spanish colonies, provided essential supplies to the fledgling British and French colonies, and devastated Spanish shipping in the Caribbean. Their most spectacular success occurred in September 1628 when Piet Heyn captured the entire Spanish treasure fleet in Matanzas Bay. He took gold, silver, and other goods worth more than 12 million guilders (approximately 4.8 million pesos). By the late 1630s, Dutch depredations had destroyed almost all Spanish commerce in the Caribbean, forever changing the balance of power in the region.[61] Unfortunately for the Dutch Republic, it did not benefit from the shift in power. Instead, after a series of wars with England and France, the Dutch were confined to a few possessions in the southern Caribbean and the northern Leeward Islands.[62]

Unlike the Dutch, who conducted most of their operations from their home waters, French buccaneers benefited from bases located in the Caribbean, especially Tortuga. Among the most notorious French buccaneers was Francois l'Olonnais, who received his first ship from the governor of Tortuga.[63] When the Spanish killed most of his crew after his ship wrecked along the coast of Campeche (Mexico), l'Olonnais became an implacable enemy of Spain. He reputedly lopped the heads off of 87 Spanish prisoners in retaliation for the mistreatment of his crew.[64] His most famous exploit was the sacking of Maracaibo and Gibraltar, Venezuela, in the spring 1667. When the residents of Maracaibo learned of his approach ahead of time, they fled the city. L'Olonnais responded by attacking Gibraltar instead. He took the town easily and extracted 10,000 pesos from the terrified citizens who knew of his reputation. Then, outsmarting the people of Maracaibo, l'Olonnais returned to the city and caught many residents who came back after he left the first time. L'Olonnais extorted 20,000 pesos and 500 cattle from those he captured on his return to Maracaibo. Each of the adventurers who participated in the mission received 70 pieces of Eight and the value of 100 more in cloth and linen. L'Olonnais' career came to a bloody end a year later when he shipwrecked once again and was killed by Indians.[65]

During the last third of the 17th century, British authorities began to take actions to curb piracy, which led to the second phase of Caribbean piracy. During this phase, which is often characterized as the "Golden Age of Piracy," the buccaneers stopped operating in large squadrons. With their safe havens curtailed or eliminated, they were unable to concentrate in large numbers as before. Instead, these pirates sailed singly or in small flotillas, preying on any ship they encountered. Since they considered not just Spain but all nations their enemies, their depredations eventually forced the Royal Navy to act to eliminate them as a threat to English commerce.

Tacit governmental support for piracy, especially in Great Britain, lost its appeal as British leaders came to realize that piracy hindered rather than furthered national goals. Spain, weakened by Morgan and the other buccaneers, no longer posed a threat to Jamaica, so the pirates were not needed for its defense. British officials shifted their attention away from stealing from Spain toward empire building. New colonies, they believed, would bring wealth to the mother country by providing raw materials and products that were unavailable at home. In the new, more ordered world that British politicians and merchants sought to establish, pirates were a liability. They interfered with trade, especially the African slave trade that provided much of the labor needed in the colonies, and endangered relations among the European nations. In a series of treaties negotiated toward the end of the century, European nations abandoned the doctrine of "no peace beyond the line," thus weakening one of the pillars of piracy, political turmoil.[66]

England began taking steps to reign in the pirates as early as the 1670s. The new governor of Jamaica, Sir Thomas Lynch, who replaced Modyford in 1671, offered pardons and 35 acres of land to any pirate willing to give up the trade.[67] Pardons were also offered to English buccaneers in 1688, 1701, and 1717.[68] The 1717 general pardon included a threat as well—a bounty was placed on all who refused to accept the pardon. Pirate hunters received £100 for captains and £20 for common pirates, both generous sums since merchant captains only earned about £65 per year.[69] By the 1680s, as agricultural-based commerce, primarily sugar, became more important to the economy of the island, public sentiment in Jamaica shifted from support to opposition to piracy. Those who chose to continue as pirates found Jamaica increasingly inhospitable. Even Jamaican merchants, who had profited greatly from the buccaneers, became ever more reluctant to trade with pirates, which further served to drive them away from their formerly secure haven.[70] New legislation, such as prohibitions against

English sailors accepting foreign letters of marque and the Piracy Act of 1699, which expedited the punishment of pirates by setting up Admiralty Courts in the American colonies, made piracy much less attractive.[71]

Increases in the number of Royal Navy ships stationed in the West Indies and American colonies also made it more difficult for the pirates. Before the 1670s, British warships were rarely stationed in the West Indies. In the 1670s, Jamaica received two frigates, Barbados got one, and a ketch was stationed in the Leeward Islands. The Admiralty did not assign any ships to the American colonies, although two warships were stationed off Newfoundland to protect that rich fishing ground. The situation changed in the 1680s. The number of ships posted to Jamaica increased to four, and two more arrived in the Leeward Islands. The American colonies finally received permanent naval components as well. One or two ships took station in the Chesapeake Bay and another in Boston.[72] Although they were not sufficient to suppress piracy by themselves, the presence of permanently assigned naval vessels served as a deterrent. As the government clamped down on the pirates, many buccaneers moved to safer hunting grounds in the Pacific or Indian Oceans, while others found new refuges in the Bahamas or the American colonies.[73]

All of those steps contributed to the eventual elimination of piracy in the West Indies. But the extermination of the pirates did not happen overnight. International conflict, such as the Nine Years' War (1688–1697)[74] and the War of the Spanish Succession (1701–1713),[75] impeded the suppression of piracy because it gave those inclined to continue pirating the cloak of legitimacy from a letter of marque. Moreover, at the end of both wars, unemployment pushed many sailors and former privateers toward piracy, causing a surge in piratical activity each time. For example, with the end of the War of the Spanish Succession, the Royal Navy discharged some 36,000 sailors, almost 75 percent of its wartime complement. Thousands more privateers found themselves out of work as well. The surplus of maritime labor allowed ship captains to cut the wages of sailors by more than 50 percent. Thus, piracy became a viable alternative for many seamen who were accustomed to violence at sea.[76]

Additionally, France did not conform to the British policy change at first. Instead, French *filibustiers* stepped up their attacks on Spain. The Marquis de Maintenon devastated the pearl trade on Margarita Island in 1676. Two years later, Michel de Grammont, along with 700 buccaneers, captured Maracaibo. Even though they held the town for 6 months, they were unable to extract much booty from its citizens because of previous attacks by l'Olonnais and Morgan.[77] Then, in 1683, Grammont and others attacked Vera Cruz. This venture was much more successful; each of the 1,000 pirates involved in the raid garnered 800 gold coins. But the assault so enraged the Spanish that they declared war on France. France quickly negotiated a peace settlement, in which France agreed to abandon the "no peace beyond the line" doctrine.[78]

French buccaneers actively supported the French crown during the Nine Years' War. In 1694, the French buccaneer Jean du Casse led an expedition against Jamaica. Du Casse burned 50 sugar plantations and captured more than 1,300 slaves. Coming on the heels of the earthquake that destroyed Port Royal in 1692, it was a devastating attack. Then, in 1697, French buccaneers and Royal troops under the command of Admiral Baron de Pointis sacked Cartagena. It was a bloody but financially rewarding venture. The French extracted some 20 million livres worth of treasure from the citizens of Cartagena although de Pointis retained control of the plunder and cheated the corsairs out of their fair share, leaving them a mere 40,000 livres worth of booty. Angered, the buccaneers returned to the city and squeezed another 5 million livres out of the survivors. Despite their success, this raid generally marks the end of the buccaneers.[79]

With the loss of their base in Jamaica and later Tortuga, many buccaneers drifted north to the Bahamas or the American colonies. Neither place offered the same advantages as Jamaica and Tortuga, but given the threat presented by Royal Navy ships stationed in Jamaica, they were viable alternatives. By the turn of the century, pirates sailed from the American colonies for the West Indies, the west coast of Africa, or the Red Sea on a regular basis.[80]

The Bahamas met, to some degree, all three of the conditions necessary for piracy to thrive. They were strategically located near the Florida Straits and Windward Passage, two of the primary outlets to the Atlantic Ocean, thus giving the pirates a geographic advantage. In addition to that, the Bahamas were privately owned. King Charles II sold the Bahamas to six of the proprietors of South Carolina in 1670. Soon thereafter, in contrast to the governor of Jamaica's attempt to rein in privateering and piracy, the governor of the Bahamas began indiscriminately selling letters of marque to English pirates and privateers. Thus, political conditions in the Bahamas facilitated piracy. But the islands, which were first settled by Puritans in the 1640s, were sparsely populated. By 1671, the population was only 700 people. Consequently, the Bahamas were a poor market for the pirates' plunder at first. But colonial American smugglers soon established trading posts on the islands, providing a voracious market for the pirates' stolen goods. Despite that limitation, the Bahamas were a relatively safe haven, far from those who might capture and punish the rovers for their acts of piracy.[81]

The American colonies also became a hotbed of piracy. While the eastern seaboard of North America did not provide easy access to the West Indies shipping lanes, fertile hunting grounds existed off the coast of South Carolina and Virginia, two of the more prosperous colonies.[82] The colonies, however, did have a favorable political climate. Rhode Island, Massachusetts, Pennsylvania, New Jersey, New York, Delaware, Connecticut, North Carolina, and South Carolina all had reputations for harboring pirates. Many of the colonial governors were involved in piracy in some way. In addition to that, the colonies were eager consumers of pirate plunder. Since the Navigation Acts increased the cost of goods imported into the colonies, many colonials willingly purchased cheap stolen goods. Moreover, other colonials, flush with cash, eagerly invested in piratical ventures, outfitting privateers and outright pirates, who operated in the West Indies and Red Sea.[83] Thus, the American colonies met the three criteria for piracy reasonably well.

The Bahamas figure into both the beginning and end of this phase of piracy. In April 1696, the 46-gun privateer *Fancy* arrived in Nassau. The captain of the ship claimed to be Henry Bridgeman, and he offered to pay the Governor, Thomas Trott, £2,000 if he allowed Bridgeman to offload his cargo in Nassau. Since Trott's annual salary was only £300, the offer was too enticing to pass up. Thus, the notorious pirate John Avery (or Henry Every) reached the relative safety of the Bahamas.[84]

The previous summer, Avery and two other pirate vessels captured the 80-gun ship *Ganj-i-sawai* (also referred to as *Gunsway*) in the Red Sea. The largest ship in the fleet of the Great Mogul of India, it was a lucrative prize, bringing the pirates an estimated £150,000. But the attack outraged the Great Mogul, and he retaliated against the British East India Company by seizing its trading posts and imprisoning its representatives. Realizing they had to appease the Indian ruler, British officials put a £500 bounty on Avery and his crew. The East India Company pledge doubled that amount for the capture of any of Avery's men. Thus, Avery and his crew were in great need of a safe haven.[85]

Although Trott welcomed Avery, his men, and their money, they could not stay in Nassau for long. Since Trott was a proprietary governor, he did not have the authority to grant the men a pardon, and the governor of Jamaica refused a £20,000 bribe to do so. Therefore, the crew decided to disperse and disappear. Some 50 crewmembers traveled to the American colonies while 44 others sailed to Ireland in two groups. None of the pirates who went to the American colonies were ever caught. Some disappeared into the frontier while others bought protection from corrupt officials. Those who went to Ireland were not so fortunate. Seven were apprehended and five eventually hung. Avery was never heard from again.[86] Still, only 7 were caught and punished out of a crew of 94. Such results convinced many mariners that the opportunity to acquire great wealth through piracy outweighed the risk of capture and death, thus piracy blossomed in the late 17th and early 18th centuries.

During the last few decades of the 17th century, collusion with the pirates was endemic throughout the American colonies. Almost every seaboard colony was involved in piracy to some extent. Public involvement was so widespread that it was difficult, if not impossible, to convict pirates in the colonies. Frustrated that many pirates escaped punishment, King William III declared that jailers would be punished for allowing them to escape.[87]

Most of the New England colonies were especially involved in piracy. Rhode Island was considered by many to be the pirate capital of the colonies. Thomas Tew, a well-known Red Sea pirate, was a prominent citizen. Even though Rhode Island had little trade with England, more European goods were available in Newport than any other place in the colonies. Massachusetts also provided support to the buccaneers. Several governors were suspected of taking bribes from pirates. Pirates sentenced to hang could avoid that fate by paying a £13 fine or accepting indentured servitude in Virginia. Governor Sir William Phips supposedly invited the corsairs of Philadelphia to move to Boston, which was another notable pirate haven. When a French pirate arrived off Boston in 1684, city merchants sent a pilot to guide him into port and helped the brigands dispose of their ill-gotten gain. The governors of Connecticut normally left visiting pirates alone because of domestic politics. Connecticut was a trading colony and needed the hard currency the corsairs brought with them. Since governors were elected annually in Connecticut, few acted against the buccaneers because doing so almost guaranteed their ouster during the next election.[88]

Pirates provided a significant contribution to the economies of the mid-Atlantic colonies. Pirates reputedly put more than £100,000 into the New York economy each year. Governor Benjamin Fletcher, his secretary, the collector of customs, and the captain in charge of the New York guard ship were all in league with the buccaneers. Fletcher sold letters of marque for £300 and protection for £100 per man. Thomas Tew, who frequented

New York as well as Newport, was seen riding in Fletcher's carriage. The center for piracy in New York was the eastern shore of Long Island. New Jersey was also a known haunt for pirates. Some residents maintained that the King's laws against piracy did not apply in New Jersey since it was a proprietary colony. In Pennsylvania, another proprietary colony, several high-level officials consorted with the brigands. Lieutenant Governor William Markham supposedly sold protection to pirates at £100 per head. Markham also allowed his daughter to marry James Brown, one of Avery's crewmen. Brown was later elected to the Pennsylvania Assembly although he was subsequently expelled. Robert Snead, a successful pirate captain, was appointed Justice of the Peace in Pennsylvania.[89] Delaware, with easy access to the markets of Philadelphia and New York, was also a popular haven for corsairs. When a crown official in Newcastle proved too energetic in pursuing locally based pirates, residents threatened to throw him into prison if he did not leave the freebooters alone.[90]

Pirates found refuge in several of the southern colonies as well. South Carolina welcomed the pirates at first, but that sentiment changed rather quickly when the buccaneers began to prey on South Carolinian merchant vessels. Charleston, the colony's foremost port, was particularly vulnerable because of a substantial sandbar that forced ships to wait until high tide to cross it. Judge Robert Quary, who later gained a reputation as a pirate hunter in Pennsylvania, was removed from office several times in South Carolina because of his association with known pirates. As acting governor, he allowed buccaneers to openly land goods in Charleston and trade with local merchants. North Carolina was a poor state that produced little of trade value. Consequently, its citizens welcomed pirate booty, which they sold at cheap prices. From the pirates' perspective, North Carolina was an excellent haven because its many coves and creeks were excellent hiding places and its shallow waters made it difficult for warships to pursue them.[91]

Although it took decades, political reform and more aggressive operations by the Royal Navy finally eliminated piracy in the West Indies. By the end of the century, most of the notorious governors were replaced by more honest officials. The laws enacted to suppress piracy also took effect. Colonial Admiralty Courts made it easier to try and execute captured pirates. Moreover, the pirates hurt themselves by shifting their hunting grounds from the Caribbean to the Atlantic seaboard. Twenty years of piratical depredations along the American coast turned many of the colonials against them. All of those developments eventually resulted in the closing of the American colonies to the pirates.

The histories of two of the most renowned pirates, Captain William Kidd and Blackbeard, illustrate those points. Although one of history's most infamous pirates, Kidd was a privateer rather than a pirate. Unfortunately for him, he got caught in the policy transformation at the end of the 17th century, was accused of piracy, and ended up hanging for something he did not do.[92] William Kidd was a successful privateer during the Nine Years' War. By the mid-1690s, he was a well-respected citizen of New York, where he lived with his wife and children. In 1695, he received another privateer commission to chase pirates and French vessels. Among his backers was the new Governor of the New York and Massachusetts colonies, Lord Bellomont. Through Lord Bellomont, four high-ranking members of the British Government, the Lord Chancellor, Secretary of State, first Lord of the Admiralty, and Chief Justice, became silent partners in the venture. King William III granted Kidd three commissions that allowed him to capture French shipping, arrest pirates anywhere in the world, and keep all the booty without going through the courts. This last commission was especially important since the King got 10 percent of the take as well.[93]

Kidd's expedition was doomed almost from the beginning. As he left London in his new ship, the *Adventure Galley*, in February 1696, some of his best crewmen were impressed into the Royal Navy. He sailed on to New York, where he filled out his crew and then left for the west coast of Africa in September 1696. Ostensibly a pirate hunter, Kidd never captured any pirates. Instead, after months of unsuccessful cruising, he captured two ships with French passes, legal prizes under his commission. The first was a Dutch-owned vessel captured in November 1697. The second, captured in January 1698, carried a rich cargo owned by Muklis Khan, a high official in the court of the Great Mogul of India. Although the *Quedah Merchant* was a legal prize, the loss of another Indian ship to English predators once again angered the Indian emperor. He threatened to expel all European traders unless his subjects' losses were repaid and the perpetrators punished. The East India Company quickly compensated the owners for their goods, paid large bribes to Indian officials, and agreed to establish antipirate patrols in the Indian Ocean.[94]

Meanwhile, unaware of the hornet's nest he stirred up, Kidd began his return voyage home. He burned the *Adventure Galley* because its hull was rotten after months in the warm Indian Ocean waters and transferred his booty to the *Quedah Merchant*, which he renamed the *Adventure Prize*. Most of his crew decided to turn pirate and remain in the Indian Ocean. The rest returned home with Kidd. When the *Adventure Prize* reached the

Caribbean island of Anguilla in April 1699, Kidd learned that he had been declared a pirate the previous November. Hoping to clear his name, he left the *Adventure Prize* in Hispaniola and sailed for Boston to meet with Lord Bellomont, his patron. But Lord Bellomont, understanding the politics of the situation, arrested Kidd and sent him to London for trial.[95]

Kidd was a victim of domestic politics. By the time he arrived in London, his backers were too busy trying to protect themselves from impeachment proceedings brought up by the opposition party to protect Kidd. His primary defense was that both prizes were legal under his commission because they carried French passes. Mysteriously, those passes disappeared after Kidd turned them over to Lord Bellomont. Soon after testifying before the House of Commons in the impeachment proceeding, Kidd was convicted of piracy and murdering a crewmember. With no proof supporting his claim, Kidd was hung on 23 May 1701, thus removing a threat to the ruling party.[96]

Blackbeard, whose name was probably either Edward Teach or Edward Thatch, was an even more notorious but equally short-lived pirate. Blackbeard ravaged the Caribbean and east coast of the American colonies from 1716 to 1718.[97] Despite his reputation, he captured few rich prizes and never harmed any captives who fell under his control.[98] After his death, when his sloop and booty were auctioned off, they only brought in £2,500.[99] Still, his activities eventually raised the ire of the governor of Virginia, who mounted an expedition against his safe haven in North Carolina. Blackbeard was brought to justice when political and military leaders worked together to eliminate a serious threat to colonial American commerce.

Like Kidd, Blackbeard started out as a privateer. In 1716, he joined the crew of Benjamin Hornigold. Hornigold quickly recognized Blackbeard's abilities and gave him command of a sloop they captured. Together, they seized six prizes off the coast of the American colonies in 1717.[100] Late that summer, Blackbeard and Hornigold parted company. Blackbeard, now accompanied by the gentleman pirate Stede Bonnet, let loose a reign of terror along the Atlantic seaboard. During a 2-week period, Blackbeard captured more than 15 vessels and made himself famous.[101]

But the tide was already beginning to turn. Blackbeard learned from his victims that two frigates, the HMS *Rose* and HMS *Squirrel*, were now assigned to Boston, the HMS *Phoenix* recently took station in New York, and the HMS *Lyme* joined the HMS *Shoreham* off the Virginia capes.[102] Then, in July 1718, Woodes Rogers arrived in the Bahamas and restored

Royal control over the islands. With the loss of the Bahamas as a safe haven, it was only a matter of time before the pirates succumbed.

Before he arrived, Rogers convinced the King to issue a general pardon for any crime committed before 5 January 1718. Proclaimed on 5 September 1717, any pirate could take advantage of the offer before 5 September 1718. Along with the pardon, the King also established bounties for anyone who spurned the pardon.[103] More than 200 of the 500 pirates inhabiting the Bahamas eventually took the pardon.[104] Among those who accepted the pardon were Benjamin Hornigold, who later completely forsook his former compatriots and became a pirate hunter, working for Rogers.[105]

Meanwhile, Blackbeard moved northward to the Carolinas. In January 1718, he met Charles Eden, the Governor of North Carolina. They quickly came to a mutually beneficial understanding. Eden pardoned Blackbeard for his crimes and allowed the pirates to keep their loot. In exchange, Eden became a silent partner in Blackbeard's ventures.[106]

After resting and refitting in North Carolina, Blackbeard set out on another cruise in March 1718. Again sailing with Stede Bonnett, Blackbeard captured several prizes in the Caribbean.[107] In May 1718, his squadron grown to four ships and 400 men, Blackbeard blockaded Charleston, completely stopping all shipping in and out of the port. One week later, Blackbeard unexpectedly left after extorting a chest of medicine from the city. He returned to North Carolina where he wrecked two of his ships and marooned most of his crew in an effort to avoid sharing his meager booty with so many people. Once again, Governor Eden gave Blackbeard a pardon for his crimes and convened an Admiralty Court that confirmed the legality of his prize.[108]

Blackbeard remained in North Carolina for several months. He married a planter's daughter and lived lavishly. Eventually, his money began to run out, so he set out on another cruise. This time, he captured a French ship carrying sugar. When he returned to North Carolina, Blackbeard claimed that he found the ship wrecked at sea and merely took over the abandoned vessel and sailed her back to North Carolina. Once again, Governor Eden played along. He convened an Admiralty Court that confirmed Blackbeard's claim. Eden received a gift of 60 barrels of sugar from Blackbeard.[109]

Blackbeard's luck finally ran out in November 1718. His blockade of Charleston concerned the Governor of Virginia, Alexander Spottswood, who feared a similar incident at the mouth of the Chesapeake Bay would devastate Virginia's economy. Consequently, in October 1718, he met with the commanders of the two British guardships, the HMS *Lyme* and HMS *Pearl*, to discuss plans to capture Blackbeard. Since both ships were too large to navigate the shallow inland waters of North Carolina, Spottswood agreed to buy two small unarmed sloops for the Royal Navy to use. Lieutenant Robert Maynard, the First Lieutenant on the HMS *Pearl*, was put in charge of the seaborne contingent. Maynard set out on 17 November 1718 with 35 sailors from the *Pearl* in his sloop and 25 more from the *Lyme* in the other sloop under the command of Mr. Hyde. Meanwhile, Captain Brand, Commander of the *Lyme*, set out for Bath by foot with a contingent of sailors. They did not reach Bath until 23 November. Before Brand arrived, in a dramatic encounter on 22 November, Lieutenant Maynard killed Blackbeard along with a dozen other pirates. He also captured 14 members of Blackbeard's crew, 13 of whom were later hanged. The Royal Navy suffered 11 dead and more than 20 wounded.[110]

Governor Eden tried to hide his complicity in the matter. In an attempt to obscure his relationship with Blackbeard, Eden accused Captain Brand and Governor Spottswood of illegally invading North Carolina. But Eden eventually gave up the 60 barrels of sugar as well as six slaves he received from Blackbeard when Lieutenant Maynard produced an incriminating letter found in Blackbeard's pocket. Despite such evidence, Eden managed to avoid prosecution, and he was able to protect his secretary, Tobias Knight, who was the primary liaison with Blackbeard, from charges of collusion with pirates.[111]

The increased presence of the Royal Navy in the West Indies and along the Atlantic seaboard helped accelerate the demise of the pirates. Beginning in 1717, the Royal Navy began stationing even more ships in the Americas.[112] From a peak of nearly 2,400 active pirates during 1719–1722, they declined to less than 200 by 1726.[113] Although many of the pirates retired into obscurity or died in combat or of disease, some 500 to 600 of them were captured and executed.[114] After years of ineffectiveness, the Royal Navy finally began to take its toll on the pirates.

In January 1722, HMS *Swallow* set out on an antipiracy cruise. On 5 February, *Swallow* spotted Bartholomew Roberts' squadron of ships off the coast of Africa. Roberts was one of the most successful pirates of this era, capturing more than 400 prizes during a career that lasted less than 3 years. When contrary winds forced *Swallow* to steer away, Roberts sent one of his ships, *Ranger* (32 guns), after what he assumed was a Portuguese merchant ship fleeing the flotilla. *Swallow* slowed to allow *Ranger* to overtake her. When the pirates finally realized they were chasing a warship, it was too late. After a short engagement, during which she suffered 26 casualties, *Ranger* surrendered. Once she secured her prize, *Swallow* returned to confront the remaining pirates. On 10 February, *Swallow* defeated Roberts' ship, *Royal Fortune* (40 guns). Roberts was killed during the action. Of his crew, 54 were executed, 37 were sentenced to work in the mines of the Royal Africa Company, 74 were acquitted, and 70 black pirates were given up as slaves.[115]

Other victories soon followed. In May 1722, HMS *Launceton* (40 guns) captured a Spanish pirate ship off Hispaniola. Of the 58 crewmembers, 41 were later executed in Jamaica. The next year, in May 1723, HMS *Winchelsea* captured the pirate captain Finn and eight crewmen on Tobago. Six of the pirates were hung in Antigua. The next month, on 10 June 1723, HMS *Greyhound* engaged two pirate ships commanded by Edward Low, a pirate renowned for his brutality, off the coast of Long Island. Although Low escaped, he never surfaced again and was either lost at sea or retired from piracy. But *Greyhound* captured Low's escort, and 26 pirates were executed on 19 July 1723.[116]

The British Government augmented the Royal Navy's effort by commissioning pirate hunters. In November and December 1715, the governor of Jamaica sent out 10 ships to hunt pirates. One of those vessels, the *Tyger*, commanded by Jonathan Barnet, captured Calico Jack Rackham in November 1720. Rackham was notable as the lover of the female pirate Anne Bonney. Another female pirate, Mary Read, was also captured on Rackham's ship. Although Rackham was executed on 27 November 1720, Bonney and Read escaped punishment by claiming they were pregnant.[117]

A few months after Blackbeard terrorized Charleston, two more pirate ships showed up off the entrance to the port and captured several merchant vessels. Alarmed by the continual attacks on the colony's commerce, the governor commissioned two privateers, the *Henry* (8 guns) and *Sea Nymph* (8 guns), to capture the pirates. Although they failed to catch the two pirates they set out after, they did capture Blackbeard's compatriot Stede Bonnet on 8 October 1718. During the engagement, 18 of the privateers and 9 pirates were killed. Bonnet and 34 of his men were captured. Despite considerable public sentiment to pardon the gentlemanly Bonnet, South Carolina officials hung Bonnet and 29 others the next month.[118]

In October 1722, the privateer *Eagle* discovered a ship careening on a deserted island. Suspecting it to be a pirate vessel, the *Eagle* closed on the ship. When the pirates began firing at the *Eagle*, she stood off and pounded the vulnerable pirate ship. Although several of the pirates escaped into the jungle, most of them remained with their ship and were captured. The privateers searched for those who escaped and eventually captured five more. During a subsequent search, the pirate captain, George Lowther, was found dead with a pistol at his side, an apparent suicide. Eleven of the pirates were later executed.[119]

Piracy in the Caribbean finally ended when two of the pillars of piracy, political turmoil and safe havens were removed. With the repudiation of the "no peace beyond the line" doctrine and government actions that made it harder to obtain letters of marque, it became increasingly difficult for the pirates to maintain a façade of legitimacy. Once they became enemies of all nations, they faced opponents such as the Royal Navy that were too powerful to successfully resist. Moreover, as the political climate changed from that of support for the pirates to opposition to their actions, their safe havens were slowly taken away from them. Without places to rest, refit, and sell their ill-gotten gains, the pirates could not sustain themselves. New legislation against piracy, pardons, rewards for their capture, and speedy trials and executions also took their toll on the pirates. By 1730, piracy in the West Indies was over. It would remain dormant until conditions allowed it to resume in the first quarter of the 19th century.

19th-Century Piracy

On 19 December 1818, the *Emma Sophia* was accosted by a Spanish privateer in the Santaren Channel. Facing a privateer armed with a swivel gun and 30 crewmen, the unarmed *Emma Sophia* surrendered without a fight. After taking over the ship, the pirates sailed the *Emma Sophia* to the Florida Keys where they expertly transferred the merchant vessel's cargo to other ships in the harbor. Once they finished offloading the cargo, the pirates ransacked the ship, looking for hidden valuables. Frustrated by not finding anything else of value, they began threatening the crew of the *Emma Sophia*. When their threats failed to produce any results, they prepared to hang one of the ship's officers from a yard arm. Before they could do so, the man jumped over the side of the ship but weighed down by his clothes, he was quickly recaptured. Despite their blood-thirsty reputation, the pirates took no further action against the crew. Later that night, the privateer set sail, leaving the *Emma Sophia* to continue on its way, minus its cargo.[120] The officer later warned that "the neighborhood of Cuba will be troubled waters until our government shall seriously determine to put down this system of piracy."[121]

Within a few months, the United States Government did act. On 3 March 1819, Congress authorized President James Monroe to dispatch naval forces south to deal with the pirates. But suppressing those pirates proved difficult because of the three conditions that facilitate piracy. As in the earlier period of Caribbean piracy, the geography of the region was favorable to piracy. Many of the pirates operated along the northern coast of Cuba or Puerto Rico, where there were many coves and creeks protected by shallow water and dangerous reefs, making them inaccessible to frigates and larger warships. The islands' dense forests grew right up to the waters' edge, which made it easy for the pirates to hide their vessels. Finally, since there was plenty of fresh water, fruit, and fish along the coast, the pirates had little difficulty sustaining themselves.[122] This was also a period of significant political turmoil. The Napoleonic Wars, the Haitian Revolution, and the Wars for Latin American Independence fueled privateering activities. Even though the United States was ostensibly neutral, American merchant vessels were vulnerable to privateers who strayed over the line into piracy. Finally, there were safe sanctuaries ashore in Cuba and Puerto Rico. Merchants and local officials tacitly, and sometimes even overtly, supported and profited from the activities of the Spanish pirates.

Suppressing piracy was also a challenge because it was such a lucrative business that it attracted more than 10,000 participants during 1820–1830. Those pirates captured about 500 vessels worth approximately $20 million in the Caribbean during that timeframe. As a point of comparison, the cost of running the United States Government in 1821, including interest payments and redemption of the public debt, was $19.785 million.[123]

Although rewarding, piracy was also a dangerous business. Even though no more than 2,000 pirates were active at any one time, US naval forces engaged about 3,000 buccaneers during the 1820s, capturing 79 ships and 1,300 pirates. The Royal Navy snared 13 pirate craft and 291 pirates. The Spanish Navy was not very active, but they still managed to catch 150 men and 5 vessels.[124] Although no estimates are available of the number of pirates killed during antipiracy operations, that number was quite substantial as well.

The United States Navy engaged pirates in the West Indies decades before Congress acted in 1819. On 1 January 1800, the 12-gun schooner *Experiment* was attacked by Haitian pirates in 10 barges while escorting 4 merchantmen. Although greatly outnumbered, the *Experiment* sunk three of the barges and drove off the rest, saving two of ships. Luckily, the crews of the two captured vessels managed to escape.[125] The hero of this battle, Lieutenant David Porter, was wounded, but he survived to fight pirates repeatedly in the Caribbean.

A few years later, after the United States bought the Louisiana Territory from France, President Thomas Jefferson expressed concern about the rampant smuggling and piracy at the mouth of the Mississippi River,

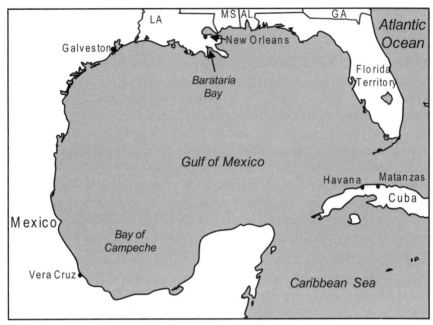

Figure 3. Gulf of Mexico.

where French and Spanish privateers and pirates operated with impunity. On 3 December 1805, he commented in his annual message that "our coasts have been infested. . . . They have captured, in the very entrance of our harbors as well as on the high seas, not only the vessels of our friends coming to trade with us, but our own also."[126] Consequently, President Jefferson decided to establish a naval station in New Orleans to combat the pirates. Captain John Shaw took command of 20 gunboats and 400 sailors in 1806. Shaw's forces were, however, ineffective because most citizens were sympathetic to the pirates and smugglers. Civil authorities were unwilling to prosecute the pirates in court and Governor William C.C. Claiborne was reluctant to help because he needed local political support.[127] (Figure 3 shows the Gulf of Mexico.)

The situation soon changed when Master Commandant David Porter arrived in New Orleans in 1808.[128] Porter, like Shaw, was stymied at first. He had to deal with local hostility, the poor material condition of his gunboats, and a shortage of sailors. On top of that, he contracted yellow fever. Meanwhile, the pirates and smugglers under Jean Lafitte prospered and grew stronger at their headquarters on Grand Terre Island in Barataria Bay. By the end of 1809, more than 30 ships and untold numbers of boats operated from Grand Terre Island.[129]

Porter realized his force was too small to take on the Baratarian pirates, but in early 1810, he got word of the arrival of three pirate vessels at the mouth of the Mississippi River and moved against them. When Porter demanded their surrender, the pirates refused. Instead, they contacted the Federal district attorney, Mr. P. Grymes, who informed Porter he did not have the right to detain the pirates. An infuriated Porter warned the pirates that, if they did not surrender immediately, he would attack. The pirates backed down and surrendered, but the battle was not yet over because the pirates had to be tried in the district court by Mr. Grymes! While the pirate crews sauntered about the city, bragging that they would be acquitted, Porter was threatened and shunned by the citizens of New Orleans. At one point, the pirates even brought suit against Porter for detaining them. Finally, after stationing marines in the courtroom, the largest of the three pirate vessels, the *Montebello*, was condemned and sold as a prize.[130] This incident highlights the difficulty of combating piracy if the pirates are favored by safe sanctuaries ashore.

Although Jean Lafitte and the Baratarian pirates continued to operate from Grand Terre Island, they were somewhat less brazen after Porter's actions. Finally, in September 1814, Porter's successor, Commodore Daniel T. Patterson, moved against Lafitte.[131] Patterson conducted a joint operation in conjunction with soldiers from the 44th Infantry Regiment. They attacked the pirate haven on 16 September, but the buccaneers got word of the operation and fled before the soldiers and sailors arrived. Even though they captured 10 pirate vessels and $500,000 worth of goods, most of the 800 to 1,000 brigands living on the island escaped.[132] But the impact of Patterson's mission was short lived; the Baratarian corsairs returned to the island and resumed operations soon after the soldiers and sailors left. The temporary nature of Patterson's operation demonstrates the importance of permanently eliminating pirate havens ashore. Commodore Patterson emphasized that point in a letter to the Secretary of the Navy in April 1815 when he wrote, "The immediate return of these people to their former mode of life will point out the indispensable necessity of keeping a small active naval force on this station in time of peace."[133]

The end of the Napoleonic Wars meant that many privateers lost their veneer of legitimacy. Some continued on as before, operating as out-and-out pirates. Others obtained letters of marque from the former Spanish colonies that revolted from Spain in 1810–1811. Many of those fledgling nations began issuing letters of marque to privateers soon after they rebelled. Even though the United States was sympathetic to the new republics, some of their privateers preyed on American shipping.[134] Even more troublesome were the actions taken by Spain in response to the successes achieved by the Latin American rebels. Spain imposed a blockade on most of the South and Central American nations. But without sufficient forces to enforce the blockade, it was merely a pretext for Spanish warships and privateers to seize neutral vessels violating the blockade. In one case, three Spanish naval ships were assigned responsibility for patrolling 1,200 miles of coastline.[135] Because of the Spanish Navy's weakness, Spanish officials used privateers to enforce the blockade. Many of the privateers focused on American shipping in retaliation for the support given to the Latin American revolutionaries. Preying on American shipping became so lucrative that other Spaniards resorted to outright piracy. Operating along the coast of Cuba and Puerto Rico, they attacked innocent vessels transiting coastal waters. Local authorities provided political cover and Spanish merchants eagerly disposed of the stolen goods at cut-rate prices. Their depredations soon began to affect American shipping, and insurance rates increased by more than 100 percent over a 1-year period.[136] Merchants, shipowners, and insurance companies clamored for help.

The Federal Government acted in response to the threat. First, as noted previously, Congress authorized President Monroe to deploy naval forces to combat pirates in the West Indies. Second, in the summer of 1819, the President sent Captain Oliver Hazard Perry, hero of the Battle of Lake Erie, on a delicate diplomatic mission to South America. Perry's job was to convince the South Americans to restrain their privateers without jeopardizing the United States good relations with those countries. His first stop was Venezuela. Although Perry's mission was a success, since Venezuela agreed to restrict the actions of its privateers and promised to pay restitution for previous losses, Perry contracted yellow fever and died on his way home. Consequently, the South American mission foundered.[137]

Meanwhile, US naval forces began operations against pirates in the West Indies. One of the first targets was Jean Lafitte. Although Lafitte received a presidential pardon as a reward for his support to Andrew Jackson during the Battle of New Orleans, he soon returned to his old ways. Lafitte moved his operation from Louisiana to Galveston, which he claimed was the capital of the province of Texas in the Republic of Mexico.[138] Galveston was a perfect location for Lafitte; it was outside of the United States yet close to New Orleans. Lafitte thrived until a combination of events did him in. First, in September 1818, Galveston was hit by a powerful hurricane that devastated the town and almost ruined Lafitte financially.[139] Second, the New Orleans station began to operate more aggressively against pirates in the Gulf of Mexico. Lafitte lost one of his newest vessels to those operations.[140] Third, increased competition with Spanish pirates made it more difficult to capture valuable prizes. Finally, in 1821, the United States Navy acted to eliminate Lafitte's haven in Galveston by sending the *Enterprise*, Lieutenant Lawrence Kearny commanding, to Galveston to root Lafitte out of his safe haven. Although Kearny did not dispute Lafitte's claim that Galveston was outside of the jurisdiction of the United States, legal constraints did not deter him from warning Lafitte that failure to leave would precipitate an attack. Lafitte acquiesced to the demand and abandoned Galveston, burning what he could not take with him.[141] With the loss of his secure base, Lafitte disappeared from the pages of history.

While Commodore Patterson's forces harried Jean Lafitte, other Navy ships commenced operations off the coast of Cuba and Puerto Rico. Initially, these were single ship missions. In 1820, the *Enterprise* (12 guns), *Nonsuch* (8 guns), *Lynx* (6 guns), and gunboats *Nos. 158* and *168* cruised the waters of the Caribbean looking for pirates. The Secretary of the Navy also directed all US Navy ships returning to the United States from Africa, the Mediterranean, and other places to sail through the West Indies as a further deterrent. Despite their presence, pirates seized 27 ships in 1820.[142]

By 1821, there were six US Navy ships assigned to antipiracy operations in the West Indies: *Hornet* (18 guns), *Enterprise* (12 guns), *Spark* (12 guns), *Porpoise* (12 guns), *Shark* (12 guns), and *Grampus* (12 guns).[143] The *Porpoise*, *Shark*, and *Grampus* each carried a large barge armed with a cannon for operations in shallow waters. Although they operated independently, they had a little more success against the freebooters. On 16 October 1821, while cruising off Cape Antonio, Cuba, *Enterprise* caught four pirate vessels robbing three US merchant ships. Since the water was too shallow for *Enterprise* to engage the pirates, Lieutenant Kearny sent five of the ship's boats in pursuit of them. The sailors rescued the merchant ships and captured 40 brigands and two of their vessels. The rest of the pirates escaped ashore.[144] A month later, *Enterprise* cleaned out a buccaneer haven near Cape Antonio. Two months later, on 21 December 1821, *Enterprise* captured another pirate ship, but once again, its crew escaped ashore.[145] The *Hornet* captured the corsair schooner *Moscow* on 29 October 1821. After escorting several merchant ships to Havana and Matanzas, *Porpoise* sailed west toward Cape Antonio. On 16 December 1821, *Porpoise*, Lieutenant James Ramage commanding, encountered the brig *Bolina*, out of Boston, and learned that pirates plundered *Bolina* the previous day. Because a shallow reef extended far from the shore, Lieutenant Ramage sent 40 men in the ship's boats to find the buccaneers.

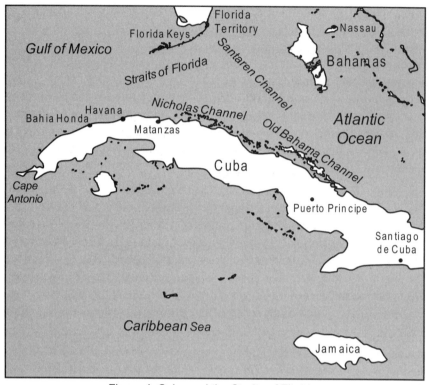

Figure 4. Cuba and the Straits of Florida.

They captured one corsair vessel and burned five others. Once again, most of the brigands escaped ashore, but the sailors caught three pirates and killed several others.[146] (Figure 4 shows Cuba and the Straits of Florida.)

Several lessons stand out from these early attempts to suppress Spanish piracy. First, the rules of engagement were too restrictive. American sailors were not allowed to land on Spanish soil, and all captured pirates were turned over to Spanish authorities. Since the Spanish were sympathetic and often worked with the buccaneers, they were usually released after a cursory trial.[147] Second, it is almost impossible to stamp out piracy if the brigands have support and sanctuary ashore. Time after time, the pirates escaped ashore, out of the reach of the American sailors. Third, the US naval squadron was not equipped with the right mix of vessels. Larger ships were ineffective pirate hunters. They needed small, oar-powered craft that could maneuver along the coast in shallow water, searching for pirates hiding in coves and creeks.

Despite the best efforts of the US forces operating in the West Indies, attacks on American shipping increased. Moreover, the pirates increasingly treated their captives harshly, torturing or killing many crewmembers. In September 1821, three American merchant ships were captured near the entrance to Matanzas harbor. The crew of one ship was beaten and the vessel was set on fire. The crewmembers managed to escape ashore in their boat. The captain and two other people were killed on the second ship. The entire crew of the third ship was killed and that vessel was also set afire. Spanish corsairs captured the *Exertion* in November 1821 and marooned the crew on a deserted island.[148] These and other outrages drove home the need for a strong, permanent naval presence in the West Indies.

Consequently, Congress authorized the establishment of a West Indies squadron in 1822. Commodore James Biddle assumed command of a powerful force, including the frigates *Macedonian* (36 guns) and *Congress* (32 guns); the corvettes *Cyane* (32 guns) and *John Adams* (24 guns); the 18 gun sloops *Hornet* and *Peacock*; the brigs *Spark* (12 guns) and *Enterprise* (12 guns); the 18-gun schooners *Alligator*, *Grampus*, *Shark*, and *Porpoise*; and gunboats *Nos. 158* and *168*. Altogether, there were some 1,300 sailors and marines in this naval force.[149]

Commodore Biddle deployed in *Macedonian* in April 1822. Upon arrival off the coast of Cuba, Biddle contacted the governor and Captain General of Cuba, Don Nicholas Mahy, and asked him to cooperate with the antipiracy operation by allowing US sailors to pursue pirates ashore. By this time, relations between the United States and Spain were strained since the United States recognized the independence of Spain's rebellious colonies the month before. In addition to that, the Spanish were concerned that American adventurers might invade Cuba in an attempt to bring it into the Union as another slave state. Consequently, Mahy demurred, replying that he was doing all that was necessary to suppress piracy in Cuba. Biddle also contacted the governor of Puerto Rico. Although he was cordial, he too denied Biddle's request. Fortunately, Biddle's request was merely a formality; the Secretary of the Navy changed the rules of engagement before Biddle departed, giving him permission to land in remote areas of Cuba and Puerto Rico while pursuing pirates.[150]

Even though the Spanish were not cooperative, the squadron vigorously pursued the Cuban pirates. In March 1822, boat crews from the *Enterprise* captured two launches and four boats in a creek near Cape Antonio. A few days later, on 6 March, the *Enterprise* apprehended 8 pirate craft and 160 buccaneers.[151] *Grampus* captured the Spanish privateer *Palmyra* during a short battle on 15 August 1822.[152] *Peacock*, Captain Stephen Cassin commanding, seized a pirate boat 60 miles west of Havana on 28 September. That afternoon, *Peacock* encountered *Speedwell*, an American merchant vessel, and learned that corsairs attacked her 2 hours earlier.

Peacock set out in pursuit. When *Peacock* reached the coast, Cassin sent 50 men in the ship's boats to search along the coast. They were unsuccessful on the 28th, but they spied a sail along the shore the next day. This time, when Cassin dispatched sailors from the *Peacock* in the ship's boats, they found their quarry and captured four schooners. Once again, most of the pirates got away on shore.[153]

It is important to note that much of the American squadron's work was performed in open boats away from the mother ship. Sailors and marines rowed for days and days, searching for pirates hiding in the many coves and inlets along the Cuban coast. One officer later recalled that he and his crew once spent 68 consecutive days in an open barge searching for corsairs along the northwest coast of Cuba.[154] While in the boats, the crews were vulnerable to attack by larger pirate vessels, subjected to the unrelenting Caribbean sun, and exposed to dangerous diseases such as yellow fever and malaria. It was slow, arduous, and dangerous work.

Despite the increased American presence, the pirate marauding continued. In May 1822, pirates plundering the brig *Aurilla* showed considerable ingenuity when they tricked the *Aurilla*'s crew into revealing all of ship's hidden money. The brigands smeared fresh chicken blood on the ship's windlass. Then, they brought the *Aurilla*'s crewmembers topside one at a time and told the sailors that they killed the other crewmen because they refused to talk. The chicken blood was a convincing prop; each sailor told the pirates as much as they knew, and consequently, the pirates found all of the money hidden on the ship.[155] Other corsairs were not as gentle with their victims. In July 1822, Spanish freebooters made the master of the British merchant ship *Blessing* walk the plank when he refused to tell them where his money was. When he tried to swim away, the pirate captain shot and killed him. Not satisfied, the pirate captain smashed the skull of the master's 14-year-old son when he could not stop crying after witnessing his father's murder.[156] By the end of the year, the *United States Gazette* estimated that almost 3,000 acts of piracy had been committed in the Caribbean and Gulf of Mexico from 1815 to 1822.[157]

Toward the end of the year, an event occurred that further galvanized American public opinion against the pirates. On 9 November 1822, Lieutenant William Allen, a War of 1812 naval hero, was killed while pursing Spanish corsairs. Allen, Commanding Officer of the *Alligator*, encountered two American sailors on 8 November while in Matanzas. They informed Allen that pirates had captured their ships and that they were trying to raise the $7,000 ransom. Allen immediately set sail toward the bay where the brigands were hiding. There, he discovered the two

American vessels as well as three pirate schooners and three more merchant vessels. Even though there were more than 100 buccaneers on their three schooners, Allen took 40 sailors and marines in the ship's boats and set out to get them. As the Americans approached the first schooner, the pirates began firing muskets and cannon at the Americans. Although he was wounded by the gunfire, Allen pressed on. The buccaneers panicked, abandoned their ship, and fled toward a second pirate schooner. Most of the pirates escaped on that vessel, but they abandoned their prizes and two schooners. Four Americans, including Lieutenant Allen, were killed and three others were wounded. At least 14 brigands were killed during the engagement.[158]

Less than a month later, the Secretary of the Navy advised Congress that the West Indies squadron needed to be expanded to improve its ability to combat the pirates. Secretary Smith Thompson recommended adding a steamboat, 10 shallow draft schooners, and 5 barges large enough to carry 40 men. Congress quickly approved the recommendation.[159]

Secretary Thompson picked Captain David Porter to command the expanded naval flotilla. Porter immediately went to work building his new command. He purchased eight small schooners: *Beagle*, *Ferret*, *Fox*, *Greyhound*, *Jackal*, *Terrier*, *Weasel*, and *Wild Cat*. Each was armed with three cannon and carried a complement of 31 personnel. Porter also acquired five large, 20-oar barges for use in the shallow waters along the coast of Cuba—the *Gnat*, *Gallinipper*, *Midge*, *Mosquito*, and *Sandfly*. The barges were particularly important since American sailors spent much of their time in open boats searching the Cuban coast for pirates. Finally, Porter procured a storeship, *Decoy*, and a steam-powered riverboat, *Sea Gull*. The *Sea Gull* was the second steam-powered vessel in the United States Navy and the first to actively serve as a warship. It was armed with five cannon.[160]

Commodore Porter and his "Mosquito Squadron" set sail on 15 February 1823. His mission was to suppress piracy, protect US commerce, and stop the illegal slave trade. He was also directed to establish relations with any foreign naval forces conducting antipiracy operations. This meant coordinating his operations with his old nemesis, the Royal Navy. Porter also benefited from an important change to the rules of engagement. He was allowed to pursue pirates ashore in inhabited areas as well as unsettled places. The only stipulation was that he had to notify local officials before he acted and assure them that his only purpose in landing was to capture pirates. This was a significant improvement over the rules with which Commodore Biddle had to comply.[161]

Porter arrived in St. Thomas in early March 1823 and immediately began deploying his forces. He sent *Shark* and three of the small schooners to patrol the southern coast of Puerto Rico. The *Fox* was dispatched to San Juan, Puerto Rico, to obtain a list of all legally commissioned privateers and a copy of their instructions. When the *Fox* entered San Juan harbor on 3 March, a shore battery fired at the ship, killing the Commanding Officer, Lieutenant William H. Cocke. Many in the American squadron believed that the Spanish fired at the *Fox* in retaliation for the capture of the *Palmyra* the previous August. But Porter, who was notorious for his temper, was surprisingly diplomatic and accepted the governor of Puerto Rico's apology for the incident. Still, Porter failed to gain the governor's cooperation with his mission.[162]

Stymied in Puerto Rico, Porter sailed to Cuba and began searching the coast for corsairs. The squadron achieved significant results almost immediately. The barges *Gallinipper* and *Mosquito* rescued an American merchant vessel on 8 April 1823. The American sailors killed two pirates and captured one other.[163] The rest of the brigands got away. Eight days later, on 16 April 1823, the two barges, along with *Peacock*, spotted a pirate felucca propelled by 16 oars near the harbor of Colorados. Although the pirates escaped, *Peacock* captured the felucca, and the buccaneers burned three other schooners before they fled.[164]

On 2 June 1823, *Grampus* rescued the crew of the American schooner *Shiboleth* after it was attacked by pirates. The brigands snuck up on the ship, killed the watch, and confined the rest of the crew in the forecastle. After they took what they wanted, the corsairs set the ship on fire. The crew managed to break out of the forecastle, but the ship was still on fire when *Grampus* arrived and rescued the remaining crewmembers. The same pirates were hunted down by Spanish dragoons after they attacked another merchant ship several days later. Once again, the buccaneers managed to escape.[165]

Also in June, *Ferret* tried to engage some pirates near Matanzas, but as its boat rowed toward the pirates, they shot a hole in the *Ferret*'s boat. The boat returned the *Ferret* before it sank, but the *Ferret*, unable to approach the buccaneers because of shallow water, sailed away in frustration. The *Ferret* soon encountered a small coastal vessel, which it commandeered. After returning to the bay to resume the attack, the *Ferret* was forced to abandon the operation because of bad weather. The next day, *Ferret* encountered a British merchant ship, which loaned the Americans a boat. When the *Ferret*'s crew returned to the spot, they only found the two boats that had been sunk by *Ferret*'s cannon fire.

On 5 July 1823, the *Sea Gull*, with the barges *Gallinipper* and *Mosquito* in tow, searched the Cuban coast for pirates. Lieutenant William Watson sent the two barges into the bay where Lieutenant Allen was killed months earlier. The Americans soon discovered a corsair schooner and launch plundering several merchant ships at anchor. Watson, who was embarked in the *Gallinipper*, immediately ordered the two barges to attack the schooner. The schooner tried to sail away, but the barges pursued the pirates to an anchorage near a village. Although they were significantly outnumbered and outgunned, the Americans stubbornly pressed home the attack. Once again, the brigands panicked and fled the ship. The Americans, yelling "Allen, Allen," showed the buccaneers no mercy. Those not cut down on the schooner were slaughtered in the water as they tried to swim ashore. Only 15 made it ashore, and the angry sailors ran down and killed 11 of them. The other four were seized by the villagers. Out of 70 to 80 corsairs, only 5 survived the American attack.[166]

By the end of the summer, the American effort to suppress piracy in the Caribbean was working. Even though piracy along the coast was still problematic, reports of piracy on the high seas waned. Porter established a virtual blockade of Matanzas, which effectively eliminated one of the pirates' most important havens. But just when it appeared that the tide was turning, yellow fever struck Porter's squadron in August. Porter withdrew most of his forces from the unhealthy Caribbean waters. Those that remained were stretched too thin, and consequently, there was a resurgence of piracy in the West Indies. Still, by the end of the year, President James Monroe was able to report that "the piracies by which our commerce in the neighborhood of the island of Cuba had been afflicted have been repressed, and the confidence of our merchants, in a great measure, restored."[167]

The British West Indies squadron, which had a few small vessels similar to the American squadron, contributed to the suppression of piracy in the Caribbean as well. British forces began actively patrolling for buccaneers in 1822. On 30 September 1822, the *Firme Union* (5 guns), a pirate felucca, attacked the sloop *Eliza* (1 gun) while cruising along the northern coast of Cuba in company with the *Tyne* (26 guns). After a running gun battle, the British boarded and captured the felucca. They killed 10 corsairs and drove the rest overboard. The British suffered two killed and seven wounded.[168] The *Grecian* (6 guns) captured the schooner *La Cata* (8 guns) on 1 March 1823 south of Cuba. Thirty pirates were killed, but only 3 were captured and almost 70 escaped.[169] Later that month, the *Tyne* and *Thracian* (18 guns) learned that the famed pirate Captain

Cayatano Aragonez in his ship *Zaragozana* (13 guns) was cruising nearby. The British ships spotted the *Zaragozana* on 31 March and gave chase. Aragonez sailed into Mata, on the eastern tip of Cuba, and anchored in the mouth of the harbor, ready to fight the British. Despite being outnumbered, British sailors rowed over to the pirate ship in their boats and captured it. Out of 70 to 80 buccaneers on board, 10 were killed, 28 captured, and the rest escaped ashore. Aragonez and the others who were captured were later hung for their crimes. The British lost only one killed and five wounded.[170]

Commodore Porter returned to the Caribbean in February 1824. This second cruise was much less successful than the first. There were few captures, and once again, the squadron was hit with another round of yellow fever in mid-spring. Porter himself contracted yellow fever for the third time. Weakened by the fever, Porter withdrew most of his force north by early July 1824.[171] In his absence, pirates, based primarily out of Puerto Rico, increased their attacks on merchant shipping. Between early July and early August, 10 incidents were reported.[172] Subsequent complaints by merchants and insurance companies led to criticism of Porter and put pressure on him to return to the Caribbean quickly and restore order.

Most of the squadron was back on station by October 1824.[173] Porter's third cruise was marred by a diplomatic gaffe involving Puerto Rico that led to Porter's removal in February 1825.[174] The only clashes with pirates of note involved the *Porpoise* and *Terrier*. In both cases, even though the American ships captured the corsairs' vessels, the crews managed to escape.[175]

The situation in the Caribbean changed for the better in 1825. During his final address to Congress in late 1824, President Monroe suggested that the United States might have to take more forceful actions against the Spanish in Cuba and Puerto Rico to end their support for piracy. Among his suggestions were hot pursuits ashore, reprisals against those assisting the pirates, and blockading ports implicated in piracy. Even though the United States did not act on any of those suggestions, fear of the American Government doing so motivated the Spanish to cooperate with the American squadron. At the same time, by 1825, Spanish opposition to the independence of the new South and Central American Republics waned. Thus, those countries stopped commissioning privateers, which took away one of Spain's primary justifications for using privateers. Finally, as the pirates were barred from the sea, they began to prey on Spanish citizens ashore. Consequently, the Spanish Army began to more actively patrol against pirates. Thus, in March 1825, when *Grampus* lured a pirate ship into attacking several armed schooners disguised as merchant ships, the Spanish Army captured those who escaped ashore and executed them.[176]

Another important reason for the eventual demise of piracy in the Caribbean was the cooperation between the United States and Great Britain. Although there was no formal agreement between the British and American commanders, both naval forces freely cooperated with one another. The most significant joint operation occurred in March 1825 when the *Sea Gull* and *Gallinipper* met the *Dartmouth*. The Commanding Officer of the *Sea Gull*, Lieutenant Isaac McKeever, learned that *Dartmouth*'s boats and two British schooners, *Lion* and *Union*, were searching the Cuban coast for pirates. McKeever transferred to the *Gallinipper* and led the combined US-British force against some buccaneers hiding near the mouth of the Sagua la Grande River. There, on 25 March, they located and attacked a corsair schooner. The allies killed 8 brigands and captured 19 more with only one slight casualty. The next day, they captured another pirate schooner although this crew managed to escape ashore.[177] Even though there were several isolated incidents over the next few years, this successful mission essentially ended active piracy in the Caribbean.

The 19th century antipiracy mission of the United States clearly demonstrates the importance of the three conditions on the growth and sustainability of piracy. Piracy was a practical endeavor in the region because of the geography. Lucrative trade routes from New Orleans, South America, and Central America passed close to the two primary pirate havens: Cuba and Puerto Rico. Pirates could wait in the relative safety and security of the coves and bays along both coasts for a victim to sail too close. Once they found a target, they darted out from their protected location and quickly captured their prey. Political turmoil during the first quarter of the 19th century facilitated piracy. First the Napoleonic Wars and then the wars for South American and Latin American independence presented opportunities for privateers and pirates. Neutrals, such as the United States, were drawn into the fray when privateers exceeded their commissions and took readily available targets. Finally, Spanish pirates and privateers were able to operate with impunity for years because of the protection afforded them by Spanish civil authorities in Cuba and Puerto Rico. The pirates had safe havens where they could refit, recruit, relax, and sell their plunder.

Piracy ended only when those three conditions were negated. Constant patrols by American and British warships eventually made piracy too dangerous. The pirates lost their justification when Spain finally accepted the independence of its former colonies in South and Central America. But it was the elimination of their safe havens ashore that finally ended piracy in the Caribbean. Once the governors of Cuba and Puerto Rico decided it was in their nations' interests to stop providing support to the pirates, the pirates were quickly put out of business.

Notes

1. Kris E. Lane, *Pillaging the Empire: Piracy in the Americas, 1500–1750* (Armonk, NY: M.E. Sharpe, 1998), 18.

2. Peter Earle, *The Pirate Wars* (New York: St. Martin's Press, 2005), 92.

3. Stefan Eklof, *Pirates in Paradise: A Modern History of Southeast Asia's Maritime Marauders* (Copenhagen: NIAS Press, 2006), 7–9.

4. Ralph T. Ward, *Pirates in History* (Baltimore, MD: York Press, 1974), 20.

5. Hugh F. Rankin, *The Golden Age of Piracy* (New York: Holt, Rinehart & Winston, 1969), 17.

6. Philip Gosse, *The Pirates' Who's Who: Giving Particulars of the Lives and Deaths of the Pirates and Buccaneers* (Boston: Charles E. Lauriat & Co., 1924), 15.

7. Captain Charles Johnson, *The History of the Lives and Actions of the Most Famous Highwaymen, Street-Robbers, etc. To Which Is Added, a Genuine Account of the Voyages and Plunders of the Most Noted Pirates* (London: Longman, Hurst, Rees, Orme & Brown, 1813), 529.

8. Earle, 90.

9. Philip Gosse, *The History of Piracy* (New York: Tudor Publishing Company, 1932), 141.

10. Ibid., 142.

11. Ibid., 141.

12. Rankin, 16.

13. Gosse, *The History of Piracy*, 1.

14. Earle, 93.

15. David Watts, *The West Indies: Patterns of Development, Culture and Environmental Change Since 1492* (New York: Cambridge University Press, 1987), 121–122.

16. Lane, 18.

17. David Cordingly, consulting ed., *Pirates: Terror on the High Seas From the Caribbean to the South China Sea* (Atlanta, GA: Turner Publishing, 1996), 17.

18. Jan Rogozinski, *A Brief History of the Caribbean: From the Arawak and the Carib to the Present* (New York: Facts on File, 1992), 38.

19. Jan Rogozinski, *Pirates! Brigands, Buccaneers, and Privateers in Fact, Fiction, and Legend* (New York: De Capo Press, 1996), 241; Rogozinski, *A Brief History of the Caribbean*, 98; Watts, 130.

20. Rogozinski, *A Brief History of the Caribbean*, 26.

21. Cordingly, *Pirates*, 26–27; Rogozinski, *Pirates!*, 153.

22. Cordingly, *Pirates*, 27–29; Rogozinski, *Pirates!*, 153.

23. Cordingly, *Pirates*, 29–30.

24. Earle, 22.

25. Cordingly, *Pirates*, 33.

26. Earle, 23.

27. Cordingly, *Pirates*, 33.

28. Rogozinski, *A Brief History of the Caribbean*, 42.

29. Ibid., 36–39.

30. Ibid., 39.

31. Cordingly, *Pirates*, 34; Rogozinski, *A Brief History of the Caribbean*, 42.

32. Rankin, 7; Gosse, *The Pirates' Who's Who*, 20.

33. Brenda Lewis, *The Pirate Code: From Honorable Thieves to Modern-Day Villains* (Guilford, CT: Lyons Press, 2008), 102–103.

34. Cordingly, *Pirates*, 34.

35. Lewis, 103–104.

36. Rankin, 7–9.

37. Lewis, 117.

38. Rogozinski, *A Brief History of the Caribbean*, 83.

39. Ibid., 90.

40. Ibid., 86.

41. There is some doubt as to the actual existence of Pierre le Grand and when he took the Spanish treasure ship. Rogozinski sets the date of the action as about 1620, which matches other developments in the vicinity of Tortuga. Gosse states that le Grand took the Spanish ship in 1665, which is well into the buccaneer era. Both authors use Alexander Exquemelin's *Buccaneers of America*, which was first published in 1678. Exquemelin does not provide a date. See Rogozinski, *Pirates!*, 194–195; Gosse, *The History of Piracy*, 147–148.

42. Rogozinski, *A Brief History of the Caribbean*, 75; Rogozinski, *Pirates!*, 339.

43. Rogozinski, *A Brief History of the Caribbean*, 85; Rogozinski, *Pirates!*, 339–340.

44. Lewis, 104–106; Rankin, 8–9; Rogozinski, *Pirates!*, 340.

45. Rogozinski, *Pirates!*, 340.

46. Lane, 103–104.

47. Rankin, 12.

48. Rogozinski, *A Brief History of the Caribbean*, 91–92.

49. Ibid., 83; Lane, 105; Douglas R. Burgess Jr., *The Pirates' Pact: The Secret Alliances Between History's Most Notorious Buccaneers and Colonial America* (Chicago: McGraw-Hill, 2008), 45–47.

50. The *Marston Moor's* name was changed to the HMS *York* after the restoration of Charles II. See http://www.ageofnelson.org/MichaelPhillips/info.php?ref=6075 (accessed 23 March 2009).

51. Watts, 122–123; Rogozinski, *Pirates!*, 235–236.

52. Ibid.

53. Ibid. Despite the Spanish complaints, when Myngs returned to England in 1665, he was knighted and promoted to Vice Admiral. Less than a year later, in June 1666, he was mortally wounded in battle against the Dutch.

54. Earle, 95.

55. Rogozinski, *Pirates!*, 227–228.

56. Rogozinski, *Pirates!*, 228; Lewis, 125–126; Gosse, *The History of Piracy*, 156–157.

57. Rogozinski, *Pirates!*, 228–229; Lewis, 127–128; Gosse, *The History of Piracy*, 157.

58. Rogozinski, *Pirates!*, 229; Lewis, 129–130; Gosse, *The History of Piracy*, 158–159.

59. Earle, 95–96.

60. Rogozinski, *Pirates!*, 229; Gosse, *The History of Piracy*, 159–160.

61. Rogozinski, *A Brief History of the Caribbean*, 59–60; Lane, 69–70.

62. Rogozinski, *A Brief History of the Caribbean*, 95; Watts, 247.

63. E.O. Hoppe, *Pirates, Buccaneers, and Gentlemen Adventurers* (South Brunswick, NJ: A.S. Barnes & Co., 1972), 97.

64. Albert Marrin, *The Sea Rovers: Pirates, Privateers, and Buccaneers* (New York: Atheneum, 1984), 58.

65. Lewis, 131–132; Hoppe, 97; Marrin, 58.

66. Rankin, 16; Watts, 246; Earle, 146–147; Lewis, 116–118.

67. Earle, 96.

68. Earle, 146, 155, and 189.

69. Earle, 189; Colin Woodward, *The Republic of Pirates: Being the True and Surprising Story of the Caribbean Pirates and the Man Who Brought Them Down* (Orlando, FL: Harcourt, 2007), 34.

70. C.H. Haring, *The Buccaneers of the West Indies in the XVII Century* (New York: E.P. Dutton & Co., 1910), 230.

71. Earle, 99–100; Gosse, *The History of Piracy*, 315–316.

72. Earle, 136–137.

73. Ibid., 99–100.

74. Also known as King William's War (1689–1697) in the American colonies.

75. Also known as Queen Anne's War (1702–1713) in the American colonies.

76. Woodward, 86.

77. Lewis, 115; Rogozinski, *Pirates!*, 144.

78. The Treaty of Ratisbon between France and Spain was signed in August 1684. See Rogozinski, *A Brief History of the Caribbean*, 98; Rogozinski, *Pirates!*, 144.

79. Rogozinski, *A Brief History of the Caribbean*, 98–100.

80. Gosse, *The History of Piracy*, 176–177.

81. Rogozinski, *A Brief History of the Caribbean*, 88–89; Rogozinski, *Pirates!*, 239–240.

82. Rankin, 42.

83. Ibid., 54–58.

84. Rogozinski, *Pirates!*, 115–116; and Woodward, 12.

85. Rogozinski, *Pirates!*, 115–116; Woodward, 20–23; Gosse, *The History of Piracy*, 179.

86. Rogozinski, *Pirates!*, 115–116, Woodward, 24–26; Gosse, *The History of Piracy*, 179–180.

87. Rankin, 63.

88. Ibid., 56–57.

89. Ibid., 54.

90. Ibid., 54–57.

91. Ibid., 54–58.

92. Gosse, *The History of Piracy*, 180–181; Rogozinski, *Pirates!*, 179–181; Earle, 119–120.

93. Gosse, *The History of Piracy*, 180–183; Rogozinski, *Pirates!*, 179–181; Earle, 119–120.

94. Ibid.

95. Ibid.

96. Ibid.

97. Rogozinski, *Pirates!*, 335–336; Earle, 193–194; Marrin, 118–127.

98. Rogozinski, *Pirates!*, 335.

99. David Cordingly, *Under the Black Flag: The Romance and the Reality of Life Among the Pirates* (New York: Random House, 1995), 191.

100. Rogozinski, *Pirates!*, 164.

101. Cordingly, *Under the Black Flag*, 207.

102. Ibid., 208.

103. Ibid., 226.

104. Ibid., 236.

105. Rogozinski, *Pirates!*, 164.

106. Ibid., 335.

107. Ibid., 335.

108. Cordingly, *Under the Black Flag*, 253–255; Rogozinski, *Pirates!*, 335.

109. Rogozinski, *Pirates!*, 335.

110. Cordingly, *Under the Black Flag*, 194–201; Woodward, 282–298; Rogozinski, *Pirates!*, 335.

111. Woodward, 296–298.

112. Cordingly, *Under the Black Flag*, 208–209.

113. Angus Konstam, *Blackbeard: America's Most Notorious Pirate* (Hoboken, NJ: Wiley, 2006), 105.

114. Earle, 207.

115. Cordingly, *Under the Black Flag*, 209–216; Rogozinski, *Pirates!*, 292–294.

116. Cordingly, *Under the Black Flag*, 217–218.

117. Ibid., 219–220; Rogozinski, *Pirates!*, 33 and 281.

118. Cordingly, *Under the Black Flag*, 220–221; Rogozinski, *Pirates!*, 32–33.

119. Cordingly, *Under the Black Flag*, 221–222; Rogozinski, *Pirates!*, 205.

120. Wheeler, 82–85.

121. Ibid., 85.

122. Gardner W. Allen, *Our Navy and the West Indian Pirates* (Salem, MA: The Essex Institute, 1929), 1.

123. Francis B.C. Bradlee, *Piracy in the West Indies and Its Suppression* (Salem, MA: The Essex Institute, 1923), 21–22.

124. Ibid., 22.

125. Allen, 2–3.

126. Ibid., 3.

127. Wheeler, 30–31.

128. Master commandant was an intermediate rank between lieutenant and captain. Master commandants typically commanded ships too small for a captain but larger than those commanded by lieutenants. The rank was later shortened to commander.

129. Wheeler, 42–43.

130. Ibid., 44–45.

131. Commodore was a courtesy title used by Navy captains when in command of multiple ships. Congress was unwilling to establish the rank of admiral in the United States Navy because of its aristocratic connotations. Consequently, captain was the senior rank in the United States Navy until 1862.

132. Wheeler, 54–58; Allen, 6–8.

133. Allen, 8–9.

134. David F. Long, *Gold Braid and Foreign Relations: Diplomatic Activities of United States Naval Officers, 1798–1883* (Annapolis, MD: United States Naval Institute Press, 1988), 51.

135. Ibid., 58.

136. Bradlee, 22.

137. Edgar S. Maclay, *A History of the United States Navy from 1775 to 1894,* vol. II (New York: D. Appleton and Company, 1894), 106–108.

138. Long, 59–60.

139. Wheeler, 78–79.

140. Ibid., 96.

141. Ibid., 96–97.

142. Allen, 20.

143. Ibid., 22.

144. Bradlee, 13.

145. Maclay, 109–110.

146. Bradlee, 15–16.

147. Allen, 20–21.

148. Ibid., 22–23.

149. Wheeler, 99.

150. Ibid., 100.

151. Allen, 27.

152. Ibid., 32–33.

153. Ibid., 35–36.

154. Bradlee, 55.

155. Wheeler, 103.

156. Ibid., 104–105.

157. Ibid., 106.

158. Bradlee, 30–31; Wheeler, 107–108.

159. Wheeler, 110.

160. Ibid., 110–111. See also the *Dictionary of American Naval Fighting Ships* (Washington, DC: Department of the Navy Naval Historical Center), http://www.history.navy.mil/danfs/index.html, for more details on individual ships.

161. Allen, 41–42.

162. Wheeler, 114–116; Maclay, 113.

163. Wheeler, 118.

164. Bradlee, *Piracy in the West Indies and Its Suppression*, 38.

165. Ibid., 41.

166. Wheeler, 125–126.

167. Ibid., 132.

168. William L. Clowes, *The Royal Navy: A History from the Earliest Times to the Present*, vol. III (London: Sampson Low, Marston and Company, 1898), 234.

169. Wheeler, 117.

170. Clowes, 235.

171. Wheeler, 138–139.

172. Allen, 60.

173. Wheeler, 140.

174. Ibid., 156.

175. Maclay, 122.

176. Wheeler, 168.

177. Ibid., 169; Allen, 84.

Chapter 3

Piracy in the Mediterranean

In 78 BC, pirates from the island of Pharmacusa encountered a merchant vessel off the coast of Caria (modern-day Turkey). The slow-sailing ship was quickly overtaken by the pirate galley, which was propelled by oars manned by slaves. When the pirates boarded the ship, most of the passengers shrank back in terror. One passenger, a young Roman nobleman, ignored the pirates and continued reading a book. His indifferent attitude infuriated the pirates. Consequently, when they began setting the ransom prices for the passengers, the pirate leader doubled the price he thought reasonable, 10 talents to 20 talents, thinking he would put the arrogant young man in his place. Instead, the Roman nobleman haughtily responded, "If you knew your business, you'd realize I'm worth at least 50."[1]

It was difficult for the young man's friends to gather such a large sum, so the pirates played host to the young noble for 38 days.[2] During that time, he interacted with the pirates in a friendly manner by competing with them in athletic exercises, reading his poetry, and practicing his oratory. The young man continually reminded his captors, however, that once he was freed, he planned on returning to Pharmacusa and getting revenge by capturing and executing the pirates. The pirates, who regarded the man as a blustering youngster, thought his threat of crucifixion quite humorous.

When the ransom arrived, the young man was sent to Miletus in Asia Minor. Once there, he took command of four war galleys with 500 soldiers and returned to Pharmacusa. As he expected, the pirates were celebrating their good fortune when he arrived and were in no condition to resist the Roman troops. The nobleman recaptured his 50 talents as well as 350 pirates. He then set out for Pergamum to get permission from the Praetor to execute the pirates. When the Praetor hesitated, the young man carried out the sentence on his own authority. But he granted 30 of the pirates a favor for their good treatment: he ordered their throats cut before they were crucified to spare them the pain of the punishment.

Who was the arrogant young Roman? Julius Caesar. Caesar had been banished from Rome by Sulla and was traveling to Rhodes to work on his oratory when he was captured by Cilician pirates. At the time of his capture, piracy was rampant throughout the Mediterranean. Despite Caesar's harsh reprisal, piracy continued to plague the Romans and all others sailing the Mediterranean Sea for many years until Rome finally acted to stamp out piracy.[3]

Piracy in the Mediterranean has deep roots. Ancient writers note that both the Greeks and Romans suffered from piratical attacks. As with other geographical areas and periods, piracy was cyclical in the Mediterranean. When political turmoil embroiled the region, piracy flourished; when strong nations exerted control over the Mediterranean, piracy waned. Thus, the decline of Rome led to an upsurge in piracy. Later, the rise of the Ottoman Empire and expulsion of the Moors from Spain resulted in a new round of piracy perpetrated by Muslims operating from North Africa. Later still, piracy rebounded in the eastern Mediterranean when the Greeks rebelled against their Ottoman masters.

Why did piracy thrive in the Mediterranean for thousands of years? Once again, specific conditions in the region facilitated piracy. The geography of the Mediterranean is favorable to piracy. Since the Mediterranean is an enclosed sea, merchant vessels normally sailed relatively close to the shore. For example, the Spanish coast from Gibraltar to Cartagena, some 300 miles long, lies within 120 miles of North Africa. Cartagena is located about 230 miles west-northwest of Algiers. Thus, Moroccan and Algerian pirates were well situated to attack merchant ships entering or leaving the Mediterranean. Similarly, the Mediterranean narrows to less than 100 miles between Tunisia and Sicily, making Tunis an ideal port for the corsairs preying on merchants trading with the eastern Mediterranean. Although it opens up east of Sicily, the Mediterranean quickly narrows to less than 250 miles between the Greek islands and Libya. And the many islands of the Greek archipelago dominate the approach to Constantinople, the capital of the Ottoman Empire.

Geography also played a part in maritime navigation. Since the Mediterranean is a relatively enclosed area, there was little need for advanced navigational techniques. Instead, mariners sailed from bay to bay and island to island. Although that made navigation simpler, it also kept merchant vessels close to shore where they were vulnerable to pirate attack.[4]

Frequent political turmoil among the Mediterranean nations also aided the spread of piracy in the region. Since the ancient Greeks were fiercely independent, a strong central Greek government never emerged to control or limit piracy.[5] As the power of the individual Greek city-states declined in the late Hellenic period (323–31 BC), piracy surged throughout the Mediterranean.[6]

Moreover, Greeks were both victims and perpetrators of the crime. Although early Greeks considered trade a less than honorable profession, no such stigma was attached to piracy. Raiding and piracy were considered manly enterprises.[7] Consequently, piracy was a common activity among the ancient Greeks, and their victims were often Greeks from other city-states. Piracy remained a legitimate enterprise to many Greeks through the 19th century, finding widespread enthusiasm in the midst of the turmoil caused by the Greek War for Independence.

Nor was Rome immune to piracy. As a land-based, agrarian nation, Rome had little interest in maritime trade. The ancient Romans ceded responsibility for maritime control to the Carthaginians and others. One of the negative outcomes of the Punic Wars (264–241 BC, 218–201 BC, and 149–146 BC) was that the defeat of Carthage put the responsibility for controlling pirates onto Rome.[8] Since the Romans were uninterested in policing the Mediterranean, piracy surged after the defeat of Carthage. The situation worsened when Rome defeated Rhodes in 167–166 BC. Rhodes' navy had suppressed piracy in the eastern Mediterranean.[9] By 100 BC, piracy posed a serious threat to Rome, even threatening to cut off grain shipments into the city.

By the time pirates captured Caesar, Rome was a trading nation, dependent upon seaborne trade for food and other products. But Rome was wracked by civil war, and the pirates grew so strong that they disrupted the flow of food into the city. Finally, in 74 BC, Proconsul Marcus Antonius was directed to subdue the corsairs. After Marcus Antonius failed to rectify the situation, Pompey was given broader powers, which he used to suppress the pirates. His commission granted him supreme command over the entire Mediterranean Sea as well as 50 miles inland. Deploying a fleet of 500 ships and an army of 12,000 infantry and 7,000 cavalry, Pompey swept the sea clear of pirates in less than 3 months.[10] Despite his success, some of the frontier areas were never fully cleared, and Rome had to maintain a strong fleet in the Black Sea and other places.[11] But as long as Rome controlled the coastline, thus eliminating safe havens, piracy was mostly eliminated. It reemerged, however, when the power of Rome began to crumble in the 5th century AD.[12] Once again, the key conditions came into play as political turmoil and the availability of safe havens made piracy a viable alternative to fishing and maritime trade.

Among history's most feared pirates were the Barbary corsairs. Based out of several small principalities along the North African coast, they preyed on shipping in the Mediterranean for more than 400 years, capturing ships, stealing cargos, and enslaving Christians. Most European nations turned to bribery, in the form of annual tribute, to limit the impact the Barbary pirates had on their commerce. From time to time, European naval powers did, however, use force to temporarily stop attacks on their merchant fleets.

To the east, Venetian and Maltese corsairs operated with impunity in Greek waters. Since they considered any non-Catholic fair prey, they attacked Orthodox Greeks as frequently as Muslim Turks. But the Greeks were not merely innocent victims; they also participated in piracy. Since provincial governors in Greece were not paid a salary during the Byzantine Empire, they raised money by allowing brigands to operate from their shores. Similar activities continued under the Ottomans after they conquered Constantinople in 1453.

Even though piracy was prevalent in the Greek islands, it rarely reached the level of notoriety achieved by the Barbary corsairs. One exception was the outbreak of piracy during the Greek War for Independence from the Ottoman Empire. During the 1820s, as the Greeks struggled to gain their independence, piracy in the Greek islands reached such a level that Great Britain, in conjunction with France and Russia, acted to end the rebellion and suppress the concurrent piracy by Greek rebels.

The Barbary and Greek pirates were so successful over such a long time that piracy became an accepted aspect of each society's economic life. Piracy among the Barbary states continued long after it was no longer economically viable because it was intrinsic to life in the Barbary nations. Piracy among the Greeks was also integral to their society, although it never reached the heights achieved by the Barbary pirates.

The three conditions that make piracy possible clearly influenced the growth and longevity of piracy among the Barbary states. They were favored by their geographic location since the relatively confined space of the Mediterranean made it easy for the corsairs to locate and attack their prey. Moreover, the Barbary pirates could always count on safe havens ashore. Since Barbary piracy was state-sponsored piracy, the political climate was always supportive. Plus there was strong support for the practice among the populace, who benefited economically from piracy. Finally, the lack of effort on the part of European naval powers to eliminate the Barbary corsairs' home bases further reinforced the legitimacy of their actions.

The Barbary rovers also highlight the conflicting definitions of piracy. Considering themselves soldiers of Islam rather than pirates, the Barbary corsairs were at war with every nation that did not pay tribute to their kingdom. Even though they signed treaties with nations, they regarded them as temporary truces that could be repudiated at their convenience. Conversely, European nations considered them pirates and treated them accordingly. Still, they did not treat the Barbary corsairs as universal enemies of society and execute them as they did the pirates of the West Indies. Instead, the Barbary pirates were often ransomed, exchanged for Europeans held by the corsairs, or employed as galley slaves.

In contrast to the state-sponsored nature of Barbary piracy, Greek piracy was a deep-rooted local practice. But it, too, depended on the three main conditions. The Greek isles were ideal for piracy. The Greek pirates could hide among the many islands and then suddenly attack merchant vessels trading with the Levant. Since piracy was intrinsic among the Greeks, a certain amount of piracy was always in the region. But political turmoil in the 1820s, caused by the Greek War for Independence, led to increased levels of piracy in the region. When the political situation stabilized, piracy quickly declined to levels acceptable to the region's naval powers. Another aspect of the intrinsic nature of piracy in the Greek isles was that the pirates could always count on safe havens ashore. When the British and French Navies attempted to suppress them, the pirates often slipped ashore and blended in with the locals. Since many locals profited from the actions of the pirates, most Greeks were reluctant to hand over their fellow citizens.

Barbary Pirates

Piracy perpetrated by the Barbary corsairs was, in many ways, vastly different from that practiced by their contemporaries in the West Indies, Greek isles, or other parts of the world. The most important and obvious difference was that it was state-sponsored piracy. In fact, piracy served as the economic foundation of the four Barbary states. Unlike other areas, the main target of the Barbary pirates was human plunder, not gold, jewels, and commercial products. Their victims were a valuable commodity that brought wealth through ransom or slavery. Finally, piracy practiced by the Barbary states differed from other regions in that it was tolerated, if not encouraged, by powerful nations, particularly Great Britain, for foreign policy reasons. Great Britain had the resources necessary to eliminate the Barbary pirates but chose not to do so because the actions of the Barbary pirates assisted Britain's foreign trade policies. Thus, the Barbary pirates survived for hundreds of years, whereas large-scale piracy in other regions existed for relatively short periods of time.

There are, however, similarities as well, for the Barbary pirates benefited from the three necessary conditions. Geography clearly helped the Barbary pirates. Even though the Mediterranean is a large body of water, it is a relatively confined space that is further narrowed by several important chokepoints. All traffic en route to or from Atlantic ports must pass through the Strait of Gibraltar. Once inside the Mediterranean, east-west trade routes necessarily pass close by the corsair cities situated on the northern coast of Africa. (See figure 5.) The Mediterranean narrows between Sardinia, Sicily, and Tunis and a second time between Crete and Tripolitania. Thus, their geographic location dominated trade routes in the Mediterranean, making it easier for the pirates to locate and attack their prey.

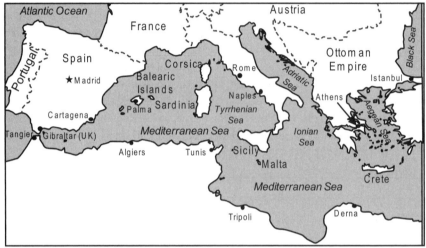

Figure 5. Barbary coast and the Mediterranean.

Geography or, more specifically, the environment also encouraged the expansion of piracy among the Barbary states. Many centuries earlier, the irrigation systems developed by Carthage and Rome fell into disrepair, allowing the desert to encroach on the arable land. By the 18th century, other than a few small strips along the coast, most of the land making up the Barbary states was arid and unsuitable for agriculture.[13] Consequently, since they were deficient in other natural resources as well and thus unable to produce the food and other necessary products, the inhabitants of North Africa sustained themselves for centuries by trading with the Europeans. They exchanged African slaves, horses, fish, hides, dates, and olive oil for European wood, metals, and cloth (silk, wool, and cotton).[14]

That commercial system collapsed in the early 16th century soon after the Spaniards drove the last of the Moors out of Spain in 1492. The Moors fled to North Africa, followed closely by the Spanish who eventually conquered all of North Africa. The Spanish imposed harsh peace terms on the Barbary states in 1510, including heavy trade duties. But peace did not last long, and by 1534, under the leadership of the Barbarossa brothers, North Africa was back in Ottoman hands. But the victory by the Turks put the Barbary states in a dilemma. They were too far from the Ottoman Empire to take advantage of its protection and now they were locked out of the European trading system as well.[15] This forced the Barbary rulers to look to other ways to sustain themselves. If they could not trade for what they needed, they had to get it some other way.[16]

The Barbary pirates' heyday occurred in the first half of the 17th century. The state built and manned corsair galleys, which operated much like European navies. During this timeframe, they were more than a match for their Christian opponents. From 1622 to 1642, Barbary corsairs captured 300 English ships and enslaved more than 7,000 English sailors.[17] At the start of that period, the Barbary states commanded significant fleets. Six large galleys and 14 sailing ships operated from Tunis. Algiers possessed a similar number of large galleys as well as 100 sailing ships, many of which were commanded by European pirates. But the power of the Barbary pirates was broken, although not eliminated, by the Venetians in 1638. One hundred years later, Algiers could only muster eight small galleys and eight more sailing ships.[18]

Although they were nominally part of the Ottoman Empire, by the end of the 18th century, the leaders of the Barbary states were semi-independent rulers.[19] Morocco was ruled by the Sultan Suleyman (Slimane). US relations with Morocco, which was the first nation to recognize the newly independent country, were fairly cordial.[20] The ruler of Algiers, who was the commander of the Algerian janissaries, was elected by a council of senior military officers.[21] The council elevated Dey Ali Hassan to the throne in 1791.[22] Yusuf Karamanli, the Bashaw[23] of Tripoli, took the throne during a bloody coup in 1795.[24] The Bey of Tunis was a hereditary title held by Pasha Hamouda.[25]

To one degree or another, all of the Barbary rulers needed the proceeds generated by piracy to maintain their positions as ruler. They did not, however, think of themselves as pirates; instead, they considered themselves at war with any nation that did not have a peace treaty with them.[26] Moreover, since they needed piracy to maintain power, piracy evolved into a state-sponsored system. Over time, piracy became the primary engine of the local economy. Captured cargos provided a source of cheap goods for local merchants. Crews and passengers were enslaved and forced to perform a wide variety of jobs, depending on their skills. The fate captives feared the most was becoming a galley slave, rowing the corsairs' boats.[27]

As piracy became more entrenched in society, it evolved into a private enterprise. Syndicates of government officials, merchants, shipowners, sailors, and small trades people invested in the galleys.[28] They profited from the goods stolen as well as the ransoms extorted from the captives and their families. Even after private syndicates took over from the state, the state continued to benefit from piracy. The Barbary rulers coerced tribute from smaller nations to prevent attacks on their country's shipping and they received a share of all profits generated by the pirate syndicates. Thus, the political climate in the Barbary states was extremely favorable toward piracy.

Finally, because of the state-sponsored nature of Barbary piracy, the corsairs benefited from secure sanctuaries ashore. Both state and commercial enterprises depended on the proceeds of piracy. There was no stigma attached to piracy; in fact, the opposite was true. Sailing with the galleys was viewed as an honorable activity. Moreover, since the corsairs preyed on infidels, the rovers were able to combine religious obligation with financial gain.

Equally as important, the Barbary corsairs faced few external threats. Although the combined naval power of Europe could have eliminated the pirates with relative ease, Europeans never made a concerted effort to do so. While it is true that individual nations mounted attacks from time to time, those nations never tried to destroy the corsair ports and thus eliminate their shore sanctuaries. Consequently, as soon as the European force left, the inhabitants resumed piratical attacks.[29]

Still, some nations did make an impact on the Barbary corsairs. Algiers signed a treaty of peace and commerce with Great Britain in 1682.[30] France and Spain negotiated a similar pact with Algiers. Fearing the consequences, the Barbary pirates tended to leave vessels from those nations alone. But the Barbary pirates felt free to attack the ships of smaller nations, such as the Dutch Republic, Austria, Denmark, and the Italian republics unless they paid tribute.[31] Soon, much of the trade in the Mediterranean was carried on British and, to a lesser extent, French ships.

Thus, France and Britain came to view the Barbary corsairs as pseudo-allies. France wanted "just enough corsairs to eliminate our rivals, but not too many."[32] French leaders realized that if the Barbary pirates were completely eliminated, France would descend to the same level as their weaker competitors. Similarly, British officials realized the strategic advantages the existence of the Barbary corsairs afforded them, especially with regard to their newly independent former colonies. Writing in 1784, Lord Sheffield suggested the following:

It is not probable that the American States will have a very free trade in the Mediterranean; it will not be in the interest of any of the great maritime powers to protect them there from the Barbary States. . . . The Americans cannot protect themselves from the latter; they cannot pretend to a navy."[33]

Thus, the Barbary pirates were sustained by the tacit support of the more powerful European nations. Piratical depredations by the Barbary states only ended when France, weary of Algerian transgressions, invaded North Africa in 1830 with overwhelming force and occupied the country. By 1847, France was in control of most of North Africa, and with minor exceptions, piracy emanating from the Barbary states ended.[34]

Lord Sheffield's words were partly correct. Soon after independence, with the cloak of British protection withdrawn, the Barbary pirates began preying on American shipping. It was almost inevitable that American ships would fall to Barbary corsairs. According to Thomas Jefferson, prior to the American Revolution, American trade with Mediterranean nations was fairly extensive. He estimated that one-quarter of the dried and pickled fish as well as one-sixth of the wheat and flour produced in the colonies was exported to the Mediterranean in 80 to 100 ships annually.[35] Once the Treaty of Paris was signed in 1783, American merchants sent ships to the Mediterranean, hoping to reestablish their trade contacts. By 1790, nearly 100 American ships sailed to the Mediterranean annually.[36]

The first Barbary nation to act was Morocco. Frustrated by the lack of progress during treaty negotiations with the United States, the Sultan of Morocco ordered his corsairs to attack. On 11 October 1784, they captured the armed brig *Betsey*. Although the Sultan did not enslave the captives, he demanded a ransom and a treaty of friendship with the United States. As a show of faith, he released the captives, ship, and cargo without payment of a ransom on 9 July 1785. The next summer, an American commissioner arrived and, within days, negotiated a treaty that ensured that American vessels could pass safely through the Strait of Gibraltar. To Congress' pleasure, the treaty cost less than the $20,000 the commissioner was authorized to spend.[37]

The next encounter with Barbary pirates did not go as well. In the summer of 1785, surprisingly, Algiers was at peace with both Spain and Portugal. With the active encouragement of the British consul in Algiers, the Algerians sailed out into the Atlantic Ocean and began taking American ships.[38] On 25 July 1785, Algerian corsairs captured the schooner *Maria*. Then, on 1 August 1785, they captured another American vessel, the

Dauphin. Unlike the Moroccans, the Algerians enslaved the 21 Americans captured during the two attacks. The Dey of Algiers demanded $1 million for a treaty of friendship. With no power to tax under the Articles of Confederation, the United States did not have the financial resources to either buy peace with Algiers or build a navy to enforce it.[39]Although renewed hostilities with Portugal soon ended the Algerian forays into the Atlantic, 21 Americans were left to languish as Algerian slaves.[40]

Over the next several years, the United States attempted to ransom the sailors and negotiate peace treaties with Algiers and Tripoli. Both attempts failed because the central government lacked, under the Articles of Confederation, the financial resources needed to ransom the captives or buy peace with the Barbary states. Despite the lack of governmental support, American vessels continued to sail the Mediterranean in relative safety by joining Spanish and Dutch convoys.[41]

Finally, in 1791, 2 years after the establishment of the Federal Government, Congress acted. Unlike the Articles of Confederation, the Constitution gave Congress the power it needed to deal with the Barbary pirates, such as full control over the Nation's commerce, the right to raise revenue through taxation, the authority to build a navy, and the power to wage war with the Barbary corsairs, if necessary.[42] In 1791, a Senate committee declared that the Nation needed a navy to protect its commercial fleet in the Mediterranean. The next year, Congress appointed a peace commission to negotiate a treaty with Algiers and the other Barbary states. Congress authorized the payment of as much as $100,000 for a peace treaty, $13,500 in annual tribute, and up to $27,000 to ransom the American captives.[43]

Unfortunately, in 1793, before the American peace commissioner arrived,[44] Britain brokered a truce between Portugal and Algiers that allowed Algerian corsairs access to the Atlantic once again. With British and American relations strained because of a recent British order-in-council that led to the seizure of more than 250 American vessels in the Caribbean, many Americans believed that the British purposely arranged the truce to set loose the Barbary rovers on American ships. Whatever the reason, the impact on American commerce was immediate. By the end of November 1793, less than 2 months after the truce was reached, the Algerians captured 11 American ships and 105 sailors. The United States was powerless to stop the havoc of the Barbary corsairs.[45]

The crisis spurred Congress to action in early 1794. American diplomats worked to reestablish peace, or at least peaceful relations, with Britain and the Barbary states. John Jay negotiated a settlement with Great

Britain that averted war. Congress authorized $1 million for a peace treaty and the release of American captives held in Algiers. The American peace commissioner, David Humphreys, was able to reduce the Dey's demands from $2 million down to about $600,000, plus an annual tribute of $21,000-worth of naval stores and a new 36-gun frigate, the *Crescent*, which was delivered in February 1798. In 1797, the cost of the treaty was estimated to be $1 million.[46] Much less was spent to gain peace with Tripoli ($56,000) in November 1796 and Tunis ($107,000) in August 1797.[47]

Meanwhile, in March 1794, Congress authorized the construction of the six frigates that became the backbone of the United States Navy in the wars against France, the Barbary pirates, and England over the next 21 years. The debate over the Navy was long and heated. In the end, opponents of the Navy inserted a provision in the bill that mandated that construction of the frigates cease if American negotiators reached a settlement with Algiers.[48] When the treaty with Algiers went into effect in March 1796, work on the frigates came to a halt, but Congress, at President George Washington's urging, authorized construction to resume on three of the six warships.[49]

With the treaties in place, business with Mediterranean nations grew rapidly. In 1799, trade with Spain and Italy amounted to $8.8 million in goods. The next year, trade with those nations almost reached $12 million.[50] But the expansion of American commerce led to increased demands for tribute by the Barbary states, particularly Tripoli.

The Pasha of Tripoli, Yusuf Karamanli, seized the throne during a bloody coup in 1795. With Tripoli in shambles, he believed that the only way he could restore his country economically was by taking prizes and extorting tribute. Thus, he began "revising" his treaties with every nation trading in the Mediterranean. Spain, Venice, and France paid the Pasha off with money, ships, and other "presents." Sweden, Denmark, the Dutch Republic, and Naples resisted and suffered numerous attacks on their shipping. Sweden and Denmark soon reconsidered their policy and began paying tribute to Tripoli as well.[51]

In April 1800, the Pasha of Tripoli, jealous of Algiers, demanded that the United States build him a frigate as well. In September, one of his ships captured two American merchant vessels, the *Betsy* and *Sophia*. Although he released the *Sophia* because it was carrying tribute to the Dey of Algiers, the *Betsy* was converted into a pirate ship and her crew was enslaved. The Pasha repudiated the existing treaty with the United States in February 1801 and demanded $250,000 and $20,000 annually for a new treaty. Finally, in May 1801, the Pasha declared war on the United States.[52]

Anticipating just such a move, President Thomas Jefferson dispatched a squadron to the Mediterranean in late spring 1801. Commodore Richard Dale's force included the frigates *President* (44 guns), *Philadelphia* (36 guns), and *Essex* (32 guns), as well as the schooner *Enterprise* (12 guns).[53] All were veterans of the recently concluded Quasi War with France. Unfortunately, since Congress had not declared war, Dale's squadron was not authorized to take action against the corsairs unless they attacked an American ship. Moreover, Dale was not allowed to seize enemy ships and retain them as prizes.[54] Thus, he was limited to passive operations such as convoys and blockading Tripoli. With only four ships in his squadron, executing both of those tasks simultaneously was problematic.

Over the next 8 months, Dale's squadron carried out its mission as best it could. Soon after he arrived in July 1801, Dale visited Tunis and Algiers. When he arrived at Tripoli on 24 July, he found the Pasha in no mood to negotiate, so Dale established a blockade of the city. One week later, while en route to Malta to pick up fresh water for the squadron, *Enterprise* encountered and defeated the enemy ship *Tripoli* (14 guns). Since he could not take *Tripoli* as a prize, the American commander, Lieutenant Andrew Sterett, stripped it of all valuable goods and released the corsair vessel.[55] Even though the blockade caused some hardship in Tripoli, it was not totally effective because ships were frequently siphoned off to escort convoys or to pick up additional supplies. Three rovers slipped out of Tripoli and captured the American merchant ship *Franklin*. Others smuggled needed food and other supplies into the city. Finally, in February 1802, with his crew's 1-year enlistments almost up, Dale returned to the United States, leaving *Philadelphia* and *Essex* to continue patrolling off Tripoli and Gibraltar.[56]

In May 1802, another American squadron set out for the Mediterranean. Commanded by Commodore Richard Morris, it included the frigates *Chesapeake* (36 guns), *Constellation* (36 guns), *New York* (36 guns), *Adams* (28 guns), and *John Adams* (28 guns).[57] Before his departure, Congress authorized President Jefferson to use the Navy to protect American interests in the Mediterranean, thus removing the Constitutional restraints that shackled the previous squadron. Morris was free to conduct offensive operations against Tripoli and seize its ships as prizes.[58]

Despite his orders and new authority, Morris executed his mission with little energy. Taking his wife and son, Morris made calls at numerous French, Italian, and Spanish ports. It took him more than a year to reach Tripoli. Meanwhile, the other ships in the squadron had some success. The *John Adams* captured the Tripolitan warship *Meshuda* (the ex-American merchant ship *Polly*) in May 1803. During that same month, Lieutenant David Porter, who later commanded the American antipiracy squadron in the West Indies, led a group of boats close to the coast to destroy a grain convoy.[59] But Morris' lack of initiative frustrated Jefferson and Congress, so he was relieved by Commodore Edward Preble, a man of much greater activity.[60]

Preble arrived off Tripoli in September 1803. Sizing up the situation, he immediately ordered a more vigorous blockade of the city. Fortunately, Preble had the ships to conduct a more effective blockade. His squadron included the frigates *Constitution* (44 guns) and *Philadelphia* (36 guns); the 16-gun brigs *Argus* and *Siren*; and the 12-gun schooners *Vixen*, *Nautilus*, and *Enterprise*. As the United States relearned during other antipiracy operations, smaller vessels were critically important because of their ability to operate closer to shore. Moreover, Preble ordered two of his ships to continuously patrol the coast of Tripoli, and he established a naval depot on Malta so that transit times for ships requiring replenishment would be less.[61]

Soon after he arrived in the Mediterranean, Preble showed his mettle by confronting the Sultan of Morocco, who was threatening war against the United States. Preble sailed into Tangier in early October 1803 with five ships and confronted the Sultan. Instead of war, the Sultan renewed his pledge of friendship without the payment of tribute.[62]

But disaster struck no longer afterward when the *Philadelphia* ran aground on 1 November while chasing smugglers along the coast of Tripoli. Unable to free himself, Captain William Bainbridge surrendered his ship. Not only did Tripoli now have 307 more American captives, it had a powerful new addition to its fleet, for soon after the Tripolitans captured the *Philadelphia*, a storm blew it off the rocks. The Tripolitans fixed the damage to the ship, refloated it, and retrieved the guns that the American crew dumped overboard.[63]

Undeterred, Preble spent the winter blockading Tripoli and planning a response. On 7 February 1804, Lieutenant Stephen Decatur entered Tripoli harbor in the captured ketch *Intrepid*, boarded the *Philadelphia* under the noses of the Barbary corsairs, and blew the ship up. Although it was a daring feat that brought great fame to Decatur and the Navy, it did little to end the war with Tripoli. In fact, the Pasha, angered by the loss of his prize and fearful of further attacks, increased the amount of money he required for peace with the United States and put the *Philadelphia*'s crew under stronger guard. But the destruction of the *Philadelphia* did restore the US strategic advantage since the *Constitution* did not have to remain on station off Tripoli to counter the threat that the larger vessel presented to the smaller American brigs and schooners.[64]

Preble had, for some time, suggested to the Navy Department that a larger force with smaller vessels was needed to defeat Tripoli. During the summer of 1804, just such a squadron was formed: 6 frigates, 6 brigs and schooners, 2 mortar boats, and 10 gunboats. Unfortunately, despite his successes, Preble was not placed in command of this expanded flotilla because of his lack of seniority. Instead, Commodore Samuel Barron was picked to command the task force.[65]

Determined to end the war with Tripoli before Barron arrived, Preble decided to attack. Since he did not have enough shallow-draft vessels, he convinced the King of Naples, who was also at war with the Barbary pirates, to loan him six gunboats and two mortar ships. The gunboats were armed with a single 24-pounder, and the two bomb ketches carried a 13-inch mortar.[66]

Preble attacked on 3 August 1804. He sent Decatur into Tripoli's harbor with six of the gunboats and the two mortar ketches. Unfavorable winds kept three of the gunboats from entering the harbor but Decatur was undeterred. With two other gunboats and the bomb ketches, Decatur wreaked havoc on the city. He was soon joined by the *Constitution*, which blasted away at the shore batteries, the town, and, most insultingly, the Pasha's castle. The Americans captured three Tripolitan gunboats, sunk one other, and damaged the rest. They also killed 52 Tripolitans and captured 56 others. Stephen Decatur's brother James was the only American killed although 13 others were wounded.[67]

Preble followed up his success with several more attacks, but the Pasha remained obdurate. In an effort to finish the fight, Preble converted the *Intrepid* into a bomb ship and sent her into Tripoli harbor during the evening of 4 September. Volunteers planned to sail the ship up to the castle and, in the midst of the Tripolitan fleet, detonate the explosive-filled vessel. Unfortunately, the ship exploded prematurely, killing the entire crew of volunteers. With the weather turning against him and his supplies running low, Preble returned to Malta with the main body to await the arrival of his replacement. In the meantime, the blockade continued.[68]

While Preble worked to defeat Tripoli using naval power, others developed plans to end the war through land operations. When Commodore Barron arrived in September 1804, he brought with him William Eaton, a former Army officer and counsel in Tunis. Earlier, Eaton convinced President Jefferson to provide assistance to

Hamet Karamanli, Pasha Yusuf's older brother. Pasha Yusuf took the throne in 1795 by killing his older brother. Although Hamet, by right of primogeniture, should have succeeded his deceased brother, Yusuf usurped the crown. Hamet was willing to sign a treaty of perpetual peace if the United States provided him $40,000 and enough military support to overthrow his brother.[69]

Eaton reached Cairo in November 1804. While he began negotiations with Hamet, others began recruiting a motley army. By the time Hamet signed the treaty with Eaton, he had an army of 400 Greeks, Levantines, and Arabs. The force also included a midshipman and a Marine lieutenant, sergeant, and six enlisted men. Eaton and Hamet set out for Derna on 6 March 1805. Along the way, 650 Arabs also joined the force. The 500-mile march took 6 weeks. After many trials and tribulations, they arrived outside Derna on 27 April. Derna's defenders felt themselves safe, but they did not count on a combined operation. On 28 April, the *Argus*, *Hornet*, and *Nautilus* entered the harbor and devastated the town. At the same time, Lieutenant Presley O'Bannon led an attack by his marines on one side while Hamet attacked from another. The defenders were quickly overwhelmed and surrendered. While Eaton was planning the next march on to Tripoli, he learned that the Pasha had finally given in. In exchange for $60,000, he surrendered the crew of the *Philadelphia* and all other American captives and agreed to stop attacking American ships.[70] Thus ended the first Barbary War.

With a small naval squadron on station, a tenuous peace held for the next few years, but the situation changed in 1807. Conflict between the United States and Great Britain over impressments and neutral rights led to an unprovoked attack on the *Chesapeake* by the HMS *Leopard* on 22 June 1807. The United States responded to that incident by withdrawing the Mediterranean squadron. From the summer of 1807 until peace with Britain was restored by the Treaty of Ghent, American merchant vessels sailed the Mediterranean at their own risk.[71]

Not surprisingly, without a naval squadron to keep them in check, the Barbary states resumed attacking American vessels and making demands for more tribute. Algiers captured three American ships in late 1807. The crew of one of the three ships, the *Mary Ann*, rallied and took the ship back from the Algerian prize crew. That, too, became a cause for complaint, for the Americans threw the Algerians overboard, which prompted the Dey to demand $16,000 in restitution.[72] As American trade ground to a halt under the Embargo Act of 1807, so too did Barbary attacks on American ships, for Americans rarely ventured into the Mediterranean after 1807.

The end of the war with England provided the United States with an opportunity to redress the situation with the Barbary states once and for all. The United States declared war on Algiers on 3 March 1815. Within a few weeks, two powerful American squadrons were en route to the Mediterranean. Commodore Decatur's squadron left first. His force included the frigates *Guerrière* (44 guns), *Macedonian* (38 guns), and *Constellation*; the sloops *Epervier* (18 guns) and *Ontario* (16 guns); three 14-gun brigs—*Firefly*, *Spark*, and *Flambeau*; and the 12-gun schooners *Torch* and *Spitfire*. Commodore Bainbridge followed with the new ship-of-the-line *Independence* (74 guns); the frigates *United States*, *Congress*, and *Java* (44 guns); and eight smaller vessels.[73]

Decatur arrived in the Mediterranean on 15 June 1815. Two days later, his squadron encountered the Algerian flagship, the *Mashouda* (46 guns). It did not take long for the *Constellation*, *Guerrière*, and *Epervier* to reduce the *Mashouda* to a hulk. Decatur's forces captured another Algerian vessel, the *Estedio* (22 guns) on 19 June. Within days of entering the Mediterranean, Decatur seized more than 500 prisoners and two prizes. He now felt he could negotiate with the Algerians from a position of strength.[74]

The American flotilla arrived off Algiers on 28 June 1815. Decatur sent the Dey a letter from the President explaining that the two nations were at war but that the United States was willing to reestablish peaceful relations if the terms were beneficial to both nations. Decatur also informed the Algerians that he would not accept any treaty that required tribute and that if he encountered any Algerian vessels, since they were at war, he would destroy them. When the Algerians tried to negotiate a cease-fire, Decatur refused. The Algerians caved in and agreed to release the 10 Americans held captive, paid $10,000 in compensation to the owners of the brig *Edwin*, and promised never to enslave American citizens. The overwhelming power Decatur brought with him resulted in equally as satisfactory treaties with Tunis, which paid $46,000 in compensation for 2 American prizes the Bey handed over to the British during the War of 1812, and Tripoli, which paid a $25,000 fine and released 10 Christian slaves. When Commodore Bainbridge arrived, his presence further reinforced the determination of the United States to deal forcefully with the Barbary corsairs. With that, the American role in the Barbary wars came to an end.[75]

But the end of the war with America did not mean that the Barbary states stopped their piratical attacks. Decatur's success motivated other nations to renegotiate their treaties with the Barbary states. The United Kingdom was the first to act. The end of the Napoleonic Wars eroded the strategic value of Barbary states as a threat to other nations' merchant shipping. Moreover, one of the primary discussions during the Congress of Vienna in 1814 dealt with ending slavery. Although the focus of the conversation was African slavery, it also renewed interest in ending the enslavement of Europeans by North Africans.[76] So the United Kingdom dispatched Admiral Edward Pellow, Lord Exmouth, to rectify the situation.

Lord Exmouth's task was to negotiate the release of all European slaves from the Barbary states. He was not authorized to use force; all he could do was pay ransoms for the captives. When he arrived off Algiers on 24 March 1816 with five ships-of-the-line and seven smaller vessels, the sight intimidated the Dey into negotiating a settlement. He agreed to peace with all European nations and accepted payments for all of his prisoners. Lord Exmouth did not, however, demand that Algiers cease piracy, thus the Dey no doubt believed himself able to resume the practice some time in the future. The British found Tunis much less amenable. After reaching the brink of battle, the Bey agreed to ransom 524 slaves, release 257 others without payment, and treat all future captives as prisoners of war rather than slaves. The Pasha of Tripoli, Yusuf Karamanli, was more agreeable. He accepted payment for 468 slaves and further agreed to abolish slavery. When Lord Exmouth returned to Algiers and tried to extract a similar promise from the Dey, he was rebuffed. With tensions high and no authority to use force, Lord Exmouth returned to England on 24 June 1816.[77]

Soon after Lord Exmouth returned, public outrage at the murder of 200 Italian fishermen and the perceived leniency of the terms obtained led to new orders for Lord Exmouth, directing him to use force, if necessary, to extract better terms from the Algerians. Lord Exmouth sailed for Algiers on 28 July 1816. His squadron included two triple-deck ships-of-the-line, *Queen Charlotte* (100 guns) and *Impregnable* (98 guns); three 74-gun ships-of-the line, *Albion*, *Minden*, and *Superb*; the frigate *Leander* (58 guns); two 40-gun frigates (*Glasgow* and *Severn*); two 36-gun frigates (*Hebrus* and *Granicus*); five sloops; and four bomb ships. When he arrived at Gibraltar on 9 August, he found a Dutch squadron, consisting of four 40-gun frigates, one 30-gun frigate, and an 18-gun sloop, in port. The Dutch commander volunteered to participate in the British campaign, further augmenting the attack force.[78]

The allied squadron arrived on 27 August. Lord Exmouth gave the Dey an opportunity to capitulate, but when the Algerians failed to respond to the allied demands, the combined squadron attacked. The bombardment lasted 8 hours, from 1400 to 2200. By 1900, many of the Algerian guns were silenced, the town was on fire, the arsenal and many storehouses were destroyed, and most of the Algerian's warships were sunk. With their ammunition almost gone, the allies left the harbor about 2200.[79]

The next morning, as the allies prepared to resume the attack, the Dey gave in and agreed to the British terms. The Algerian leader released 1,642 slaves, including 18 British citizens; agreed to abolish slavery; returned $382,500 in ransom money to Naples and Sardinia; apologized to the British consul for his mistreatment over the previous few days; and accepted peace terms with the Netherlands.[80] The cost of success was heavy: the British suffered 128 killed and 690 wounded, while the Dutch lost 13 killed and 52 wounded. The British fired almost 40,000 rounds, and the Dutch fired over 10,000 rounds, resulting in more than 4,000 casualties on the Algerian side.[81]

Despite that drubbing, piracy among the Barbary states did not end until the 1830s when France invaded North Africa. There were isolated incidents in 1817 and some of the smaller European nations, such as Sweden, Denmark, Portugal, and Naples, continued to pay tribute to the Barbary states as late as 1827. But the situation changed in 1827 when a dispute between the French consul and the Dey of Algiers provoked France. At first, France limited its response to a blockade, but when the Dey expelled the French consul in August 1829 and fired on his ship as he left under a flag of truce, France responded by invading Algeria. A French fleet carrying 37,000 troops arrived at Algiers on 13 June 1830. Within weeks, the powerful French ground force defeated the Algerians and invested the city. Algiers fell on 4 July. Finally, Barbary piracy was eliminated.[82]

The actions against the Barbary pirates demonstrate that piracy is ultimately a land problem. Despite strong naval actions by the United States and Great Britain, piracy emanating from the Barbary states did not end until the corsairs were conquered by the French Army. In the case of the Barbary kingdoms, the three pillars of piracy, geography, political instability, and safe havens, were not easily disrupted by naval operations alone. The geography, of course, remained the same, and naval power was unable to change the political situation in the three principalities. But the Barbary corsairs did respond to land operations. Thus, Eaton's invasion of Tripoli caused the Pasha to finally agree to terms. Although the American and British Navies eventually forced the Barbary rulers to accept treaties ending piracy, they did not stop preying on other nation's shipping until France eliminated their safe havens ashore by permanently occupying them.

Greek Piracy

The Greek Revolution began on 25 March 1821. Once it started, nearly all of Greece rose up against its Ottoman rulers. Within days, the entire Morea[83] was in rebellion, and within 6 weeks, the rebels killed virtually all of the 25,000 Turks living in the region.[84] By the end of the year, most of the Morea was free of Turks and the uprising spread onto mainland Greece.

Many of the early leaders of the rebellion were bandits. Brigands, or *klefts*, were an offshoot of an irregular militia (*armatoli*) that served the Ottoman rulers for many years. When the Sultan withdrew his patronage in the late 18th century, they became opponents of the Ottoman Empire. Forsaken by the Sultan, the militias turned to thievery to support themselves.[85] They lived in bandit villages, called *kleftochoria*, high in the mountains where the Turks rarely ventured. Since almost four-fifths of Greece was mountainous, the bandits suffered little outside interference.[86] Thus, topography made brigandage a viable and common occupation throughout the country.

Despite their unlawful activities, most Greeks held the *klefts* in high esteem. Their opposition to the Turks caused many people to consider the brigands heroes rather than villains. They were protectors of the people and defenders of the Orthodox Christian faith against its heathen oppressors.[87] Consequently, when the *klefts* rebelled, most Greek peasants followed their lead. Virtually overnight, the entire nation went *sto klari* (became brigands).[88] Bandit tactics and behaviors influenced and shaped the conduct of warfare on land.

Similarly, the Greek effort at sea soon lapsed into piratical practices as well. As with banditry ashore, piracy was considered an honorable profession by the Greeks. Many of the commanders in the new Greek Navy were former pirates.[89] Moreover, since the Greek Government was chronically short of cash, it was unable to pay its sailors or adequately supply its ships. Always in need of money, food, and supplies, the navy viewed prospective missions as commercial ventures and expected to profit from them. Without plunder, the navy could not exist, and without an opportunity for plunder, it would not fight.[90]

Although piracy was a nuisance from the beginning of the war, European naval forces kept it in check for awhile. But Austrian support for the Ottomans soon led to retaliation by the Greeks against Austrian shipping. By 1824, the lack of monetary support from the rebel government, the relatively easy profits that could be attained through piracy, and despair as the Egyptian fleet turned the tide against the Greeks at sea pulled many more Greek sailors into piracy. Even more concerning, most of the Greek pirates were not particularly discerning about who they attacked. A contemporary historian recounted that "it was a common saying among them that they were at war with Turkey, Egypt, Barbary, Austria, and France."[91] But piracy builds its own momentum, and by 1825, Greek pirates began to prey on British, American, and other nations' shipping as well.

As with brigandage on land, Greece's geography played an important role in the success of piracy in the eastern Mediterranean. (See figure 6.) Its many islands were perfect bases for pirates, who could hide along the coast and then quickly swoop down on their unsuspecting victims as they passed within range. Psara, for example, was ideally situated to disrupt both Turkish commerce and naval operations. Located in the central Aegean, Psara is only about 80 miles from Smyrna (present-day Izmir, Turkey), which was an important Turkish commercial port, and all ships en route to the Dardanelles had to pass within 50 miles of the island. Similarly, sailors from Skiathos, Skyros (Skiros)*, and Skopelos[92] attacked ships trading with the Ottomans with impunity and defied the Greek Government to stop them. Although many sailors from Spetsai served the revolution with distinction, Spetsai was also a notorious pirate haven.[93]

Greek pirates used fast, three-masted vessels called mistikos. Each mistikos carried about 40 men and one bow-mounted gun. Their mistikos' shallow draft allowed the pirates to avoid detection by hiding in small creeks and coves along the coast. If pursued too closely, the Greek corsairs abandoned their small vessels and escaped ashore, blending into the local populace.[94]

Once they were ashore, Greek pirates benefited from widespread support and assistance. Greek support for piracy at sea paralleled acceptance of banditry on land. Greek citizens participated in piracy by providing safe havens for the corsairs, disposing of their plundered goods, repairing or replacing their damaged vessels, and giving the pirates access to supplies and naval stores. Their active support of the brigands made suppressing Greek piracy a difficult task.[95]

Thus, the three pillars of piracy came into play during this episode of piracy in the eastern Mediterranean. The geography of the Greek islands

---

*Names in parenthesis are present-day names of islands.

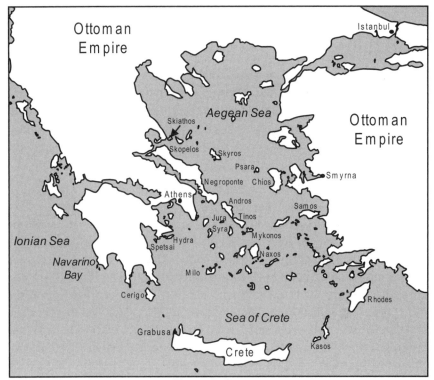

Figure 6. Greece.

greatly facilitated piracy. Since the islands sat astride the shipping lanes to Istanbul, Smyrna, Egypt, and cities in the Levant, they were outstanding bases for Greek corsairs. The islands provided the pirates with easy access to lucrative targets and readily available places to hide. The Greek Revolution also triggered considerable political turmoil, which the pirates used to their advantage. The Ottoman Empire no longer policed Greek waters, and the revolutionary government of Greece was too weak to exert any meaningful control. Thus, Greek pirates were able to act with impunity throughout much of the war. Finally, Greek corsairs benefited greatly from safe havens ashore. The Greek tradition of brigandage, whether on water or ashore, legitimized their actions. Moreover, with the Greek economy in shambles, piracy was one of the most rewarding enterprises available to Greek sailors and merchants. Few Greeks, therefore, willingly turned in their compatriots who engaged in piracy.

Despite the horrific atrocities the Greeks and Turks perpetrated on one another during the war, Greek pirates rarely treated their captives harshly. Since merchant crews seldom resisted, the Greeks usually confined their actions to beatings. This is in stark contrast with the behavior of the Caribbean pirates of the 19th century, who often killed or tortured their victims.[96]

Much like the Greek Army, the Greek Navy was an ad hoc organization. Individual islands contributed forces to an operation as they saw fit. Each island selected its own captains and admirals, and they retained control of their own ships. Although there was a nominal head of the combined naval force, as a practical matter, each islands' commanders could, and often did, act independently.[97]

Notwithstanding those organizational challenges, the Greeks had many advantages at sea when compared to the Ottomans. Some of the Greek islands, such as Spetsai, Psara, and Hydra (Ýdra), were maritime powers in their own right. Although the Greeks did not have a navy when the war began, the rebels controlled about 300 armed merchant vessels employing some 12,000 Greek sailors. More than half of those ships and crews came from Spetsai, Psara, and Hydra.[98] Moreover, because of the threat posed by piracy in the Mediterranean, those ships were well armed and their crews were well trained. Conversely, the loss of the Greek islands severely crippled the Ottoman Navy. The Ottoman Empire was a land-oriented empire. It relied on its subjugated peoples, primarily the Greeks, to man and operate its navy. Loss of the Greek islands severely hampered the Ottoman Navy's ability to man its ships during the war. Thus, when the Turkish fleet put to sea in 1821, it was manned by an inexperienced and diverse mix of sailors drawn from all parts of the Ottoman Empire.[99]

During the first few years of the rebellion, the Greeks reigned supreme at sea. Ottoman admirals were reluctant to confront the Greeks and often remained in port. With little to fear from the Turkish Navy, the Greeks turned their attention to commerce raiding. They attacked coastal vessels operating between the Dardanelles Straits and Egypt. Although their primary targets were Turkish merchant ships, they also took ships of other nations, especially Austria. They generally left British, American, and French ships alone, but even those nations suffered attacks by Greek pirates from time to time.[100] Since the United States and most European nations supported the revolution, they were willing to tolerate a limited amount of piracy.[101] By the end of 1822, piracy and privateering were so lucrative that many of the best Greek ships preferred to act as commerce raiders rather than join the fledgling nation's navy.[102]

The situation on both land and at sea changed markedly in 1824 when Sultan Mahmud decided to call on his vassal, Mohammed Ali, Pasha of

Egypt, for help. The Sultan realized that he needed command of the sea to defeat the Greeks. Since the Ottoman Navy was not up to the task, he decided to use Mohammed Ali's French-built and French-trained fleet to do so.[103]

The Egyptians began their campaign in June 1824. On 19 June, 200 Egyptian warships and transports set sail carrying 18,000 troops.[104] That same day, an independent Egyptian squadron landed 3,000 troops on Kasos, from which Greek ships had preyed on Egyptian merchant vessels for more than 3 years. The island was poorly defended so the Egyptians quickly overran it, killing 500 seaman and taking 2,000 women and children into slavery. The Egyptians moved against Psara next. Although they put up a better fight, the residents of Psara were no match for the Egyptians either, and some 8,000 people were killed or carried off into slavery.[105] A series of inconclusive naval battles in the late summer and fall of 1824 kept the Egyptians from invading Crete, but on 24 February 1825, the Egyptians landed on the southern tip of the Morea.[106] With that, the tide of the war turned against the Greeks.

Although the Greeks continued to struggle, the course of events in 1825 and 1826 gave them little hope for success.[107] Anarchy prevailed throughout the country and the surrounding waters. In September 1826, six Greek Navy ships mutinied and turned to piracy, claiming they were driven to do so because of the lack of support by the rebel government.[108] Greek turmoil and Ottoman ineffectiveness at sea led to an "administrative no-mans' land in the eastern Mediterranean."[109] There are estimates that more than one-quarter of the Greek population was involved in piracy by this time.[110]

The large number of Greek vessels involved in piracy and the broad geographic area over which they ranged threatened to bring trade in the eastern Mediterranean to a halt. Although their actions were contrary to the established rules of international law, the Greeks considered any ship trading with the Ottoman Empire, regardless of the cargo it carried, as fair game. More and more British vessels fell victim to the Greek pirates. The most notorious corsair base was Grabusa (Gramvoússa). Pirates from there reputedly captured 487 merchant ships, 93 of which were British.[111] Throughout the Greek isles, more than 150 British ships were attacked between March 1825 and October 1827.[112] But the impact of the pirates went well beyond merely capturing and plundering of merchant ships. Since the pirates were willing to take whatever they could get for their stolen goods, pirate plunder depressed the prices of legal merchandise and drove many legitimate merchants out of business.[113]

By the 1820s, American trade with the Levant was fairly substantial. Although the American colonies were not allowed to trade directly with the Levant, American merchants quickly established commercial relations with the Levant after the American Revolution ended. Trade with the Levant grew steadily until, by 1820, it averaged $1 million per year.[114] The *Spark* became the first American warship to visit a Middle Eastern port when it sailed into Smyrna in 1820. The Greek Revolution did not, at first, greatly affect American trade with the region. That changed in 1825 with the general breakdown of authority in the eastern Mediterranean. In May of that year, an American ship was plundered by Greek pirates. [115]

Concern for American commerce prompted President Monroe to dispatch the most powerful naval force in the country's history to the Mediterranean in early 1825 to protect American interests there.[116] Merchant ships were only safe if they sailed in armed convoys, and even then, it was risky to transit Greek waters. Despite the presence of the American squadron, two more American ships were taken in 1826, which led to the establishment of an American convoy system later that year.[117] US Navy ships escorted merchant vessels from Smyrna to Malta, allowing ships of all nations to join the convoys.[118]

But even convoys did not always deter the Greek corsairs. They merely adopted other tactics, such as picking off stragglers separated from the main body of the convoy at night or as the result of bad weather.[119] During a convoy in September 1827, boat crews from the *Porpoise* saved a British vessel sailing with the convoy. The *Porpoise* left Smyrna bound for Malta in company of 11 merchant ships, only 5 of which were American. While transiting through the Doro Passage (Stenón Kafiréos), the winds died and the convoy drifted apart.[120] At that moment, 200 to 300 pirates in five vessels from Andros and Negroponte (Évvoia) attacked the *Comet*, which had lagged behind in the calm air. As the buccaneers towed *Comet* away, *Porpoise* gave chase using her oars. When it became apparent that *Porpoise* could not overtake the pirates, 40 sailors were dispatched in the ship's boats to deal with them. Rowing strenuously, the American sailors caught up with the *Comet* and, in a sharp fight, recaptured the vessel and killed 80 or 90 corsairs.[121]

The fortunes of three American brigs that left the *Porpoise*'s convoy demonstrate the dangers all merchant ships ran. They left the convoy near Chios (Khios). Soon thereafter, one was attacked and robbed of its cargo. The crewmembers of the second merchantman abandoned their ship before the brigands could capture them. Only the third vessel reached its next port unscathed.[122]

The cruise of the *Warren* during 25 September through 6 December illustrates the activities conducted by American warships in the Levant. On 25 September, *Warren* escorted a group of American merchant ships from Smyrna to a point about halfway to Sicily, some 200 miles west of Cerigo (Kýthira). *Warren* captured a boat with 15 brigands on board and a pirate brig armed with 16 guns off Grabusa on 4 October. Over the next 3 weeks, *Warren* patrolled the sea between Crete and Cerigo (Kythira), occasionally escorting merchants vessels transiting the area. *Warren* received word that Greek corsairs attacked two American ships, the *Rob Roy* and *Cherub*, and went looking for the victims to provide assistance. While searching for *Cherub*, *Warren* encountered a 10-gun pirate brig near Argenteero (Kimolos). *Warren* attacked and sunk the brig, but the brigands escaped ashore into the mountains. She located the *Cherub* at Syra (Syros) Island on 28 October. When *Lexington* arrived later that evening, *Warren* left *Cherub* in her charge and resumed her patrol. The next day, *Warren* discovered the Austrian brig *Silence* adrift after being robbed of her cargo and sails. *Warren* towed *Silence* back to Syra and left her in *Lexington*'s care as well. *Warren* captured a large, 40-oar pirate boat on 30 October while cruising off Mykonos (Mikonos). When she entered the port of Mykonos on 1 November, *Warren* discovered some of the property stolen from *Cherub*, *Rob Roy*, and *Silence*, including sails, rigging, and opium. After returning the sails and other property to the merchant ships at Syra, *Warren* began cruising around Andros Island. Boats from the *Warren* were sent to explore the coast of the island on 7 November. The boats returned 2 days later with a captured pirate boat. They also burned a second boat. *Warren* continued cruising around Andros and Jura (Yiaros) until 18 November when she sailed into Milo (Milos) Island's harbor. While off Andros, some of the inhabitants returned to *Warren* a boat, cannon, and tools stolen from *Cherub*. On 30 November, *Warren* got underway with two American ships and six other vessels en route to Smyrna. The convoy arrived in Smyrna on 6 December without incident. It was a busy cruise. In a little over 2 months, *Warren* captured or destroyed seven pirate vessels, rescued three merchant ships, found some of their stolen cargo and other property, escorted two convoys, and patrolled hundreds of miles of ocean.[123]

Many other nations stationed substantial naval forces in the eastern Mediterranean as well, including the United Kingdom, France, Austria, the Netherlands, and Sardinia. However, there were several reasons why those naval contingents never combined to crush the Greek pirates. First, despite the large number of warships in the region, there were never enough vessels to successfully suppress Greek piracy. Second, a majority of the naval officers tasked with suppressing piracy were sympathetic to the Greek cause and were reluctant to react harshly to Greek actions. Moreover, Britain, France, and Russia were not eager to suppress piracy since it served as one of the most important pretexts for their eventual intervention in the war. Therefore, cultural, geographic, and diplomatic considerations worked together to retard efforts to suppress piracy in Greek waters.

Austria, which was one of the few European nations not supportive of the Greeks, reacted aggressively to Greek piracy. Austria's opposition to the Greek Revolution was based on two important considerations. First, since Russia, Austria's traditional enemy, backed the Greeks, Austria naturally became a supporter of the Turks. Second, and perhaps even more important, the Austrians viewed Greek nationalism as a threat to their own empire, which was cobbled together among peoples of many nationalities.[124]

Believing that the Austrians were in league with the Ottomans, the Greeks enthusiastically attacked Austrian merchant vessels. The Austrians responded by sending a large naval contingent to the Levant. In 1826, 22 Austrian ships operated in Greek and Turkish waters. Because of the hostility between the Greeks and Austrians, the Austrians resorted to force more often, whether to prevent acts of piracy or to punish villages that provided support to pirates, than did the other navies operating in the Mediterranean. For example, the Austrians landed on Mykonos in July 1826 in retaliation for a pirate attack. They burned three boats, destroyed a house, and forced the villagers to pay a fine. A few days later, on 22 July, the same Austrian force attacked Tinos and captured a Greek corvette and brig, which they held for ransom. A month later, the Austrians bombarded and then assaulted Naxos in retaliation for two attacks on Austrian vessels.[125] Despite such efforts, the Greeks continued to prey on Austrian shipping.

The Austrian squadron actually outnumbered the Royal Navy forces in the Mediterranean in 1826. The British Mediterranean Fleet was only assigned 13 warships in 1826. Of those 13 ships, 8 were sloops and small frigates, the ships most useful for antipirate operations. Following the pattern used against the Caribbean pirates, the British used their small boats to engage the corsairs close to shore. For example, in April 1826, sailors in boats from the sloop *Alacrity* destroyed 3 pirate vessels, killed 40 pirates, and captured 70 more near Psara. Although the *Alacrity* suffered only five wounded, such actions were not always easy. When the frigate *Sibylle* sent its boats to recapture a Maltese vessel taken by two mistikos off the coast of Crete in June 1826, the British sailors were bloodily repulsed. As they approached the cove into which the buccaneers fled, several other pirate crews ambushed the British, killing 14 and wounding 30 others.[126] As in the Caribbean, crews spent many hours in small boats, searching for and chasing brigands. One captain stated that his crew chased five pirate vessels for almost 20 miles before giving up.[127] But the British did not have enough ships to effectively counter the pirates. Consequently, the British sloops and frigates were stretched thin and unable to stem the tide.

Some Greeks believed that the more piracy occurred, the greater the likelihood of allied intervention. They may have been right. By the spring of 1827, serious negotiations were underway between Britain, France, and Russia to settle the terms for intervention in the war. In the meantime, Admiral Sir Edward Codrington took command of the Mediterranean Fleet in February 1827 with orders to put a damper on piracy. Soon after he arrived, he met with Greek leaders in Napoli de Romania (Náfplio) and warned them that they had to end the piracy plaguing the region if "unpleasant consequences were to be avoided."[128] Codrington also received additional ships, more than doubling his force by the end of 1827. Just as important, 19 of Codrington's ships were sloops and small frigates.[129]

Meanwhile, the allies agreed to terms and signed the Treaty of London on 6 July 1827. One explicit justification for the treaty was the need to suppress piracy and protect the commercial interests of the three signatory nations, the United Kingdom, France, and Russia. The treaty did not necessarily guarantee independence for Greece; instead, it proposed establishing Greece as a tributary state under Turkish rule. But a secret article also directed the allies to enforce an armistice if either side chose not to participate. In the instructions sent to the British, French, and Russian admirals, the admirals were directed to treat the Greeks as friends if they accepted the armistice. The admirals were also authorized to prevent resupply of Turkish and Egyptian forces if the Turks failed to abide by the treaty.[130] When the Ottoman and Egyptian commanders resisted the restraints placed on them by the allies, the allies pulverized the Egyptian and Turkish Fleets at Navarin Bay on 20 October 1827. With the loss of their fleet, the war was effectively over for the Ottomans since they could not control the sea and were thus unable to resupply or reinforce their forces in Greece.[131]

Navarin Bay demonstrated to the Greek Government what would happen to them if they failed to comply with the allies' demand that they stop piracy. To head off further action, the president of Greece asked the allies to eliminate the most galling pirate haven—the island of Grabusa near Crete. Grabusa was a perfect pirate haven. Its citadel was almost impregnable, and its harbor was difficult to blockade because of the winds and current. But it was a place of little significance until some 6,000 Christians, driven off Crete by the Turks, took refuge on the island in August 1825. With no means to support themselves, the refugees turned to piracy. Their first foray occurred in February 1826 when the raiders extorted $5,000 from a French ship. Over the next 2 years, the corsairs of Grabusa captured 486 more vessels. They soon developed a highly organized structure, much like a joint stock company, to distribute the booty. Each inhabitant owned shares of the venture and was rewarded accordingly. The community received one-fifth of all the spoils. Soon, 20 brigs and schooners and almost 60 smaller craft were operating from the island. Even worse, they were later joined by some of the best Greek warships, which abandoned the cause for plunder and profit.[132]

An allied squadron, including three British frigates, two British sloops, and two French corvettes, sailed into the harbor of Grabusa on 31 January 1828. There, they found 14 Greek ships and two prizes. Most of the other pirates fled Grabusa because of rumors of allied retribution. Commodore Sir Thomas Staines demanded that the pirates surrender immediately. When they failed to do so, his flotilla opened fire and destroyed most of the pirate ships.[133] Although this action destroyed the naval power of the island, Staines still had to reduce the citadel and capture the pirate leaders. Over the next month and a half, through negotiation and subterfuge, Staines managed to accomplish that task as well without combat. Once he gained control of the fortress and evacuated all the inhabitants, Staines' soldiers, sailors, and marines demolished the citadel, rendering it useless.[134]

Around the time that Commodore Staines finished with Grabusa, the Greek Navy moved against having the pirates operate from the island of Sporades. In early March 1828, the Greek frigate *Hellas*, accompanied by two gunboats, seized 78 armed craft on the island without incident. The Greek Government kept 37 of the boats and destroyed the rest. None of the pirates were, however, prosecuted by the government.[135]

Although there continued to be isolated acts of piracy in the eastern Mediterranean, those two actions essentially ended piracy in the Greek islands. As in other regions and eras, Greek piracy flourished because of the three conditions that facilitate piracy: favorable geography, political turmoil, and sanctuaries ashore. Once the political situation stabilized and the Greek Government neutralized the corsairs' island sanctuaries, piracy diminished to acceptable levels. But it took operations ashore, such as the capture of Grabusa and the destruction of the havens on Sporades, to remove the pirates' support system and demonstrate that the cost of continued acts of piracy was worse than pursing other means of support. Therefore, naval power alone was not sufficient to end piracy in the Greek isles.

Notes

1. Philip Gossse, *The History of Piracy* (New York: Tudor Publishing Company, 1932), 5.

2. Gosse estimated that 50 talents was the equivalent of £12,000, which is approximately $850,000 in current dollars.

3. Gosse, *The History of Piracy*, 4–8.

4. Ralph T. Ward, *Pirates in History* (Baltimore, MD: York Press, 1974), 22.

5. Ibid., 20.

6. Ibid., 29.

7. Ibid., 18.

8. Ibid., 33–34.

9. Ibid., 37.

10. Ibid., 41–44.

11. Ibid., 45.

12. Robin Fowler, "Pirates of the Mediterranean: Pillaging and Plundering in Ancient Times," *Suite101.com*, 21 May 2007, http://ancient-culture.suite101.com/article.cfm/pirates_of_the_mediterranean (accessed 29 January 2009).

13. Ward, 115.

14. Frank Lambert, *The Barbary Wars: American Independence in the Atlantic World* (New York: Hill and Wang, 2005), 31.

15. Ibid., 32–33.

16. Gregory Fremont-Barnes, *The Wars of the Barbary Pirates; To the Shores of Tripoli: The Rise of the US Navy and Marines* (Oxford: Osprey Publishing, 2006), 16–17.

17. Peter Earle, *The Pirate Wars* (New York: Thomas Dunne Books, 2005), 41.

18. Ward, 118.

19. Fremont-Barnes, 16.

20. Lambert, 51.

21. Ibid., 35; Ward, note 2, 123.

22. Lambert, 73–74.

23. The title Bashaw is a variation of Pasha and is used by a head of government with the added role of military commander. See Ward, note 2, 123.

24. Lambert, 90.

25. Ibid., 93. Bey means governor and is also an honorific for persons of equivalent rank to a governor. See Ward, note 2, 123.

26. Ibid., 123.

27. Lambert, 37–38.

28. Earle, 51.

29. Ibid., 71.

30. Fremont-Barnes, 19.

31. James A. Field, *America and the Mediterranean World, 1776–1882* (Princeton, NJ: Princeton University Press, 1969), 29.

32. Earle, 73.

33. Field, 32.

34. Fremont-Barnes, 85–86.

35. Lambert, 32.

36. R. Ernest Dupuy and William H. Baumer, *The Little Wars of the United States* (New York: Hawthorn Books, 1968), 28.

37. Fremont-Barnes, 32; Lambert, 58–59.

38. Field, 33.

39. Fremont-Barnes, 32–33; Lambert, 59–61.

40. Field, 33.

41. Ibid., 34.

42. Lambert, 71–72.

43. Dudley W. Knox, *A History of the United States Navy* (New York: G.P. Putnam's Sons, 1936), 58; Lambert, 73.

44. John Paul Jones was the first commissioner, but he died before he could carry out his mission. Likewise, the second appointee, Thomas Barclay, also died before he even left the United States. In the meantime, the Dey of Algiers died and was replaced by Ali Hassan, who decided he needed to take a hard line against the United States to solidify his position as Dey. See Lambert, 73–74.

45. Ibid., 73–76; Field, 37.

46. Knox, 60; Field, 37; Lambert, 81.

47. Knox, 60.

48. Ibid., 58–59; Field, 37.

49. Knox, 60.

50. Dupuy and Baumer, 30; Knox, 61.

51. Lambert, 90–92.

52. Knox, 61–62; Lambert, 92.

53. Knox, 62.

54. Fremont-Barnes, 39.

55. Dupuy and Baumer, 36–37.

56. Fremont-Barnes, 41.

57. Knox, 63.

58. Lambert, 132–133.

59. Dupuy and Baumer, 41.

60. Lambert, 133.

61. Knox, 63–64; Fremont-Barnes, 44.

62. Dupuy and Baumer, 44; Knox, 64.

63. Lambert, 140–141; Fremont-Barnes, 46; Knox, 64.

64. Lambert, 143–145; Fremont-Barnes, 47–49; Knox, 65–66; Dupuy and Baumer, 46–49.

65. Lambert, 146; Dupuy and Baumer, 52.

66. Dupuy and Baumer, 49.

67. Lambert, 147; Fremont-Barnes, 49–52; Dupuy and Baumer, 49–51; Knox, 70–72.

68. Lambert, 148–149; Fremont-Barnes, 53–55; Dupuy and Baumer, 53; Knox, 73–74.

69. Field, 52–53; Lambert, 146–147; Fremont-Barnes, 56–57.

70. Field, 53–54; Lambert, 150–153; Fremont-Barnes, 58–62; Dupuy and Baumer, 55–59.

71. Field, 56–57.

72. Lambert, 177–178.

73. Fremont-Barnes, 76–77; Dupuy and Baumer, 61–62.

74. Fremont-Barnes, 76–77.

75. Fremont-Barnes, 77–79; Dupuy and Baumer, 63–64.

76. Fremont-Barnes, 80.

77. Ibid., 81.

78. William L. Clowes, *The Royal Navy: A History From the Earliest Times to the Present*, vol. VI (London: Sampson Low, Marston and Co., 1901), 226–227.

79. Ibid., 227–229; Fremont-Barnes, 83–85.

80. Clowes, vol. VI, 229; Fremont-Barnes, 84–85.

81. Clowes, vol. VI, 227.

82. Fremont-Barnes, 85–87.

83. The Morea was another name used for the Peloponnese Peninsula.

84. W. Alison Phillips, *Modern Europe, 1815–1899, Period VIII*, 2d ed. (London: Rivingtons, 1902), 136.

85. W. Alison Phillips, *The War of Greek Independence, 1821–1833* (New York: Charles Scribner's Sons, 1897), 10.

86. Douglas Dakin, *The Greek Struggle for Independence, 1821–1833* (Berkeley, CA: University of California Press, 1973), 17.

87. Phillips, *The War of Greek Independence,* 10.

88. Dakin, 60.

89. Earle, 225.

90. C.G. Pitcairn Jones, ed., *Piracy in the Levant, 1827–28: Selected From the Papers of Admiral Sir Edward Codrington, KCB* (London: Navy Records Society, 1934), xvii; Dakin, 74–75.

91. Thomas Gordon, *History of the Greek Revolution*, vol. II (Edinburgh: William Blackwood, 1832), 477.

92. These islands are part of the Sporades Islands in the northern Aegean Sea.

93. Gordon, 478–479.

94. Earle, 226–227.

95. Gordon, 479.

96. Earle, 227.

97. Dakin, 74–75.

98. Ibid., 74.

99. Phillips, *Modern Europe,* 137–138.

100. Dakin, 100.

101. Earle, 225.

102. Dakin, 100.

103. Ibid., 121.

104. Phillips, *The War of Greek Independence,* 156–157.

105. Dakin, 122.

106. Phillips, *The War of Greek Independence,* 168.

107. Dakin, 184.

108. Earle, 226.

109. David F. Long, *Gold Braid and Foreign Relations: Diplomatic Activities of United States Naval Officers, 1798–1833* (Annapolis, MD: United States Naval Institute Press, 1988), 200.

110. Phillips, *The War of Greek Independence,* 253.

111. Gordon, 486.

112. Earle, 226.

113. Ibid.

114. Field, 125.

115. Edgar S. Maclay, *A History of the United States Navy From 1775 to 1894*, vol. II (New York: D. Appleton and Company, 1894), 125.

116. Peter M. Swartz, "US-Greek Naval Relations Begin: Antipiracy Operations in the Aegean Sea" (Alexandria, VA: Center for Naval Analysis, Center for Strategic Studies, June 2003).

117. Field, 127.

118. Swartz.

119. Gordon, 479.

120. A passage between the islands of Negropont (Evvoia) and Andros.

121. *A Naval Encyclopedia* (Philadelphia, PA: L.R. Hamersly and Co., 1881), 314–315.

122. US Congress, *On the Expediency of Sending Two Additional Sloops-of-War to the Mediterranean Sea, for the Suppression of Piracy by the Greeks*, 20th Cong., 1st sess., no. 361, 11 March 1828, http://www.ibiblio.org/pha/USN/1828/18280311Piracy.html (accessed 18 February 2009).

123. Ibid.

124. R.C. Anderson, *Naval Wars in the Levant, 1559–1853* (Princeton, NJ: Princeton University Press, 1952), 509.

125. Ibid., 508–509.

126. Clowes, vol. VI, 251.

127. Earle, 248.

128. Jones, xxviii.

129. Ibid., xxv. Of the 13 ships assigned to the British Mediterranean Fleet in 1826, there were the seven sloops, one sixth-rate frigate, four fifth-rate frigates, and one third-rate ship-of-the-line. Because of their shallow draft, the sloops and the *Talbot*, a sixth-rate frigate, were useful antipiracy vessels. By the end of 1827, there were 27 ships in the Mediterranean Fleet, including six fourth-rate or better ships-of-the-line, six fifth- or sixth-rate frigates, and 15 sloops.

130. Dakin, 182–183. After the battle, Admiral Codrington received significant public criticism, and the battle was officially labeled an "untoward event." Codrington steadfastly maintained that he merely followed his orders. Since Prime Minister George Canning died on 8 August 1827, a little over a month

after he sent Codrington his orders, there was considerable uncertainty about what, exactly, the admiral was authorized to do. Although he was never officially reprimanded for the destruction of the Ottoman Fleet, Admiral Codrington was recalled to Britain in the summer of 1828 and never given another sea-going command. See also Clowes, vol. VI, 261.

131. Dakin, 226–230.
132. Gordon, 482–486.
133. Clowes, vol. VI, 261–262.
134. Gordon, 490–796.
135. Ibid., 496–497.

Chapter 4

Asian Piracy

Asia encompasses a broad geographic range and a wide variety of cultures. However, whether in the Persian Gulf, among the islands of Southeast Asia, or along the coast of China, piracy found the right conditions to flourish: geography, political instability, and safe havens ashore. Moreover, piracy prospered in many eras, not just the periods under consideration in this chapter. As noted earlier, pirates from the Persian Gulf raided the Sumerians more than 4,000 years ago and Hammurabi outlawed piracy in his code.[1] There are written records referring to piracy during the Chow (Zhou) dynasty in China, which lasted from 1122 to 221 BC, as well.[2] Although similar records do not exist among the Malays, piracy in the islands no doubt goes back equally as far.

Once again, geography played a crucial role in the development of piracy in Asia. Both the Arabs and Malays benefited from major chokepoints: the Strait of Hormuz for the Arabs and the Strait of Malacca for the Malays. The Arab pirates, who were based on the Arabian Peninsula, could easily control the Strait of Hormuz. Southeast Asian pirates based on Sumatra or the Riau Archipelago were in a position to dominate the Strait of Malacca. The thousands of islands in the region provided the pirates excellent places to hide and to wait for victims. Although there is no comparable chokepoint for Chinese pirates, they too benefited from favorable geography. China's long coastline and many rivers gave the pirates innumerable places to hide. Moreover, China was so large that the central government could not easily control the entire country, so pirates often acted with impunity along the frontier.

Political instability also played an important role in Asian piracy during the 19th century. There was conflict between the Arab pirates and their nominal ruler, the Sultan of Oman. The rulers who emerged after the destruction of the empire of Malacca were not strong enough to regulate the Southeast Asian pirates. Even though China had a centralized government, by the 19th century, the Manchu dynasty was in decline and unable to exert control over its periphery.

Finally, in all three geographic areas, safe havens existed, which made piracy feasible. Piracy was integral to the lives of many Arabs and Malays, who essentially lived on the water. Piracy supplemented their income. Since it was woven into the fabric of their lives, those involved in piracy found ready havens ashore where they could rest, refit, and expend their plunder. Chinese piracy was not as integrated into the primarily agrarian society. Still, Chinese pirates found ready markets for their stolen goods, often through the good offices of corrupt officials.

Piracy in the Persian Gulf

The Portuguese were the first European mariners to enter the Persian Gulf in force in the modern period. They dominated the Gulf from the early 16th century until the arrival of the British and Dutch in the early 17th century. With help from the East India Company, Shah Abbas of Persia drove the Portuguese out of their stronghold on Kharg Island in 1622. From that point onward, British commercial interests grew in importance even as Portuguese fortunes declined.[3] But the Persian Gulf remained a strategic afterthought to British policymakers for almost 200 more years.

During the late 18th century, particularly after the death of the Shah Karim Khan in 1779, Persia lost control of the Gulf. The result was increased competition and conflict among the various coastal tribes of the Persian Gulf. That conflict devolved into raiding and, in British eyes, piracy.[4] Arab corsairs based on the western coast of the Arabian Peninsula ranged far out into the Indian Ocean, threatening British shipping there as well as in the Persian Gulf.

The increase in piracy negatively impacted British trade in the region. Since the East India Company's trade in the Persian Gulf was relatively limited, it made no effort to suppress piracy in the Gulf. But independent British merchants, known as "country traders," were affected. These country traders developed fairly substantial and lucrative trade relationships in the Gulf.[5] They exchanged British manufactured goods for pearls, Persian silks, and specie that were used in the China trade. Even though the Arabs normally left the well-armed East India Company vessels alone, they sometimes attacked the smaller, more vulnerable country traders. British merchants, of course, condemned such transgressions and pressed both the British Government and East India Company to take action.[6]

The strategic outlook also changed at the beginning of the 19th century. Because the Persian Gulf was one of the primary mail links between the United Kingdom and India, the pirates impinged on official Britain when they attacked British mail ships.[7] Even more important, the French expedition to Egypt (1798–1801) and France's short-lived alliance with the Shah of Persia (1807–1809) raised the threat of French invasion through India's northwest territories. British policymakers began to view the Persian Gulf as a buffer zone, protecting India's western flank.[8]

The death of the Sultan of Oman in November 1804 led to further aggression against British merchant shipping in the Gulf. At the time of the

Sultan's death, the British were actively pursuing an alliance with Oman. East India Company leaders realized that Oman, because of its location at the entrance to the Persian Gulf, was perfectly situated to restrict French and Dutch access to the Gulf. But Britain's relationship with Oman put it at odds with one of the tribes most involved in piracy. The al-Qawasim[9] were nominal vassals of the Sultan of Oman, but when he died, they reneged on their allegiance and broke away from Oman.[10] Britain became a de facto enemy of the al-Qawasim. But that circumstance had distinct advantages since suppression of piracy in the Gulf not only would appease merchant and shipping interests in Britain but also would enhance Great Britain's strategic relationship with Oman.

All three conditions that facilitate piracy are readily apparent when considering the Persian Gulf. The al-Qawasim were ideally situated geographically to perpetrate acts of piracy. The tribe's territory included some 25 coastal towns on the western side of the Arabian Peninsula from the tip south to Dubai.[11] Its main port was Ras al-Khaymah,[12] which is located some 50 miles from the northern tip of the Arabian Peninsula. At that point, the Strait of Hormuz is only about 30 miles wide. Thus, the al-Qawasim could easily control traffic entering or leaving the Persian Gulf. The decline of Persian control of the Gulf and the death of the Sultan of Oman led to political turmoil, which facilitated piracy in the Gulf. Furthermore, since the United Kingdom was fully involved in the Napoleonic Wars, the British lacked the resources to aggressively respond to piracy in the Persian Gulf. Since the al-Qawasim depended on the sea for their existence, whether by trading, harvesting pearls, or raiding, there was considerable land-based support for their piratical activities within their territory as well. (Figure 7 shows the Persian Gulf and the Gulf of Oman.)

The attacks began in the last quarter of the 18th century. In December 1778, six al-Qawasim vessels attacked a British ship carrying official dispatches. After a running battle that lasted 3 days, the British ship succumbed and was taken to Ras al-Khaymah as a prize. Encouraged by their success, the al-Qawasim assaulted two more British vessels the next year. The most significant incident occurred in October 1797 when the al-Qawasim stormed the East India Company cruiser *Viper* while in port in Bushehr.[13] Although the company ship drove off the attackers, *Viper* suffered 32 casualties out of a crew of 65.[14]

After they broke away from Oman, the al-Qawasim began levying tolls on all shipping entering or leaving the Gulf. When the British refused to pay the toll, the al-Qawasim retaliated by raiding British shipping.[15] They captured two British ships in 1804 and attacked a 24-gun East India Company cruiser in January 1805.[16] There was a short respite after the

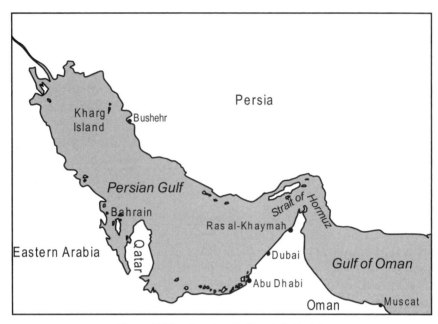

Figure 7. The Persian Gulf and Gulf of Oman.

Omanis, led by the British Resident in Muscat, blockaded the main al-Qawasim fleet in Ras al-Khaymah and forced them to submit.[17]

The truce did not, however, last long. In the meantime, the al-Qawasim continued to consolidate their power. By 1808, the al-Qawasim fleet numbered some 63 large vessels, 810 small dhows, and 18,000 to 25,000 fighters.[18] In April 1808, two al-Qawasim dhows attacked another East India Company ship, the *Fury* (6 guns).[19] Once the summer pearling season ended,[20] the al-Qawasim resumed the war against the United Kingdom. The violence quickly escalated. When they captured the East India Company schooner *Sylph* (8 guns) in October 1808, the pirates killed 22 crewmembers. Only the captain survived. Wounded when the Arabs took the ship, the captain hid in a storeroom below deck and was rescued when the HMS *La Nereide* (38 guns) recaptured the *Sylph* as the raiders sailed her back to Ras al-Khaymah.[21] The next month, some 40 al-Qawasim dhows entered the Indian Ocean and wreaked havoc on British and Indian shipping. Within a short time, they captured 20 merchant vessels and shut down commerce along the western coast of India.[22]

This proved too much for the East India Company to accept so, in September 1809, a combined land and naval force was dispatched to the Persian Gulf to deal with the pirates. The force included 2 Royal Navy frigates, 8 East India Company cruisers, 1 East India Company bomb ketch, and 1,300 soldiers, half of whom were Europeans.[23] Its primary objective was Ras al-Khaymah, which was assaulted and captured on 13 November 1809. Company soldiers sacked the town and burned 60 dhows trapped in the harbor.[24] Later, the British force attacked two al-Qawasim strongholds in Persia: Linga and Luft.[25]

British operations against the al-Qawasim pirates demonstrate the difficulty of trying to eliminate piracy using primarily naval forces. Although the British inflicted a substantial amount of damage on the al-Qawasim, the impact of the 1809 expedition was limited. Once the British returned to India, the al-Qawasim quickly recuperated. By the fall of 1813, al-Qawasim dhows once again hunted for prey off the coast of India. Further pirate cruises were conducted in the spring and fall of 1814. The al-Qawasim acted even more aggressively in the Persian Gulf, attacking two American, one French, and three Indian ships.[26] In 1816, the British sent another expedition to punish the pirates, but it was even less effective because the naval force limited its actions to merely bombarding Ras al-Khaymah.[27] During the 1817–1818 trading season, the situation was so bad that convoys were used to mitigate the risk of attack.[28]

By the end of 1818, the situation was ripe for a more forceful response to the pirates. By that date, the British successfully concluded two wars in India, the Pindari and Mahratta Wars, and now had sufficient forces available to mount a more substantial attack on the al-Qawasim. Major General Sir William Grant-Keir organized and led this expedition. His force included 1,450 European soldiers and 2,100 Sepoys; the HMS *Liverpool*, a 50-gun frigate, and the HMS *Curlew*, an 18-gun brig; and a 14-gun East India Company cruiser. The HMS *Eden* (24 guns) and seven East India Company warships were already in the Persian Gulf and joined the task force once it arrived in the Gulf.[29]

The British force anchored off Ras al-Khaymah on 4 December 1819. The troops landed southwest of the town and advanced to within 300 yards of the city walls. There, they erected entrenchments and set up artillery to bombard the fortifications. The bombardment continued for 2 days. By 6 December, it was clear that the 12- and 18-pounders were not powerful enough to knock down the town's walls, so sailors brought two 24-pounders ashore. They began firing on 8 December and continued until Grant-Keir's troops assaulted Ras al-Khaymah on 9 December. Meanwhile, the Arabs abandoned the city, so the troops entered unopposed. Over the next few days, the British force occupied itself by destroying the town's fortifications and burning all of the dhows in the harbor.[30]

Over the next few weeks, realizing the power of the British force, all of the leading sheiks traveled to Ras al-Khaymah and submitted to General Grant-Keir. On 8 January 1820, they signed the General Treaty of Peace.[31] The most pertinent provisions of this treaty required all signatories to suppress piracy and refrain from killing captives.[32] If they failed to do so, other parties, that is, the United Kingdom, could step in and take action. From this point forward, acts of piracy in the Persian Gulf declined precipitously. Moreover, when they did occur, the local sheik acted quickly to punish the deed before the British stepped in to rectify the situation.[33]

British antipiracy operations in the Persian Gulf clearly demonstrate the need to eliminate shore havens. The first two British expeditions were of limited value because the land element was either insufficient or nonexistent. Even though the first expedition captured Ras al-Khaymah and destroyed several more towns, its impact was short lived because the British force soon sailed away. Once they were gone, the Arabs resumed acting as they had before the British arrived. The second expedition, which made no attempt to conduct operations ashore, was totally ineffective. Only the third expedition, which included a substantial land component, was successful. This force had enough troops to insinuate that the British were there to stay and intimidate many Arab groups, not just the al-Qawasim, into signing the General Treaty of Peace.

East Indies Piracy

Spices such as nutmeg, pepper, cinnamon, ginger, and cloves were highly prized commodities for thousands of years. Before the 16th century, such spices were only available to Europeans through overland caravan routes terminating in the Levant. That changed in the 16th century when the Portuguese reached the East Indies. The Portuguese began bringing back spices by ship around the Cape of Good Hope. The desire to obtain a share of the spice trade was a significant motivation for the exploration and subsequent colonization of the East Indies by other European countries.[34] Once the Dutch and English joined in the competition, the number of ships sailing to the Malay Archipelago in search of spices increased from a couple each year to 11 per year during 1600–1630.[35] By the late 18th century, spice imports into Europe tripled.[36] Although the potential for profit was great, trading with the East Indies was risky. Commenting on the risks in 1796, a British merchant noted that, if piracy was suppressed, trade would become more regularized and profitable.[37]

Piracy in the East Indies proved, however, difficult to suppress. As with other regions, it flourished because of the three conditions that make piracy possible. The pirates of the Malay Archipelago benefited from favorable geography. Some 17,500 islands make up modern-day Indonesia, which lies at the heart of the geographic region under consideration. Moreover, Indonesia has almost 34,000 miles of coastline. Even today, with all of our modern technology, it is impossible to effectively patrol such a vast coastline.[38] There are also a limited number of passages through which vessels heading east toward the Spice Islands and China can transit. Thus, ships laden with valuable cargo were funneled into confined areas, making them more vulnerable to attack. The Malay pirates used their geography to their advantage. Because of the chokepoints, they knew where to look for potential prizes. While they waited for their quarry, the pirates hid in the many coves, bays, and inlets dotting the coast of the East Indies islands. When they spotted a likely target, usually a ship becalmed or aground in the shallow coastal waters, the pirates swooped down on it in their swift boats and quickly boarded and plundered it.[39] (Figure 8 shows Sumatra and the Malacca Strait.)

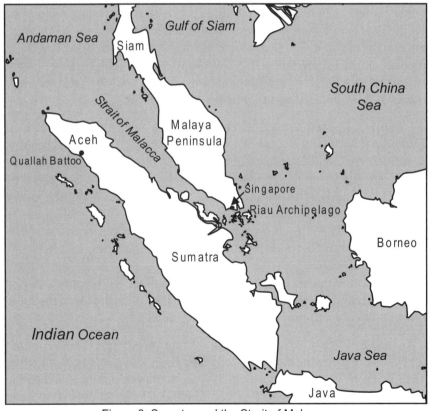

Figure 8. Sumatra and the Strait of Malacca.

The region also suffered from political instability, making it ripe for piracy. The Portuguese destroyed the Malay Empire of Malacca in the early 16th century. A series of relatively weak small kingdoms took its place. For example, in the early 19th century, the Sultan of Johor was nominal ruler of the Riau Archipelago. Piracy was rife in the islands of the Riau Archipelago, which dominated the southern end of the Strait of Malacca. Since the Sultan was unable to exert control over the many local chiefs, they operated as they pleased most of the time.[40] Similarly, the Sultan of Acheen ruled the northwestern coast of Sumatra, known as the "pepper coast." Although he was strong enough to maintain his independence from the Europeans, he had little control over most of his subjects.[41] Thus, political instability made it easier for the Malay pirates to operate with impunity.

The Malay pirates also benefited from safe havens ashore. Piracy was an integral part of life in the East Indies. In the Riau Archipelago, an annual cycle of commercial activity and piracy evolved. From February to April, islanders busied themselves collecting agar-agar, an edible algae they traded with the Chinese. In early summer, when the southeast monsoon set in, the islanders turned to piracy. They remained at sea through October, ranging throughout Southeast Asia and the Indian Ocean in search of plunder. After a short rest, the cycle resumed in February.[42] Since piracy was deeply woven into life in the islands, the pirates were afforded safe places to rest, replace their losses, and dispose of their plunder.

For many years, the East Indies pirates avoided the heavily armed European vessels. But as the volume of trade expanded in the 19th century, so did the temptation to attack European and American vessels. The first American ship to visit the pepper coast was the brig *Cadet* out of Salem in 1789.[43] When other American merchants learned that the *Cadet* turned a 700-percent profit on that voyage, they too turned their sights onto the East Indies.[44] By 1812, 29 American ships sailed to the Orient each year. The pace quicken after a lull due to the War of 1812. From 1815 to 1820, American merchants sent, on average, 39 ships per year to the Orient. President James Monroe considered this commerce so important that he sent the *Congress* to the Orient in 1819 to protect US merchant ships from pirates.[45]

One of the most successful Malay pirates was Raga, who terrorized the Makassar Strait for more than 17 years. Raga first garnered attention in 1813 when he captured three British vessels and personally executed the captains of all three ships. The British responded by sending two sloops to chastise the pirate. When one of the warships, the *Elk*, destroyed several of Raga's vessels and killed many of his crewmen, he swore vengeance against the British. A contemporary observer claims that, through 1830, Raga captured more than 40 European ships and murdered the captains and crews of each one.[46]

The East India Company responded to the transgressions of Raga and others half-heartedly, sending a rag-tag collection of vessels to the Malacca Strait to deal with the pirates. These included schooners, yachts, flat-bottomed boats, and other small craft. But the heart of the British antipiracy flotilla was a 6-gun brig and a 12-gun schooner.[47] Hamstrung by the lack of resources, Royal Navy and East India Company naval commanders had little impact on the situation until 1830 when Rear Admiral Edward Owen arrived. Owen soon determined that the indifference with which local officials treated the piracy problem was, in part, due to their lack of success against the corsairs. Consequently, he instituted several changes in tactics that proved moderately successful. Owen decided to focus on destroying the brigands' boats and controlling the coastline. When British forces engaged pirates, they allowed the brigands to escape, but they seized and destroyed the corsairs' vessels. Without their boats, the pirates were unable to prey on merchant shipping. He also constructed small forts and established small boat patrols near the mouths of rivers known to serve the brigands. By controlling the pirates' egress points, Owen's forces prevented the brigands from putting to sea and attacking commercial vessels. By the mid-1830s, after Owen departed, his initiatives waned and piracy surged in the region.[48]

East Indian piracy eventually provoked the United States into using military force against the brigands. Malay pirates attacked an American merchant ship, the *Friendship*, while anchored off the coast of Quallah Battoo, Sumatra, on 7 February 1831. A boatload of armed Malays boarded the *Friendship*, killing three crewmen and wounding three others, while the captain and four other crewmen were ashore negotiating with the inhabitants of the village. Four sailors escaped the massacre and joined the captain, Charles Endicott, and his party who were saved by a Raja from a neighboring village. The Americans rowed to Muckie, some 25 miles away, and enlisted the help of three other American vessels. When the American merchant ships arrived at Quallah Battoo, the Raja refused to release the *Friendship* and return the goods plundered from it. The Americans used their guns to drive the Malays away from the *Friendship* and then boarded the ship without incident. The pirates stole all of the ship's navigational instruments, trade goods, opium, and $40,000 in hard specie.[49]

When word of the incident reached the United States in the summer of 1831, President Andrew Jackson ordered the Navy to investigate the affair and, if necessary, to secure restitution and ensure that the transgressors were punished. The 44-gun frigate *Potomac*, under the command of Commodore John Downes, left the United States on 26 August 1831. Downes' orders authorized him to attack the village, reclaim the stolen goods, and punish the murderers if his inquiry confirmed Endicott's story and the village Raja refused to cooperate. By the time Downes arrived at Quallah Battoo on 5 February, he had decided to ignore the first part of his orders, directing him to look into incident before acting. Convinced that the Malays were guilty, Downes attacked Quallah Battoo without warning on 6 February 1831. Early that morning, 282 sailors and marines assaulted four of the forts defending the town. Within hours, more than 100 Malays, including the Raja, were dead. The Americans suffered only 2 dead and 11 wounded. The next day, *Potomac* fired several broadsides into the village, which prompted the Malays to surrender and submit to Downes. He warned the inhabitants that, if they attacked another American ship, the United States would respond with even more force. A few days later, he sailed into a neighboring village and delivered a similar message. After learning of Quallah Battoo's fate, the Raja of that town as well as several surrounding villages precipitously promised to treat American ships as friends.[50]

Even before the *Potomac* returned home, Downes' actions caused considerable political turmoil in Washington. The aftermath of the Quallah Battoo mission underscores the difficulty of dealing harshly with pirates. The *Daily National Intelligencer*, an anti-Jackson newspaper, severely criticized Jackson for making war without Congressional approval. While the newspaper agreed that the Federal Government had the right to punish the pirates, it maintained that only Congress had the authority to declare war and it considered the action at Quallah Battoo warfare. Downes' actions put Jackson in a bad spot. Jackson did not reveal that Downes failed to comply with his orders, instead arguing that the punishment was justly deserved. With current international law ambiguous, this incident highlights one of the potential pitfalls facing modern naval forces if they use lethal force against modern-day pirates.

Although he severely punished the pirates, the impact of Downes' actions was short lived and a second incident occurred in August 1837. The *Eclipse*, from Salem, was taking on pepper off Trabangan, when a group of armed Malays were allowed on board. They quickly killed the captain and an apprentice. Several other crewmen were wounded but allowed to escape by climbing the rigging or jumping overboard. Those who escaped ashore were saved by the Raja of Trabangan. The pirates stole 4 cases of opium and 18 casks of Spanish dollars.[51]

Before news of that incident arrived, President Martin Van Buren dispatched another naval force to the Orient to check on the situation in Sumatra and elsewhere. Commodore George Read set sail from Hampton Roads on 6 May 1838 on the *Columbia*, a 50-gun frigate. *Columbia* was accompanied by the sloop *John Adams* (30 guns), a veteran of the West Indies antipiracy campaign. While visiting Colombo, Ceylon (Sri Lanka), in early December, Read learned of the attack perpetrated on *Eclipse*. He immediately set out for Sumatra, arriving there on 22 December. Learning from Downes' mistake, Read did not act precipitously. Instead, he tried to negotiate with the Raja of Quallah Battoo. After 3 days of discussion, Read determined that the Raja was stalling and decided to act. The next day, Christmas 1838, he bombarded Quallah Battoo. The inhabitants surrendered within a half hour and Read refrained from further attack. Read then sailed over to the village of Muckie, where some of the chief instigators of the crime lived. Once again, negotiations failed, so Read attacked Muckie on New Years' Day 1839. After a brief bombardment, 320 sailors and marines landed on the beach and laid waste to the town. Read then transited to the third town involved in the crime, Susu. When he got there and discovered its miserable condition, Read refrained from attacking the village. Instead, he forced the ruler of Susu, along with many of the other local rulers, to promise not to attack American vessels in the future.[52]

By the mid-1830s, piracy was on the rise in the Malacca Strait. In May 1833, Singapore merchants estimated the value of their trade at 2 million Spanish dollars. That trade, along with the commercial traffic that did not stop in Singapore, acted as a magnet for pirates. Singapore officials estimated that 40 to 50 pirate vessels were operating in the strait.[53] When the world descended into an economic depression in the 1830s and 1840s, suppression of the East Indian pirates took on new importance because of the impact it had on trade.[54] Losses to piracy depressed prices and discouraged merchants from trading with the East Indies.

Any attempt at suppressing piracy in the region was complicated by the United Kingdom's treaties with the various Malay Sultans. Most of the treaties prohibited British interference in local affairs. Since many of the Sultans gave support and cover to the pirates, intervention would infringe on the treaties.[55] By the mid-1830s, piracy in the Malacca Strait became so obtrusive that the British began to act unilaterally. The *Harrier* (18-guns) eradicated two pirate settlements in the Strait of Malacca in 1834. Two years later, boats from the *Andromache* located and destroyed three pirate proas operating in the strait. During a running battle on 30 May 1836 that lasted long into the night, British sailors killed 113 Malays and captured 9 while sustaining no casualties themselves. Disregarding Dutch protests, the British then moved against Galang Island in the Riau Archipelago. Even though they killed only a few brigands, the British razed three villages and burned dozens of proas. By smashing the corsairs' havens, the British put a significant damper on further pirate attacks in the Strait of Malacca.[56]

Similarly, British forces led by Captain Henry Keppel and James Brooke, who had used intrigue to become a native official known as the Raja of Sarawak, conducted a series of expeditions against the pirates operating along the northern coast of Borneo in the 1840s. Brooke and Keppel agreed that the most effective way to counter the pirates of Borneo was to destroy their strongholds far upriver. The first expedition set out up the Saribas River in July 1843. The mixed British and native force traveled up the river in eight boats. Over the next 9 days, the British-led force captured and destroyed three fortified villages. By 17 July, all of the tribes along the river submitted to Brooke. The next year, in August 1844, the pair led another expedition against a different pirate tribe. This time, they captured 4 forts, seized 60 brass cannon, burned numerous villages, and destroyed several hundred boats. This campaign broke the power of the pirate leader, Raja Seriff Sahib, who went into hiding. There were several more engagements with the pirates of Borneo in 1846. Still, those actions were not enough to convince the pirates to stop their piratical activities, so in July 1849, Brooke and a large British force under Commander Arthur Farquhar set out to subdue the Dyak pirates. During the Battle of Bantung Maru, 31 July 1849, the British force trapped the pirates and smashed their fleet. Perhaps as many as 800 pirates were killed and 60 vessels were destroyed. Although isolated instances of piracy continued to occur, the pirates of Borneo never recovered from this defeat.[57]

The American and British actions against the Malay pirates demonstrate the necessity of cleaning out pirate havens ashore. Both the Americans and British struck the pirates where they were most vulnerable: their shore bases. It is never easy to detect, identify, and destroy pirates at sea. The geography of the Malay Archipelago made that task even more difficult. Consequently, antipiracy forces eliminated their shore havens and thus neutralized the pirates.

Even though the impact of the first American expedition was short lived, and there were several more unsuccessful attacks on American ships in the 1840s, no more American merchant ships were taken by Malay pirates after the second expedition. Some of the credit for neutralizing the Malayan brigands must go to the vigorous American response to the attacks. But changing political conditions also contributed to the decline in attacks. The Dutch took control of Sumatra in 1846 and set up trade restrictions that prevented Americans from freely trading with the Sumatrans. By the mid-1850s, the once vigorous pepper trade had withered away to almost nothing. With little reason to visit Sumatra, few American merchant ships exposed themselves to the risk of Malay piracy after the mid-1850s.[58]

Similarly, the British campaigns in the Strait of Malacca and Borneo succeeded because they attacked the pirates in their lairs. But the success Brooke and Farquhar achieved was tainted by the high number of casualties inflicted on the native pirates. Both men were severely criticized in Parliament and in public.[59] Their subsequent treatment underscores the challenges of dealing harshly with pirates. Even though such actions might be effective, public backlash might render them moot.

Chinese Piracy

Late one afternoon, a heavily armed junk got underway from Hong Kong en route to Swatow (Shantou), 180 miles to the north. Later that evening, when the winds died, the vessel dropped anchor to wait for better sailing conditions. While at anchor, the junk was accosted by pirates, who quickly overran the ship. After locking the passengers and crew below deck, the pirates sailed south toward Macao. The next morning, the pirates tied the hands and feet of all but one of the 83 passengers and crewmembers and flung them overboard to drown. They only spared a 12-year-old boy, who they put to work as their servant. The pirates pulled into a small cove north of Macao and disposed of the junk's cargo. Then, they burned the junk, and breaking up into smaller groups, they returned to Hong Kong. Seven of the pirates, along with the young boy, took a ferry from Macao to Hong Kong. The boy managed to tell the ferry's captain what had happened, and the captain notified the Hong Kong police, who captured the seven pirates. When the boy's story was corroborated by one of the passengers who managed to avoid drowning, the pirates were tried and executed.[60]

That story encapsulates much of the piracy rampant along the coast of China in the 19th century. Chinese piracy was frequently perpetrated against Chinese rather than foreign vessels. It was a bloody affair; if ransoms were not forthcoming, Chinese pirates frequently murdered their victims. Much of the piracy occurred in the vicinity of Hong Kong and Macao. And it conformed to the three conditions for piracy. The coast of China is inundated with many small coves, harbors, creeks, and inlets.

These served as excellent hiding places for pirates, who darted out and attacked coastal vessels. China was in the vortex of political turmoil throughout much of the 19th century as the ruling Manchu dynasty slowly collapsed. Consequently, there were many safe locations from which the pirates could operate. Local officials, situated far from the centers of Chinese power, often protected the pirates and profited from their activities. Thus, the pirates were able to safely dispose of their plunder; repair their ships; and rest, recuperate, and recruit without fear of capture.

The first American ship to sail to China was the *Empress of China*, which arrived at Canton, China, on 28 August 1784.[61] American trade with China grew gradually throughout the late 18th and early 19th centuries. From 1804 to 1812, on average, 29 American ships sailed for Asia. Between 1815 through 1820, that number increased to 39 ships.[62] In 1832, 30 American ships set out specifically for China.[63] By 1820, American trade with China exceeded that of all nations except the United Kingdom.[64] In 1832, that trade amounted to more than $1.5 million in exported goods and $5.3 million in products imported from China.[65] Thus, protection of foreign trade from piracy, whether in Chinese waters or in other parts of the Far East, was an increasingly important task. (Figure 9 shows Hong Kong, Macao, and Canton.)

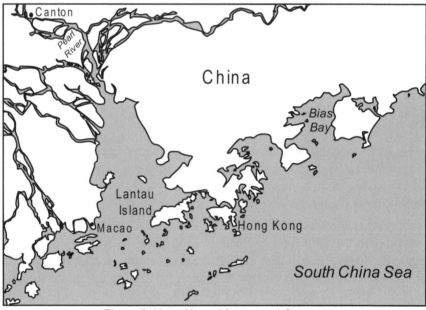

Figure 9. Hong Kong, Macao, and Canton.

Although trade with China was even more important to the United Kingdom, it was a decidedly one-sided affair at first. The China trade, primarily tea, began expanding in the mid-18th century. The British East India Company imported 15 million pounds of tea from China in 1785.[66] Because of their vast internal market, Chinese officials viewed trade with Great Britain with indifference. Everything they needed, most Chinese believed, could be produced from within.[67] Even more frustrating to foreign diplomats, Chinese officials refused to deal with other nations on equal terms. They believed that China was the Middle Kingdom, suspended between heaven and earth. Consequently, since the Emperor was superior to all other rulers, Chinese officials treated foreign dignitaries as social and political inferiors. This caused considerable friction between Great Britain and China. It also meant that China would not countenance direct foreign trade because it was beneath them. Instead, all trade was conducted between middle men (*co-hong*) in one port—Canton. Foreign merchants feared offending the Chinese and precipitating a prohibition against foreign trade altogether, so they were reluctant to challenge Chinese conditions.[68]

One of the primary consequences of the Chinese mind-set was that Chinese officials insisted on receiving silver for their tea instead of trading for other goods they believed they did not need. That policy quickly led to a trade surplus that reached $26 million during 1800–1810.[69] But the British soon developed a substitute for silver—opium. Although the Emperor forbade the importation of opium in 1730, imports continued to grow steadily. More than 1,000 chests[70] of the drug were imported into China in 1773.[71] Imports of opium grew to 34,000 chests in 1836. More important for the British, China's trade surplus was transformed into a trade deficit of $38 million by 1836.[72] But increased trade meant more pressure to protect the sealanes from pirates. By the mid-19th century, this became a main concern of both the British Government and Royal Navy.

As in other parts of the world, many ordinary Chinese citizens living along the coast participated in petty piracy. Temporary, seasonal piracy was common because sea conditions prevented most fishermen from working more than 120 to 150 days per year. During the summer months, when fishing was difficult and dangerous, many fishermen turned to low-level piracy. Taking advantage of the southerly winds, they sailed north and pillaged along the coast until the winds shifted in the fall. Such patterns led to the integration of piracy into the framework of coastal society, thus making it possible for pirates to blend back into society once the cruise was over.[73]

Chinese piracy remained relatively inconsequential until the early 19th century when a vast pirate confederacy emerged. The impetus for the formation of this confederation was civil war in Vietnam—the Tay-son Rebellion. The Tay-son rebels recruited Chinese pirates to augment their naval forces during the war.[74] When they were not fighting the deposed Vietnamese ruler's forces, the pirates preyed on Chinese vessels in the Gulf of Tonkin. By 1796, the pirates were so successful that the Chinese Government could no longer ignore their activities. But when a squadron of gunboats tried to crush the pirates the following year, the government forces were routed.[75] (Figure 10 shows the Hainan Island and the South China Sea.)

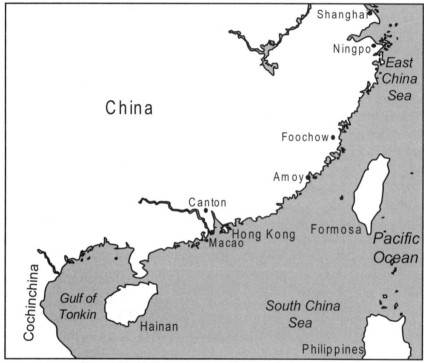

Figure 10. Hainan Island and the South China Sea.

When the Tay-son Rebellion ended in defeat in 1802, the pirates returned to Chinese waters and began attacking native shipping. Outnumbering the government forces more than three to one, the pirates soon gained control of most of the southern coast of China.[76] By 1809, the pirates threatened Canton itself.[77] Fighting for the Tay-son rebels had taught the pirates many valuable lessons. They were no longer loose gangs of petty pirates; they had become well organized both operationally and logistically. They were also much more skilled in combat than the government forces sent to suppress them.[78] At first, the various pirate groups competed with one another for prizes, but in 1805, seven pirate leaders joined forces, creating a confederation that, at its height, encompassed more than 2,000 vessels of all sizes.[79]

China's military was poorly organized and unable to effectively counter the pirates. Since the Chinese Government was concerned about rebellion originating on the periphery of the empire, it was reluctant to concentrate military power along the seacoast. Instead, it parceled out small units of soldiers in guard houses along the coast to protect against raiders. Moreover, China did not have an established fleet. Instead, it dispersed its naval forces among several independent naval districts that could not combine or coordinate their operations. Additionally, there were rules governing the size of vessels, which, in turn, limited the size of naval vessels because the Chinese did not build specific naval craft. Since the pirates did not comply with those rules, Chinese naval vessels were consistently smaller than and outgunned by the pirates.[80] The result was that Chinese Government forces could never concentrate enough combat power to overwhelm the pirates and suffered a series of defeats during the first decade of the 19th century. By the end of the decade, government forces were afraid to put to sea.[81]

Unable to defeat the brigands, Chinese provincial leaders attempted to co-opt the pirates instead. Government officials implemented a "pardon and pacification" policy, in which any pirate who agreed to stop piracy received a pardon, money, and, if so desired, an appointment in the military or as a servant.[82] Even though they continued to suffer defeats at sea, the pardon and pacification policy eventually worked, and by June 1810, the last of the corsair fleets were defeated by former pirate leaders.[83]

But the final victory against the pirates came much too late, for attacks on American and British flagged vessels opened the door for foreign naval involvement in the region. An American schooner, the *Pilgrim*, was captured in 1808 and its crew held for ransom.[84] Five more US ships suffered attacks in 1809. By the summer of that year, it was clear that the government was unable to control the corsairs, and foreigners became concerned that the pirates might shut down all trade with China.[85] Thus, in September 1809, when Chinese officials approached the "barbarians" in Macao for help, the Europeans were ready to act. The Chinese hired the British ship *Mercury*, which was armed with 20 cannon and manned by 50

American merchant sailors, to confront the pirates. Later that same month, the Chinese leased six Portuguese warships to use against the pirates.[86] While those forces were not able to defeat the brigands either, they set the precedent of foreign intervention against pirates in Chinese waters.

Acts of piracy in Chinese waters eventually drew a response from the navies of both the United States and Great Britain. The first US warship to visit China was the frigate *Congress* (36 guns), which arrived in November 1819. But her mission, protecting American commerce from piracy by convoying them out of the region, went unfulfilled because American merchants, fearful that accepting the *Congress'* protection would offend the Chinese and precipitate a trade ban, refused to join any convoys. *Congress*, therefore, returned to the United States in May 1821 with little to show for her effort.[87] By the time the sloop *Vincennes* (18 guns) arrived in 1830, after years of growing pirate activity, the attitude of American merchants toward naval intervention was much different. American merchants requested annual visits by a warship, and from the mid-1830s onward, the United States maintained at least one warship in Far Eastern waters to look after American interests. The East Indies Squadron was formally established in 1841.[88]

The Royal Navy increased its presence in Chinese waters during the 1830s as well. That decision was due in part to the increase in piracy in the region. The antipiracy mission fell to the Royal Navy in 1834 when the East India Company's monopoly on trade with China expired. From 1715 until 1834, the East India Company was responsible for Anglo-Chinese relations. The company's powerful East Indiamen and warships made the presence of Royal Navy warships in Chinese waters unnecessary.[89] Very few Royal Navy ships visited China during that period. Like American merchants, the East India Company complied with the Chinese prohibition against foreign warships entering China's territorial waters because of fear that failing to do so might trigger a trade ban.[90] But British warships were disinclined to follow such rules, which led to conflict between China and Great Britain when the Crown took over responsibility for relations with China in 1834.

During the first few years after the expiration of the East India Company's monopoly, the British Government maintained a hands-off approach. But an increasing number of incidents in the second half of the 1830s led to a change in that policy. By the early 1840s, Chinese brigands not only were attacking native craft but also were targeting British, American, and European vessels. On 26 March 1841, they attacked the British vessel *Blenheim* and killed three British citizens.[91] The British responded by dispatching the sloop *Pylades* (18 guns) to the Chusan Archipelago where she captured three pirate junks.[92] Eventually, a permanent squadron consisting of one ship-of-the-line, one frigate, five sloops, and one steamship was established. A second frigate was added to the squadron in 1853.[93]

More attention was also paid to pirate hunting because it was potentially profitable. The British Parliament passed "An Act for Encouraging the Capture or Destruction of Piratical Ships and Vessels" in June 1825. This act paid a bounty of £20 for each pirate killed or captured and £5 for any pirate that was on the pirate vessel at the time of the attack who later escaped.[94] So, there were significant monetary incentives to seek out and kill the brigands, even if they were hiding in Chinese territorial waters.

The Chinese state had other problems in this period, with political turmoil threatening to overwhelm the Manchu dynasty in the 1840s and 1850s.[95] Friction between China and Great Britain burst into outright hostility in 1839 when the new Governor General of Canton, Lin Tse-hsu, tried to enforce the Emperor's edict against the importation of opium into China. After 2½ years of desultory warfare, the British forced the Chinese to submit. Among the reasons for the war, in Britain's view, was the right to carry out and defend legitimate trade.[96] The Treaty of Nanking, which ended the war, opened four more ports to British trade and ceded Hong Kong to Great Britain.[97]

A second, far more serious, war broke out in 1856. This time, the French teamed up with the British to punish the Chinese. After a delay caused by the Indian Mutiny, an Anglo-French task force assembled in Hong Kong in December 1857. The allies quickly took Canton. After they threatened to assault Peking, the Chinese agreed to negotiate. The Treaty of Tientsin, completed in June 1858, seemed to acknowledge political equality between China and the victors. It allowed for the establishment of a permanent residency in Peking, opened five more ports to trade, and allowed foreign travel in China with a passport. But the Chinese continued to equivocate, and the allies responded by marching on Peking. When they broke through the Chinese river defenses and began bombarding the city, the Chinese finally gave in.[98]

Those two wars, plus the Taiping Rebellion, which raged from 1850 until 1864, tore the country apart and critically wounded the Manchu dynasty. The turmoil created by the wars greatly facilitated the proliferation of piracy in Chinese waters. It was difficult to tell who was a rebel and who was a pirate. With the central government unable to respond, pirates acted with growing impunity.

The acquisition of Hong Kong was problematic for the British. On the one hand, Hong Kong had an excellent harbor that could be developed for the Royal Navy and British merchants. On the other hand, many Chinese corsairs operated in or near Hong Kong. Hong Kong merchants and shopkeepers provided those pirates with substantial assistance. They furnished them with arms, ammunition, supplies, and information. In exchange, the merchants and shopkeepers bought the pirates' stolen goods at cut-rate prices.[99] Thus, the British were now responsible for controlling piracy in the waters surrounding Hong Kong.

Although the Governor of Hong Kong could prosecute pirates captured within 3 miles of shore and the Royal Navy could apprehend them on the high sea, corsairs operating within China's territorial waters were subject only to Chinese laws. Since it was clear that the Chinese did not have the ability to suppress piracy in their territorial waters, this posed a dilemma for the British because the Treaty of Nanking did not grant Great Britain the right to pursue pirates in those waters.[100] Chinese determination not to extend any further privileges to the British resulted in restrictive rules of engagement for the Royal Navy. At the insistence of the British Superintendent of Trade, Vice Admiral William Parker ordered his captains to refrain from attacking possible pirate vessels unless they personally observed a piratical act.[101] The result was an upsurge of piracy after 1842.

By 1846, the Admiralty Board considered piracy such a problem that it advised the Commander of the East Indian and China Station, Rear Admiral Samuel Hood Inglefield, that "suppression of the system of Piracy prevailing on the Coast of Fukien as far as it may be practicable to accomplish it, is an object of great importance to our commercial interests and to the improvement of our relations with China."[102] Soon, the new British commander, Rear Admiral Francis A. Collier, eased up on the requirement to personally observe an act of piracy before taking action. To allay Chinese concerns, Collier tried to work with the Chinese whenever he could.[103] Thus, the conditions were set for a more aggressive response to the pirates in the late 1840s and 1850s.

There were plenty of opportunities for action and British and American naval forces frequently operated together against Chinese pirates. In 1849, the United States sloop *Preble* (16 guns), operating in support of British naval forces, helped capture 57 junks and destroy two pirate havens.[104] The British sloop *Pilot* (16 guns) spent the entire summer of 1849 looking for pirates along the east coast of China.[105]

British and American forces conducted a successful campaign against the Chinese pirate Shap-ng-tsai and his associate Chui-Apoo in 1849.

110

Chui-Apoo murdered two English officers in February 1849 in Hong Kong, thus bringing down the fury of the Crown on him. The British brig *Columbine* (12 guns), with help from the paddle-wheel sloop *Fury* (6 guns), the Peninsula and Orient Company steamer *Canton*, and boats from the HMS *Hastings*, destroyed Chui-Apoo's fleet during two encounters on 28–29 September 1849. British forces destroyed 23 pirate junks and killed an estimated 400 of the 1,800 pirates engaged.[106]

One month later, in October 1849, *Columbine*, caught up with Shap-ng-tsai. Shap-ng-tsai's pirates devastated the southern coast of China in the spring and summer of 1849. He even had the temerity to attack a British-owned junk off Hainan in June. Accompanied by a Chinese official and eight imperial warships, *Columbine* went in search of Shap-ng-tsai. The coalition force finally caught up with Shap-ng-tsai and his pirates on 20 October. Over the next 2 days, British and Imperial Chinese forces destroyed 58 pirate ships, including Shap-ng-tsai's, and killed some 1,700 pirates with the loss of only one man. Both Shap-ng-tsai and Chui-Apoo escaped. Shap-ng-tsai was eventually pardoned and co-opted into the Chinese bureaucracy while Chui-Apoo was captured and committed suicide while in jail.[107]

Despite the successes achieved in 1849, pirate attacks continued. The *China Mail* reported pirate attacks on a weekly basis. A British official complained that "there does not appear to have been any piracy committed on a grand scale, but the seas continue to be infested by a class of rovers who are fishermen, traders, or Pirates, as it serves their turn." The British squadron in Chinese waters, while successful, was too small to be effective, and it had too many responsibilities to provide continual protection to any one location.[108]

After a short interlude caused by the First Opium War, antipiracy operations resumed in 1853. In May of that year, the *Rattler* (11 guns), a screw-propelled sloop, engaged seven corsair junks and an eighth vessel near Namquan. The pirates had recently captured a merchant convoy and were waiting there for their prizes to be ransomed. Gunfire from the *Rattler* sunk the pirate commander's junk and one other vessel, which disheartened the pirates. The other junks beached themselves, and the brigands tried to escape ashore. But angry peasants on the beach hunted down and killed most of the pirates. One group seized a nearby junk, murdered the crew, and tried to escape upriver. The *Rattler*'s cutter caught up with the pirates, but when the British sailors tried to board the junk, an officer and two sailors were killed and the survivors were driven off. The *Rattler*'s commander reported that they killed 500 pirates; captured 84 guns, 4 junks, and 1 lorcha; and sank 2 junks and burned a third.[109]

By 1854, civil disturbances sparked by the Taiping Rebellion added to the piracy problem in China. The Pearl River was almost impassable for Chinese vessels, and even foreign ships were attacked while trying to make the transit up river to Canton. Conditions were almost as bad in Shanghai.[110] When Commodore Matthew C. Perry withdrew the East Indies Squadron from China so he could make a more impressive showing in Japan, his action caused an uproar in the American merchant community. To appease the merchants, Perry leased a British-owned steamboat, the *Queen*, and left her behind to protect American commercial interests. The *Queen* was manned with 20 American and 10 Chinese sailors and armed with 4 small guns. Its first commander was Lieutenant Alfred Taylor from the side-wheel steamer *Mississippi* (10 guns).[111] Later that year, Lieutenant George H. Preble was detached from the sloop *Macedonian* (36 guns) and given temporary command of the *Queen*.[112]

With the situation becoming more serious each day, the British decided to act. Since they expected most of the encounters to occur in Chinese territorial waters, the Governor of Hong Kong asked the Chinese to join the coalition against the pirates. Chinese officials agreed and sent a high-ranking official and a war junk to participate in the operation. American and Portuguese naval forces as well as Chinese merchants also contributed to the operation. By November 1854, the British had gathered together a task force consisting of the screw-propelled sloop *Encounter* (14 guns), the paddle-wheel sloop *Barracouta* (6 guns) and the paddle-wheel sloop *Styx* (6 guns), a launch from the *Winchester*, and the pinnace from the *Spartan*. Other vessels included the *Queen*, the Portuguese *Amazon*, two Peninsula & Orient Company steamers hired by Chinese merchants, and the Chinese war junk.[113]

One of the first actions by the newly established coalition force occurred in early November when the *Queen* discovered a large group of corsairs anchored in Taiho Harbor on the north side of Lantau Island. Since the *Queen* was unable to close with the pirates because of shoal water, Preble returned to Hong Kong and requested assistance from Rear Admiral Sir James Stirling. Admiral Stirling sent the *Encounter* and some armed boats to help. *Encounter* used her guns to drive the brigands off their ships. Boarding parties in the armed boats captured and burned 17 pirate vessels.[114]

Following that mission, Admiral Stirling led seven allied vessels against the Chinese corsair Aw-ung, who was thought to be hiding near Khulan (Coulan) on a nearby island. The allies attacked the brigands on 11 November 1854, destroying 50 junks, razing 3 villages, and smashing

3 shore batteries. Although the coalition force killed 90 pirates, its losses were light. Only one American, a sailor off the *Macedonian*, was killed.[115]

In February 1855, the British brig *Bittern* (12 guns) rescued the British schooner *Zephyr*, which was held captive on the River Min near Wanchew. The sailors captured 3 pirate junks and 64 corsairs. Eight or nine other vessels got away.[116]

Later, Preble commanded two more missions against brigands in the vicinity of Shanghai. In June 1855, Preble led an armed party on the towboat *Confucius* to Foochow and Ningpo. Along the way, they escorted a convoy of 250 junks carrying timber and successfully engaged five pirate vessels. The next month, Preble joined a British expedition against corsairs operating in the Yellow Sea. Once again, Preble sailed on the *Confucius*. This time, the allies aborted the mission after their support vessel, the coal brig *Clown*, foundered in heavy seas.[117] (Figure 11 shows Nanking (Nanjing), Shanghai, and Ningpo (Ningbo).)

The British sloop *Racehorse* (18 guns) discovered a pirate flotilla while searching the Chinese coast between Amoy and Foochow. The

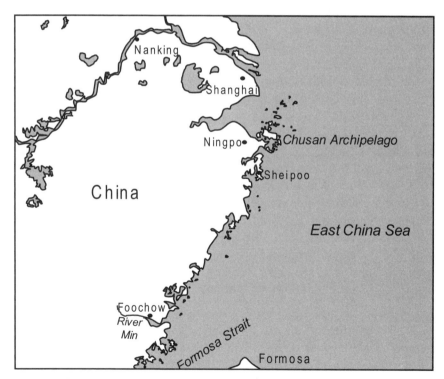

Figure 11. Nanking (Nanjing), Shanghai, and Ningpo (Ningbo).

next day, 26 June 1855, a cutter from the *Racehorse* captured one of the corsairs' vessels and burned it. That afternoon, two more pirate junks were engaged. One was captured and the other burned. A captured lorcha was liberated and returned to Amoy.[118]

A few weeks later, on 4 July 1855, *Racehorse* captured a pirate junk. Unfortunately, during the same engagement, *Racehorse* suffered nine casualties while trying to capture a larger junk. As the sloop's gig pulled up alongside the pirate ship, a stinkpot was dropped into the gig, igniting the ammunition in the boat. All nine sailors were blown out of the boat. While all nine crewmen were recovered, seven received severe injuries, two of whom subsequently died. Meanwhile, the vessel approached the junk unnoticed and blasted away at the corsairs. With their ship full of holes, the brigands ran it ashore to prevent it from sinking. Most of the pirates were either killed or drowned. Those who survived were captured by *Racehorse*'s crew or villagers living nearby.[119]

In late July 1855, three trading junks and a fourth vessel were captured by pirates while under escort by the armed steamer *Eaglet*. When *Rattler* learned of the incident, she went in search of the pirates. *Rattler* located the pirates in Khulan Harbor, scene of a battle the previous November. Unfortunately, *Rattler* was unable to engage the brigands because she drew too much water to enter the anchorage and did not have enough small boats to take on the pirates. Consequently, *Rattler* returned to Hong Kong and requested assistance from the *Powhatan*. *Rattler* got underway on 3 August, towing three small boats from the *Powhatan* that were manned by 100 American sailors and marines and armed with a howitzer. The next morning, 4 August, the shallow-draft *Eaglet* took both the *Rattler*'s and *Powhatan*'s boats under tow and steamed into the anchorage. When a private vessel tried to escape, the *Rattler*'s pinnace and the *Powhatan*'s cutter moved to cut it off. Just as the two boats rowed out of view, the rest of the small flotilla discovered the main pirate force—36 war junks. Although the corsairs directed heavy cannon fire toward the allies, it was ineffective. But the aim of the British and American sailors was not. They sank six vessels and captured 14 large junks although 16 smaller ones escaped. They also liberated seven junks. Two of the junks could not be salvaged and were burned along with the 14 captured pirate vessels.[120]

The *Bittern* continued operations against the pirates during the summer of 1855. Over the last 2 weeks in August, *Bittern* engaged a pirate fleet composed of 30 to 40 vessels and destroyed 20 of them. On 19 August, *Bittern* attacked corsairs in the Gulf of Leotung (Liaodong Wan) and sank eight vessels. Most of the brigands fled south, and *Bittern* caught up with

13 of the pirate ships the next day and captured or sank 11 of them. Finally, on 30 August, *Bittern* discovered one more pirate vessel from the original flotilla and destroyed it as well.[121]

A few weeks later, on 18 September 1855, *Bittern*, along with the hired armed ship *Paoushun*, engaged 22 pirate vessels near Sheipoo. During a sharp fight that lasted more than an hour, *Bittern* devastated the corsair fleet. After the battle, *Bittern* determined that only one of the 22 vessels was seaworthy, so her crew destroyed the rest of them. Some of the brigands tried to flee ashore but they were killed by peasants from neighboring villages. The commander of the *Bittern* noted that, since the mandarin in Sheipoo was almost totally helpless, the village near where the corsairs were discovered, which he described as "thoroughly piratical," was clearly a haven for the pirates.[122]

Despite those efforts, piracy remained a problem throughout the 1860s. But a series of measures implemented by British and Chinese authorities reduced piracy to acceptable levels by the end of the decade. The Treaty of Tientsin, which ended the Second Opium War, granted the British the right to enter Chinese waters in pursuit of pirates.[123] Later, the United States received similar concessions from the Chinese.[124] More important, the new Governor of Hong Kong implemented reforms in 1866 that ended Hong Kong's role as a haven for brigands. Helping pirates in any way, whether by providing them with arms and supplies, protecting them, or receiving their plunder was a violation of the law and subjected the violator to heavy penalties.[125] Although the British organized a coalition antipiracy task force, including Chinese, American, Dutch, Portuguese, and Prussian ships in the mid-1860s, by the end of the decade, the British sought to disengage from antipiracy operations.[126] Instead, they tried to provide the Chinese with the military and administrative tools necessary to do the job themselves. For example, in 1869, the Chinese received two gunboats for use against pirates. They also ordered three small armed steamers that same year.[127] While one cannot claim that corsairs no longer roamed Chinese waters, these measures made it possible for the United Kingdom to scale back its antipirate activities after 1870.

Piracy in Chinese waters flourished because of the three primary pillars. There was favorable geography. Much of the piracy was concentrated in the approaches to Canton. Those waters are filled with small islands, bays, coves, and inlets, all of which made ideal hiding places for pirates. China also suffered from political turmoil throughout much of this period. The Chinese fought two wars with the United Kingdom and, in between the two wars, was wracked by rebellion. Chinese pirates profited from those circumstances. One of the benefits was safe havens ashore. In many areas, local officials were unable to effectively govern, thus allowing the pirates to act with impunity. But their most important haven was Hong Kong. Until the reforms of the late 1860s, pirates freely walked the streets of the colony. They were able to resupply, gather intelligence, and dispose of their plundered goods there. Thus, for much of the 19th century, conditions in China made piracy a profitable venture.

But the story of antipiracy operations in China also underscores other conditions that limited the viability of piracy. One of the most important was that pirates did not always operate in friendly or benign environments. On more than one occasion, British and American officers reported that villagers attacked and killed the brigands who tried to escape ashore. Therefore, Chinese pirates, unlike their Greek and Arab contemporaries, could not always count on safe havens ashore. Moreover, British and American actions to suppress piracy occurred during the transition from wind power to steam power. This was an important development, for the antipirate naval forces had a significant technological advantage over their foes whenever steamships were added to the mix. Since British and American naval forces often engaged the pirates in rivers or in shallow bays, where it is difficult to maneuver sailing ships, steam-powered vessels provided them with a decided advantage. The war against Chinese corsairs also demonstrated the superiority of British and American weapons, tactics, and discipline, which enabled them to defeat much larger pirate forces with minimal losses. Unlike earlier antipirate campaigns, the British and Americans had the right ships and tactics from the beginning.

Thus, the battle waged by British and American naval forces against the Chinese pirates serves as a bridge between modern antipiracy operations and those of the age of sail. Even though the pirates had the advantages of geography, political turmoil, and sanctuaries ashore, the British and Americans were able to limit the scope of their actions. Technology, not overwhelming force, enabled them to do so.

Notes

1. Ralph T. Ward, *Pirates in History* (Baltimore, MD: York Press, 1974), 1–2.

2. Philip Gosse, *The History of Piracy* (New York: Tudor Publishing Co., 1932), 265.

3. Middle East Research and Information Project, "Neo-Piracy in Oman and the Gulf: The Origins of British Imperialism in the Gulf," *MERIP Reports*, no. 36 (April 1975): 4.

4. L.E. Sweet, "Pirates or Polities? Arab Societies of the Persian or Arabian Gulf, 18th Century," *Ethnohistory* 11, no. 3 (Summer 1964): 265.

5. Country traders were East India Company officials acting in a private capacity or Indian merchants operating under license by the East India Company, which found it expedient to allow private merchants to conduct external trade, especially the ever growing opium trade with China. See C.M. Turnbull, "Country Traders," in *Southeast Asia: A Historical Encyclopedia From Angkor Wat to East Timor*, Ooi Keat Gin, ed. (Santa Barbara, CA: ABC-CLIO, 2004), 389–390; C.E. Davies, "Britain, Trade and Piracy: The British Expeditions Against Ras Al-Khaima of 1809–10 and 1819–20," in *Global Interests in the Arab Gulf*, Charles E. Davies, ed. (New York: St. Martin's Press, 1992), 36.

6. "Neo-Piracy in Oman and the Gulf," 4.

7. Patricia Risso, "Cross-Cultural Perceptions of Piracy: Maritime Violence in the Western Indian Ocean and Persian Gulf Region During a Long Eighteenth Century," *Journal of World History* 12, no. 2 (Fall 2001): 2.

8. James Onley, *The Arabian Frontier of the British Raj: Merchants, Rulers, and the British in the 19th Century Gulf* (Oxford: Oxford University Press, 2007), 35.

9. This tribe is also referred to as the Joasmees and Jowasim in various sources.

10. J.B. Kelly, *Britain and the Persian Gulf, 1795–1880* (Oxford: Clarendon Press, 1968), 105.

11. Sweet, 271.

12. Ras al-Khaymah, which is sometimes identified as Ras-al-Khyma, Ras al-Khaimah, and Ras al-Khaima, is located in what is now the United Arab Emirates.

13. Bushehr may also be spelled Bushire or Bushir.

14. Gosse, *The History of Piracy*, 255–256.

15. Onley, 44.

16. Kelly, 106.

17. Gosse, *The History of Piracy*, 257.

18. Kelly, 111.

19. Gosse, *The History of Piracy*, 257.

20. The Arabs traditionally honored a truce during the summer months when they harvested pearls. Raiding resumed during the winter months. See Sweet, 275.

21. Gosse, *The History of Piracy*, 257–258.

22. Kelly, 114.

23. Ibid., 116.

24. Gosse, *The History of Piracy*, 263.

25. "HMS Caroline," *Michael Phillips' Ships of the Old Navy,* http://www.ageofnelson.org/MichaelPhillips/info.php?ref=0460 (accessed 15 January 2009). Linga (Bandar-e Lingeh) is located on the mainland of Persia. Luft (Laft) is located on the island of Jazireh-ye Qeshm.

26. Kelly, 129–132.

27. Gosse, *The History of Piracy*, 264; Kelly, 133–134.

28. Kelly, 137.

29. Ibid., 149.

30. "HMS Liverpool," *Michael Phillips' Ships of the Old Navy,* http://www.ageofnelson.org/MichaelPhillips/info.php?ref=1348 (accessed 14 January 2009).

31. Kelly, 154–156.

32. Risso, 11.

33. Kelly, 205–208.

34. The terms East Indies and Malay Archipelago will be used interchangeably in this chapter. *The CIA World Fact Book* defines the Malay Archipelago as the modern-day nations of Brunei, Indonesia, Malaysia, Papua New Guinea, and the Philippines and their surrounding waters. See *The CIA World Fact Book* (Washington, DC: Office of Public Affairs, 2008), https://www.cia.gov/library/publications/the-world-factbook/appendix/appendix-f.html (accessed 23 February 2009).

35. Anthony Reid, "An 'Age of Commerce' in Southeast Asian History," *Modern Asian Studies* 24, no. 1 (February 1990): 9.

36. Ibid., 7.

37. H.R.C. Wright, "The Anglo-Dutch Dispute in the East, 1814–1824," *The Economic History Review* 3, no. 2 (1950): 231.

38. *The CIA World Fact Book.*

39. Proas are wooden boats of 35 to 50 feet displacing some 6 to 8 tons. They were typically armed with one or two small bow-mounted cannon and four swivel guns on both sides. They carried crews of 20 to 30 men. See Charles Ellms, *The Pirates Own Book: Authentic Narratives of the Most Celebrated Sea Robbers* (Philadelphia, PA: Thomas, Cowperthwait, & Co., 1837), 106.

40. David Cordingly, consulting ed. *Pirates: Terror on the High Seas From the Caribbean to the South China Sea* (Atlanta, GA: Turner Publishing, 1996), 189.

41. David F. Long, *Gold Braid and Foreign Relations: Diplomatic Activities of United States Naval Officers, 1798–1833* (Annapolis, MD: United States Naval Institute Press, 1988), 252.

42. Cordingly, *Pirates: Terror on the High Seas*, 190.

43. Charles O. Paullin, *American Voyages to the Orient, 1690–1865: An Account of Merchant and Naval Activities in China, Japan, and the Various Pacific Islands* (Annapolis, MD: United States Naval Institute Press, 1971), 43.

44. Long, 252.

45. Paullin, 23.

46. Ellms, 107–108. See also Gosse, *The History of Piracy*, 285–286.

47. Cordingly, *Pirates: Terror on the High Seas*, 193.

48. Ibid., 194–195.

49. Paullin, 44–45; Long, 252–253.

50. Paullin, 45–53; Long, 253.

51. Paullin, 79; Long, 256–257.

52. Paullin, 79–83; Long, 256–258.

53. Cordingly, *Pirates: Terror on the High Seas*, 195.

54. Nicholas Tarling, *Imperial Britain in South-East Asia* (London: Oxford University Press, 1975), 66.

55. Ibid., 58.

56. Cordingly, *Pirates: Terror on the High Seas*, 196–198.

57. Ibid., 198–205; Gosse, *The History of Piracy*, 288–294; and William L. Clowes, *The Royal Navy: A History from the Earliest Times to the Present*, vol. VI (London: Sampson Low, Marston and Co., 1901), 332–336; 362–363.

58. Long, 259–260; Max Boot, *The Savage Wars of Peace: Small Wars and the Rise of American Power* (New York: Basic Books, 2002), 49.

59. Cordingly, *Pirates: Terror on the High Seas*, 205.

60. Captain H.C. St. John, RN, *Notes and Sketches From the Wild Coasts of Nipon, With Chapters on Cruising After Pirates in Chinese Waters* (Edinburgh: David Douglas, 1880), 279–282.

61. Paullin, 9.

62. Ibid., 23.

63. Robert E. Johnson, *Far China Station: The US Navy in Asian Waters, 1800–1898* (Annapolis, MD: United States Naval Institute Press, 1979), 3.

64. Paullin, 23.

65. Johnson, *Far China Station*, 3.

66. Peter Lowe, *Britain in the Far East: A Survey From 1819 to the Present* (London: Longman, 1981), 9.

67. Donald MacIntyre, *Sea Power in the Pacific: A History From the Sixteenth Century to the Present Day* (New York: Russell and Co., 1972), 62.

68. Long, 208.

69. Lowe, 10.

70. A chest of opium contained 140 to 160 pounds of the drug. See MacIntyre, 64.

71. Ibid.

72. Lowe, 10.

73. Cordingly, *Pirates: Terror on the High Seas*, 214–215.

74. Dian H. Murray, *Pirates of the South China Coast, 1790–1810* (Stanford, CA: Stanford University Press, 1987), 35.

75. Ibid., 43–45.

76. Cordingly remarks that just before the formation of the confederation, some 70,000 pirates operated 400 junks along the coast of China. See Cordingly, *Pirates: Terror on the High Seas*, 222.

77. Ibid., 234.

78. Ibid., 222–225.

79. Murray, 91.

80. Grace E. Fox, *British Admirals and Chinese Pirates, 1832–1869* (London: Kegan Paul, Trench, Trubner & Co., 1940), 84.

81. Cordingly, *Pirates: Terror on the High Seas*, 232.

82. Murray, 114.

83. Ibid., 144.

84. Ibid., 85.

85. Ibid., 132.

86. Cordingly, *Pirates: Terror on the High Seas*, 235.

87. Dudley W. Knox, *A History of the United States Navy* (New York: G.P. Putnam's Sons, 1936), 145–146.

88. Long, 209.

89. Fox, 25–26.

90. Ibid., 30.

91. Ibid., 88.

92. Ibid., 89.

93. Ibid., 60–61.

94. Ibid., 85–86.

95. The First Opium War (1840–1842), the Taiping Rebellion (1850–1865), and the Second Opium War (1856–1860).

96. MacIntyre, 84–91.

97. The treaty ports were Canton (Gangzhou), Amoy (Xiamen), Foochow (Fuzhou), Ningpo (Nanjing), and Shanghai. See Long, 212.

98. MacIntyre, 103–107.

99. Fox, 94.

100. Ibid., 90–91.

101. Ibid., 98–99.

102. Ibid., 102.

103. Ibid., 105.

104. Long, 218.

105. Fox, 107.

106. Ibid., 107–108.

107. Ibid., 107–109.

108. Ibid., 122.

109. Clowes, vol. VI, 385–386.

110. Fox, 123.

111. Johnson, *Far China Station*, 67–68.

112. Long, 218.

113. Fox, 123–125.

114. Johnson, *Far China Station*, 77.

115. Ibid.

116. Fox, 130–131.

117. Johnson, *Far China Station*, 78.

118. Clowes, vol. VI, 388.

119. Ibid., 388–389.

120. Ibid., 389–390; Long, 218; Johnson, *Far China Station*, 79.

121. Clowes, vol. VI, 390; Commander E.W. Vansittart to Rear Admiral Sir J. Stirling, letter dated 2 September 1855, in *Allen's Indian Mail and Register of Intelligence for British and Foreign India, China, and All Parts of the East*, vol. XIV, January–December 1856 (London: Wm. H. Allen and Co., 1856), 48–49.

122. Clowes, vol. VI, 390; Vansittart to Stirling letter, 49–50.

123. Fox, 143.

124. Ibid., 145.

125. Ibid., 156–159.

126. Ibid., 175.

127. Ibid., 183.

Chapter 5

Modern Piracy

The headlines read "Somali Pirates' Unexpected Booty: Russian Tanks"[1]; "Ship Seized by Somali Pirates Carrying 33 Russian Tanks"[2]; and, more ominously for the pirates, "US Navy Watches Seized Ship With Sudan-Bound Tanks."[3] In an unprecedented act on 25 September 2008, Somali pirates captured the MV *Faina*, a Ukrainian freighter carrying 33 T-72 tanks and other weapons. Explaining the event, the pirates' spokesman, Sugule Ali Omar said, "We saw a big ship, so we decided to capture it, and later we discovered that it was carrying tanks. That made us happy because we got a chance to demand more money."[4] They did indeed demand more money—$35 million at first. But the opportunity for more money also sparked a crisis that resulted in increased international pressure to end piracy emanating from Somalia. As one intelligence official noted, they "might get more than they bargained for."[5]

This was the Somali pirates' most brazen attack up to that point. The pirates seized the ship on Thursday, 25 September 2008, some 200 miles off the Somali coast and sailed it into Somali territorial waters near Hobyo.[6] The international reaction was swift. The USS *Howard* arrived in the vicinity of the MV *Faina* later that same day and began continuous surveillance of the ship.[7] According to Rear Admiral Kendall Card, commander of the task force that monitored the *Faina*, *Howard*'s mission was to ensure that no weapons left the ship. Admiral Card recalled that it was made quite clear to the Somalis that the task force was in Somali territorial waters under the authority of the United Nations and that it would sink any vessel that tried to offload the *Faina*'s military cargo.[8] The seizure of the *Faina* changed the game. Almost immediately, Russia announced that it was sending a warship to the area to protect Russian merchant vessels.[9] Soon, other nations sent ships to the region as well. Some came under the auspices of NATO or the European Union. Others, such as China, India, and Japan, came to protect their individual nations' interests.

Seemingly oblivious to the scrutiny, the pirates settled in and waited to collect their ransom. On 23 October, almost a month into the standoff, the pirates' spokesman reiterated that they would hold the ship as long as it took to get the money they demanded. Sugule Ali Omar asserted that "they are not worried at all. They are comfortable and ready to wait."[10]

Conditions were not as pleasant for the hostages. The *Faina*'s captain died of a heart attack soon after the ship was taken. The rest of the crew survived, but their living conditions were grim. The Somali freebooters locked them in a single room and only let them out once or twice each week. Water and food were in short supply, and they lived in constant fear of their guards. When the Americans demanded that the crew be brought topside to be observed and checked out, the *Faina*'s sailors thought they were about to be executed.[11]

Finally, even the pirates began to tire of the drama, and they lowered their ransom demand. After several more rounds of talks, at long last, they agreed to release the ship for $3.2 million. On Thursday, 5 February 2009, the ship's owners delivered the cash to the modern-day buccaneers via parachute. Once they collected their money, the pirates left the ship and, after 5½ months of captivity, the *Faina* was free.[12] Soon thereafter, *Faina* departed the area under an American escort and arrived at its original destination, Mombasa, Kenya, on 12 February 2009.

According to Secretary of the US Navy Gordon R. England, "The seas are un-policed and unregulated and, therefore, attractive to those who want to exploit and abuse them."[13] Although he made that comment in 2004, nothing has occurred over the last 6 years to undermine the validity of that statement. In fact, the late 20th and early 21st centuries, rather than the late 16th and early 17th centuries, may be the real "Golden Age of Piracy." Estimates are that the buccaneers of the West Indies captured about 2,400 ships during 1716–1726 or about 218 per year.[14] By way of comparison, the International Maritime Bureau (IMB) reported 3,521 pirate attacks over the last 11 years (1998–2008), an average of 320 per year.[15] If, as the IMB and others suggest, 50 to 90 percent of all attacks are not even reported, then the comparison looks even more dramatic.[16] Clearly, piracy has emerged as a real problem over the last three decades.

The Emergence of Piracy in the Late 20th Century

The history of international awareness of and concern with modern piracy dates back to the early 1980s. The International Chamber of Commerce established the International Maritime Bureau in 1981. Although its primary responsibility was countering maritime fraud, it soon started working to counter other types of maritime crime, such as piracy.[17] During a 1983 meeting of the Maritime Safety Committee of the International Maritime Organization (IMO), the UN agency responsible for legislation to "improve the safety and security of international shipping," Sweden raised concerns about the prevalence of piracy off the coast of West Africa. Sweden had a strong trading relationship with Nigeria—oil and raw materials for Swedish machinery—but piratical acts were damaging that trade. Since the Nigerian Government was unable to rectify the situation, Sweden turned to the United Nations.[18] Responding to Sweden's concerns, the IMO adopted a resolution in November 1983 that urged governments to "take, as a matter of the highest priority, all measures necessary to prevent and suppress acts of piracy and armed robbery against ships in or adjacent to their waters, including strengthening of security measures."[19] The resolution, *Measures to Prevent Acts of Piracy and Armed Robbery Against Ships*, also requested nations to report incidents of piracy to the IMO. With this measure, piracy achieved visibility at the international level for the first time in many decades.[20]

Despite the IMO request that nations report incidents of piracy, few did. Only West Germany, Japan, and Greece submitted reports on a regular basis.[21] In a 1983 report to the IMO, the IMB postulated four reasons why nations or shipowners might forgo reporting incidents:

1. Negative press reports of pirate attacks might hurt a nation's commerce.

2. Reporting incidents might anger local officials, leading to retaliatory actions by local officials.

3. Merchant mariners might refuse to sail into danger areas or demand hazardous duty pay, thus increasing costs for shipowners.

4. Evidence of piracy might lead to increased insurance costs.[22]

In addition to these reasons, which remain valid today, many shipping companies cite the costs associated with investigations and court proceedings as reasons to avoid reporting attacks. Every day that a vessel remains in port while law enforcement officials investigate an incident costs the shipping company $25,000 or more.[23] Moreover, it is often difficult and expensive for witnesses to return to foreign countries to testify during court proceedings. Thus, many shipowners encourage, and even direct, their masters to refrain from reporting pirate attacks.

Despite those concerns, the number of reported incidents rose in the early 1990s. That increase, coupled with the belief that the reports did not accurately reflect the true scope of the problem, convinced many in the shipping industry that they needed a better reporting mechanism. In October 1992, the Regional Piracy Center, an agency of the IMB, began operations in Kuala Lumpur, Malaysia.[24] Malaysia was chosen as the site of the new center because Southeast Asia was the region most affected by piracy at the time. But officials in several regional countries reacted negatively to the establishment of the center, apparently concerned that the center's name, Regional Piracy Center, reflected negatively on their nations and might harm their country's commercial interests. Even though the center's name was changed to the Piracy Reporting Center (PRC) in 1997, regional nations remain ambivalent about the PRC.[25]

The PRC is a piracy information clearinghouse. Merchant ships victimized by piracy report incidents to the PRC. The center, in turn, issues piracy and armed robbery reports via voice communications, ensuring mariners are aware of incidents and danger areas. At the same time, it provides assistance to victims, shipowners, and law enforcement agencies. The PRC has, on several occasions, provided law enforcement agencies with vital intelligence that led directly to the apprehension of the criminals. Finally, the PRC publishes weekly updates on pirate activity over the Internet as well as comprehensive quarterly and annual reports.[26] Although self-reporting by victims has increased the number of incidents reported, the IMB still suspects that no more than half of all occurrences are reported to the PRC.[27]

Even more basic to the problem of reporting and understanding modern-day piracy is the contentiousness surrounding the definition of piracy. There are two competing definitions. The United Nations Convention on the Law of the Sea (UNCLOS), which was enacted in 1982, narrowly defines piracy as:

> a.   Any illegal acts of violence or detention, or any act of depredation, committed for private ends by the crew or the passengers of a private ship or a private aircraft, and directed:
> 1) On the high seas, against another ship or aircraft, or against persons or property on board such ship or aircraft;
> 2) Against a ship, aircraft, persons or property in a place outside the jurisdiction of any state;
> b.   Any act of voluntary participation in the operation of a ship or of an aircraft with knowledge of facts making it a pirate ship or aircraft;
> c.   Any act of inciting or of intentionally facilitating an act described in subparagraph (a) or (b).[28]

According to the United Nations, piracy can only occur on the high seas. A criminal act committed in territorial waters is not piracy. It is, instead, "armed robbery against ships," which the United Nations defines as "any unlawful act of violence or detention or any act of depredation, or threat thereof, other than an act of 'piracy,' directed against a ship or against persons or property on board such ship, within a State's jurisdiction over such offences."[29]

What makes the UN's narrow definition of piracy problematic is the phrase "high seas." Territorial waters, which were generally limited to 3 nautical miles prior to UNCLOS, were extended to 12 nautical miles by the convention. A second 12-mile zone, the contiguous zone, further extended the control of coastal nations out to 24 miles. The contiguous zone is not necessarily part of the high seas, where countries can act to suppress piracy, because UNCLOS allows nations to enforce their customs, immigration, and sanitary regulations within this zone. Finally, UNCLOS permits nations to establish an exclusive economic zone, up to 200 miles from the coast, within which they can regulate fishing and control the exploitation of resources under the seabed such as oil and gas. Both the contiguous and exclusive economic zones introduce ambiguity into the definition of high seas and thus piracy because some legal theorists argue that neither zone constitutes the high seas.[30]

Meanwhile, the IMB defines piracy much more broadly. According to the IMB, piracy is "an act of boarding or attempting to board any ship with the apparent intent to commit theft or any other crime and with the apparent intent or capability to use force in the furtherance of that act."[31] Thus, the IMB reports and tracks any attack, or attempted attack, whether in port, at anchor, or underway as an actual piratical incident.

The problem is that the definition of piracy under UNCLOS transforms most acts of piracy into armed robbery against ships since a majority of the incidents do not take place on the high seas. Instead, as in the days of the buccaneers and Barbary corsairs, contemporary pirates generally operate close to shore, within the territorial waters of sovereign nations, where they can hide from potential victims until they strike and more easily avoid law enforcement authorities. In 2003, for example, only 27 percent of the 445 reported incidents occurred on the high seas.[32] Of the 210 incidents that occurred while underway, only 58 percent took place in international waters.[33]

For both the victims of the crime and those charged with suppressing it, the distinction between acts of piracy on the high seas and armed robbery of ships at sea in territorial waters is a "distinction without difference."[34] There is little difference between being assaulted by Somali pirates in the Indian Ocean, hundreds of miles beyond Somali's territorial waters, and being accosted by pirates in Indonesian territorial waters in the Strait of Malacca. But under the UN's definition, the first is piracy while the second is not. More important, other nations can legally act against the former but not the latter.

Regardless of the definition, piracy encompasses a wide range of actions, from petty theft in port to permanently stealing a ship. There is, however, a significant difference between the level of violence associated with petty theft conducted in port or at anchor and piracy against ships underway. Criminal attacks on ships in port are typically less violent than attacks while underway. The pirates usually want to get on and off the ship quickly so they target things they can easily access and steal. For example, they might take paint, rope, spare parts, electronic equipment, or the personal effects of crewmembers. Since they are opportunistic and quick, these incidents do not normally bring the perpetrators much plunder, but they seldom result in violence unless confronted by crewmembers who resist.[35]

Conversely, pirate attacks while underway are more difficult to execute and their target is frequently the ship itself, its cargo, or the crew. While 90 percent of the pirate attacks in port were successful in 2003, only 58 percent of the attempted boardings were successful while underway. Moreover, in 2003, attacks at sea tended to be more violent. During the 235 incidents that occurred in port in 2003, there were only two deaths and two more crewmembers went missing. During the 210 underway attacks, 19 crewmembers were killed and 38 more are still missing. There were also 13 hijackings involving 193 hostages.[36] It is, therefore, clear that incidents while underway are of a different order of magnitude when compared to incidents in port.

The types of pirate attacks that are routinely carried out while underway include low-level armed robbery, long-term ship seizures, hijackings, and ship theft. Low-level armed robbery involves temporarily taking over a ship and forcing the crew to give up valuable personal items and the ship's safe. The attacks normally occur between midnight and 0400. The victims are usually underway at speeds up to 15 knots. The pirates approach the merchant ship in high-powered speedboats from the stern, thus masking the ship's radar. Four to 10 pirates scramble over the side of the ship using grappling hooks or bamboo poles. Their primary objective is the safe in the master's cabin. If they cannot open it, they often seize crewmen and coerce them into opening the safe and giving up personal items such as cash, jewelry, watches, credit cards, binoculars, cameras, electronic equipment, and medicine. Consequently, they may use some level of violence to intimidate crewmembers into complying with their demands. The attack is usually over in 15 to 20 minutes, even if they fail to steal anything. Still, this type of attack requires greater sophistication than incidents of petty theft because it requires speedboats and weapons.[37]

A long-term ship seizure is similar to low-level armed robbery except for the objective, which is to take the ship's cargo. The pirates may transfer the cargo to another vessel at sea or sail the prize to a safe port and offload the cargo there. Hijackings involve taking an entire ship and holding the vessel, cargo, and crew for ransom. Finally, there have been cases of pirates stealing ships, disposing of their cargos, and falsely registering the stolen vessels so that they can be used for other activities. Again, all of these attacks involve greater levels of violence and, at times, murder of the innocent crew.[38]

Piracy is an international crime, but measures to suppress it often rely on national efforts rather than international actions largely because of concerns about national sovereignty. The regions of the world most often plagued by piracy today are usually controlled by developing nations. Like the Spanish in Cuba and Puerto Rico in the 1820s, many of those countries are reluctant to allow other nations to pursue pirates into their territorial waters because doing so could potentially undermine their sovereignty over those areas. Modern-day pirates understand that and take advantage of those concerns by attacking vessels in international waters and then scurrying back into territorial waters for protection.

Piracy began to increase in the mid-1990s. According to the IMO, up through 1994, an average of 42 acts of piracy occurred each year worldwide (see table 1). Over the next 4 years, 1995–1998, the average increased to 216 per year. Another spurt occurred in 1999, pushing the annual total to 300 for the first time. Over the last 10 years, the average number of pirate attacks increased further to 332.

Why has piracy grown so much over the last two decades? One of the most important explanations is simply opportunity. In an increasingly interconnected global economy, with more than 80 percent of all freight shipped by sea, many more ships at sea are available as targets.[39] Many of those vessels must transit chokepoints such as the Malacca Straits, the Strait of Bab el-Mandeb, and the Strait of Hormuz to deliver their goods to the United States, Europe, Japan, China, and other places. Chokepoints not only concentrate potential targets into a limited area, but they also force merchant ships to slow down to safely navigate those heavily trafficked areas, thus making them even more vulnerable to pirates. Because shipowners have reduced the size of their crews over the last several decades, it is also easier for modern-day buccaneers to approach and board merchant ships undetected. Hard times economically, the reallocation of maritime surveillance assets from antipiracy to antiterrorism missions, lax port and coastal security, and political corruption all factor in as well.

Table 1. Incidents of Piracy, 1984–2008

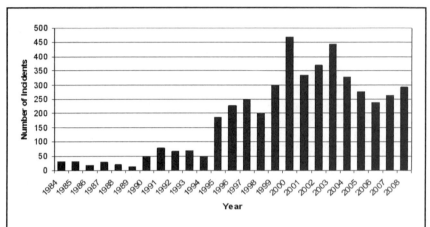

From: The 1984–1994 data comes from the Martin N. Murphy, *Small Boats, Weak States, Dirty Money: Piracy and Maritime Terrorism in the Modern World* (London: Hurst & Co., 2008), 61; the 1995–2002 data comes from the Murphy, 62; the 2003–2008 data comes from *Piracy and Armed Robbery Against Ships, Annual Report, 1 January–31 December 2008* (London: International Chamber of Commerce, International Maritime Bureau, January 2009), 5–6.

Finally, the easy accessibility of weapons gives the pirates the firepower necessary to take on larger, harder, targets.[40]

Despite the upsurge in piracy incidents, shipping companies have shown surprisingly little interest in adopting measures to counter the pirates. Among the options available are Secure-Ship, a collapsible nonlethal 9,000-volt electric fence that surrounds the ship; Long-Range Acoustic Device (LRAD), which directs a high-pitched tone at intruders; and water cannons.[41] Shipping companies could also arm their crews or hire armed security guards to protect their ships, but those measures have the potential to be dangerous, costly, and complicated legally. The commander of the US Fifth Fleet, Vice Admiral Bill Gortney, is a proponent of using armed guards. He maintains that companies hire armed guards to protect their assets ashore so they should also do so to protect their afloat assets.[42] But many people in the shipping industry worry that such actions might prompt the pirates to use more force, thus further endangering the crews.[43] Furthermore, guards are expensive. Unarmed guards cost $12,000 to $18,000 for a 3- to 5-day transit.[44] Armed guards, some of whom will even provide their own escort vessels, cost from $10,000 to as much as $200,000 per transit.[45] Even if shipping companies employ them, there is no guarantee that guards will be effective. Despite the presence of unarmed guards using LRAD, Somali pirates captured the chemical tanker Biscaglia on 28 November 2008. When it was apparent that their actions did not deter the brigands, the guards abandoned their charges and jumped over the side of the ship. They were later rescued by a German Navy helicopter.[46] Shipping companies could also train and arm their crews, but again, they run the risk of escalating the level of violence during hijacking attempts. Moreover, there are significant legal hurdles to overcome, since many countries do not allow mariners to bring arms into port. Both Indonesia and Malaysia initially opposed the use of armed guards in the Strait of Malacca although they eventually relented.[47]

Another reason why shipowners are reluctant to invest in defensive systems is that the costs of piracy, whether cargo theft, ransom, or increased insurance and labor costs, are miniscule when compared to overall world maritime trade. Analysts estimate the cost of piracy ranges anywhere from $500 million to $25 billion.[48] The IMB calculates the cost to be $1 billion to $16 billion per year. Even the largest of those numbers, $25 billion, is dwarfed by the estimated total of $7.8 trillion in world maritime commerce in 2005.[49] Although kidnapping and ransom insurance policies have increased in cost almost tenfold, to about $30,000 per trip through the Gulf of Aden, it is still cheaper than transiting around the Cape of Good Hope.[50] A Norwegian company that recently stopped sending its fleet of 100 vessels through the Gulf of Aden reported that doing so is costing the company $30,000 each day.[51] Diverting an oil tanker from Saudi Arabia around the Cape of Good Hope to the United States instead of through the Suez Canal adds 2,700 miles to the trip, costs an extra $3.5 million in fuel costs each year, and results in only five annual transits instead of six.[52] Since insurance spreads risk, even at the higher rates, it is cheaper than paying for armed guards or diverting vessels around the southern tip of Africa. Thus, there is little incentive for maritime businesses to invest in countermeasures that may or may not be effective.

But piracy is not just an international crime, it is also a local problem. For example, over the last 5 years, the average number of reported incidents of piracy worldwide was 280. In 2004, almost 47 percent of all incidents occurred in Southeast Asia while less than 5 percent of the total took place along the coast of east Africa. By 2008, a new trend emerged, which demonstrates the local nature of piracy. In 2008, 44 percent of all pirate attacks occurred off the eastern coast of Africa, primarily Somalia.[53] Meanwhile, piracy in Southeast Asia, declined to 16 percent of all incidents. World attention, therefore, shifted to the pirates of Somalia (see table 2). These two regions—Southeast Asia and Somalia—are the areas most plagued by modern-day pirates.

Table 2. Piracy Attacks by Region, 2003–2008

Region/Nation	2003	2004	2005	2006	2007	2008	Totals
Pacific Ocean	0	1	0	0	2	0	3
	0.0%	0.3%	0.0%	0.0%	0.8%	0.0%	0.2%
Far East (South China Sea)	31	19	20	11	14	18	113
	7.0%	5.8%	7.2%	4.6%	5.3%	6.1%	6.1%
Southeast Asia	158	154	102	77	64	47	602
	35.5%	46.8%	37.0%	32.2%	24.3%	16.0%	32.6%
Indian Ocean	87	34	39	55	34	24	273
	19.6%	10.3%	14.1%	23.0%	12.9%	8.2%	14.8%
Arabian Gulf	3	3	10	5	7	0	28
	0.7%	0.9%	3.6%	2.1%	2.7%	0.0%	1.5%
East Africa	29	15	53	29	66	129	321
	6.5%	4.6%	19.2%	12.1%	25.1%	44.0%	17.4%
West Africa	64	58	27	32	54	60	295
	14.4%	17.6%	9.8%	13.4%	20.5%	20.5%	16.0%
Europe	1	0	0	1	1	1	4
	0.2%	0.0%	0.0%	0.4%	0.4%	0.3%	0.2%
South America	45	27	13	25	18	12	140
	10.1%	8.2%	4.7%	10.5%	6.8%	4.1%	7.6%
Central America	3	1	1	0	0	0	5
	0.7%	0.3%	0.4%	0.0%	0.0%	0.0%	0.3%
Caribbean	23	16	11	4	3	2	59
	5.2%	4.9%	4.0%	1.7%	1.1%	0.7%	3.2%
United States	1	1	0	0	0	0	2
	0.2%	0.3%	0.0%	0.0%	0.0%	0.0%	0.1%
World Totals	445	329	276	239	263	293	1,845

From: *Piracy and Armed Robbery Against Ships, Annual Report, 1 January–31 December 2008* (London: International Chamber of Commerce, International Maritime Bureau, January 2009), 5–6.

Southeast Asian Piracy

The increase in piracy in Southeast Asia in the 1990s was sparked by the growth of international commerce, especially seaborne trade. Today, 80 percent of the world's trade is transported by sea. More than 46,000 merchant vessels ply the seas.[54] The United States is the world's largest trading nation, and a large portion of that trade is conducted with Asia, especially Japan, South Korea, and China.[55] As China's economy exploded in the 1990s, increasing almost fivefold from 1990 to 2000, merchant shipping to and from China also increased.[56] Along with trade came piracy as the number of targets available to the modern-day buccaneers in the Strait of Malacca and Indonesian waters increased as well.

As with other eras and geographic areas, the conditions facilitating piracy came into play in Southeast Asia. Geography is of critical importance. Southeast Asia is home to one of the world's most important chokepoints—the Malacca Strait. More than 50,000 ships, almost 25 percent of the world's shipping, transit through the strait each year.[57] (See figure 12.) Virtually all of the oil delivered to Japan, China, and South Korea, about 10.3 million barrels of oil, passes through the strait each day.[58] Moreover, it is estimated that some 10,000 boats fish the plentiful fishing banks in the strait every day. In addition, more than 80,000 people cross the strait daily on other business.[59] Thus, the Strait of Malacca, just as it was 150 years earlier when Great Britain sought to suppress piracy in the region, is a fertile hunting ground for pirates.

But Southeast Asian piracy is not confined to the Malacca Strait. The Phillip Channel and Singapore Strait, which separate Malaysia and Singapore from Indonesia's Riau Archepelago, are rife with piracy as well. Incorporating more than 17,500 islands, modern-day Indonesia is

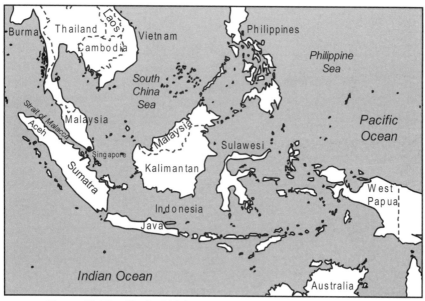

Figure 12. The Strait of Malacca, Indonesia, and Southeast Asia.

a pirate paradise (figure 13). Indonesia has more than 34,000 miles of coastline that provides countless coves, harbors, creeks, and other places from which Indonesian pirates operate.[60] Similarly, Malaysia has more than 2,900 miles of coastline, making it another regional nation with many remote locations for pirates to hide.[61] Since more than 200 merchant ships as well as numerous small boats transit through the region each day, the waterways are congested.[62] As in the Malacca Strait, the heavy traffic, narrow channels, and shallow waters force merchant vessels to slow while transiting the Phillip Channel and Singapore Strait, making them all the more vulnerable to attack. Therefore, the geography of Southeast Asia provides the pirates with a concentrated target area and thus increased opportunities for plunder.

Political conditions also facilitate piracy in Southeast Asia. Piracy is a regional issue, and countering it requires cooperation among the three regional states affected by the crime—Indonesia, Malaysia, and Singapore. Unfortunately, such cooperation is not always forthcoming because of sovereignty issues. Pirates operating from one nation can, within minutes,

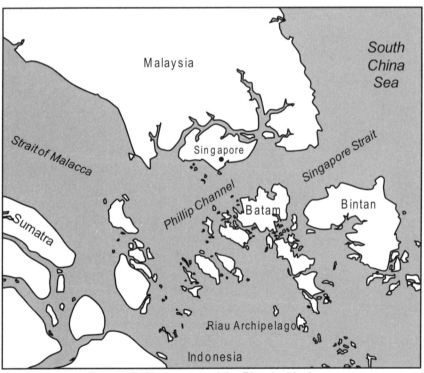

Figure 13. Singapore and the Riau Archipelago.

cross into the territorial waters of another country, attack a ship, and then flee back into their home waters, free from pursuit by maritime law enforcement officials from the victim state. Or the brigands can capture a ship in one nation's waters and sail it into another's territory to dispose of the booty, all the while controlled by bosses in a third country.[63] The permeability of national borders at sea makes it easy for pirates to operate in the region.

Unfortunately, Indonesia has done relatively little to suppress piracy in its territorial waters. Part of the problem is resource based—the Indonesians do not have the resources necessary to effectively police their more than 17,000 islands. But the other part of the problem is that Indonesia does not consider piracy to be as great a threat to its security and economy as other countries do to theirs.[64] Unlike Singapore and Malaysia, Indonesia is not a shipping terminus and thus benefits little from the massive amount of trade that passes through the region each year.[65] Moreover, Indonesian officials view the Aceh rebels' criminal activities, arms, people, and merchandise smuggling, and illegal fishing, which costs Indonesia more than $4 billion each year, as much greater threats.[66] Therefore, it stands to reason that Indonesia has put more emphasis on those problems that more directly affect its security and economy.

By contrast, as an island nation dependent on foreign trade, Japan has been greatly concerned with piracy in the region since the mid-1990s. Japan imports 70 percent of its food by sea. Virtually all of Japan's trade with Europe, Africa, Australia, and the Middle East passes through the region. And almost all of its oil imports come through the Malacca Strait. Thus, suppression of piracy in Southeast Asia is important to Japan's economic security.[67]

Political instability and corruption have also allowed pirates based in Indonesia to thrive. With the fall of the Suharto dictatorship in 1998, Indonesia moved into a period of political uncertainty, which was further exacerbated by the 1997 Asian financial crisis and the 2004 Asian tsunami. Despite these challenges, Indonesia has slowly moved toward democracy.[68] But corruption, which was rampant under Suharto, remains a problem. There were numerous reports almost 25 years ago that Indonesian naval and maritime police forces moonlighted as pirates.[69] Despite the passage of time and the change of regime, similar criminal activities remain a concern today. Royal Malaysian Marine Police openly complain that Indonesian naval units supplement their pay through part-time pirating.[70] Such corruption does two things. First, dishonesty among elected officials and members of the security forces undermines the legitimacy of the elected government.[71] Second, it damages Indonesia's relations with its regional partners, Malaysia and Singapore. Good relations between the three countries are crucial if piracy is to be stopped in the Malacca Strait and surrounding waters.

Finally, piracy continues to flourish in the region because the brigands have secure sanctuaries among the many islands of Indonesia. Most of the pirates preying on the Phillip Channel and Singapore Strait are based on the island of Batam, which is part of the Riau Archipelago, 9 miles south of Singapore. During the economic boom of the 1980s, tens of thousands of Indonesians flocked to the island looking for work. When the bubble burst and they lost their jobs, many turned to criminal activities such as piracy to make a living.[72] With its direct access to the shipping lanes in the vicinity of Singapore and a readily available pool of labor, Batam became a hotbed for piracy in the region. In the northern portion of the Malacca Strait, the primary culprits are brigands operating out of the Sumatran province of Aceh. This province has been wracked by a separatist insurgency for a number of years, making it an area ripe for piracy.[73] Thus, in both areas, piracy reemerged because the three conditions necessary for piracy to exist—geographic location, political instability, and safe havens—were present and available for the pirates to exploit.

One of the first-known cases of modern-day piracy in the region occurred on 20 May 1981 when a Liberian-flagged tanker was attacked in the Phillip Channel.[74] During the early part of the decade, Indonesian pirates refrained from attacking Indonesian-flagged vessels, apparently hoping that by doing so they could avoid the attention of Indonesian authorities.[75] Despite that self-imposed limitation, Indonesian pirates were extremely active in the months following the initial attack. They assaulted 21 ships in the Phillip Channel and many more while at anchor in the vicinity of Singapore, stealing money and other personal property.[76] Most of the attacks were random, opportunistic assaults involving petty theft. That pattern continued throughout the remainder of the decade.

During the 1990s, Southeast Asia averaged 99 incidents per year.[77] As the Indonesian pirates became more organized during the decade, they began to carry out long-term ship seizures and ship theft. Those attacks require more arms, personnel, and organization. Because the pirates had to seize control of the prize, acts of violence against crews also increased.[78]

An example of long-term ship seizure occurred in August 1991 in the Singapore Strait when 25 pirates boarded and took over the *Sprintstar*. While securing the ship, the pirates killed the chief officer. The rest of the crew was imprisoned on board while the freebooters transferred the ship's cargo, worth some $3 million, to another vessel. The *Far Trader*, a small cargo ship carrying food, textiles, electronics, and cigarettes, suffered a similar fate in December 1992. Armed pirates locked up the crew and diverted the vessel to Thailand, where they conveyed the ship's $7 million cargo to another ship. Although the IMB did not report any long-term ship seizures in 1993, there were nine more during 1994–1997.[79]

Then, in April 1998, a gang of pirates tried to steal the tanker *Petro Ranger* outright. The tanker, which was carrying $1.5 million worth of diesel and jet fuel, was captured on 16 April east of Malaysia. The pirates locked up the crew and sailed the ship toward southern China. While underway, the pirates painted a new name on the ship—*Wilby*—to match recently obtained Honduran registration. Six days after they seized the *Petro Ranger*, the brigands offloaded most of the diesel fuel into two smaller tankers that the gang had stolen earlier. The small tankers were apparently used to smuggle the stolen fuel into Hainan Island. Soon after one of the small tankers returned with the sale proceeds, both *Wilby* and the small tanker were detained by the Chinese Marine Police, who suspected them of smuggling. The Chinese eventually figured out the situation and arrested the pirates. They released the *Petro Ranger* and the crew but kept the money and the rest of the cargo as evidence. The pirates, who bragged to the *Petro Ranger*'s captain that they were working with some senior Chinese naval officers, were not prosecuted for their crimes. Instead, they were deported to Indonesia where Indonesian officials released them without investigating the case.[80]

China figured prominently in most of the major organized pirate incidents in the mid-1990s. Hijacked ships often surfaced in Chinese ports where they were sold or Chinese officials tried to force the owners to pay for the release of their property. International pressure finally forced China to suppress corruption among government officials and to crack down on black market activities, which eliminated one of the primary markets for stolen vessels.[81]

Then, in November 1998, one of the most notorious incidents of piracy occurred in Chinese waters when pirates captured the MV *Cheung Son* and brutally murdered all 23 crewmembers. After killing the crew, the brigands disposed of their victims by attaching weights to their bodies and dumping them over the side. Although neither the ship nor its cargo was ever found, a few days later, Chinese fishermen pulled up six bodies, thus exposing the crime. Chinese authorities eventually discovered incriminating photographs of the pirates carousing in the midst of the dead crewmen while questioning a suspect. In December

1999, a Chinese court convicted 38 men of hijacking the MV *Cheung Son*, 13 of whom were sentenced to death and executed in January 2000. The *Cheung Son* executions and the stiff prison sentences handed out to another group of pirates around the same time seems to have put a damper on pirate activity in the vicinity of China.[82]

Although there were no long-term seizures or thefts of commercial vessels from October 2002 until late September 2005, piratical actions in the region did not stop. Instead, the brigands shifted their attention to softer targets such as tugs and barges. Since tugs are slow with a low freeboard, they are easy to board and capture. Moreover, their cargoes, especially palm oil, are valuable and relatively easy to dispose of. Pirates hijacked 22 tugs and tows between September 2001 and September 2005.[83]

Two of those attacks occurred in February and March 2005. On 28 February, pirates boarded a tug in the Malacca Strait and took the captain and chief officer hostage. They held them for a week before releasing them. Similarly, pirates attacked the Japanese tug *Idaten* on 14 March 2005 while it was towing a crew barge with 154 personnel on board. This was a more violent attack, during which the pirates fired at the pilot house to force the tug to stop. Four pirates boarded the vessel and took three crewmembers hostage. Five days later, they transferred the hostages onto a Thai fishing boat.[84]

The northern part of the Malacca Strait was relatively free of piracy until mid-2001 when an Indonesian tanker was attacked. The *Tirta Niaga IV* suffered an engineering casualty and anchored off the west coast of Aceh. While the crew was making repairs, brigands assaulted the ship, robbed the ship's safe and crew, and took the master and second officer hostage. They soon let the second officer go, but the pirates kept the captain and eventually extorted $30,000 in ransom for his release.[85]

The success of the attack on the *Tirta Niaga IV* served notice to others that kidnapping for ransom was a lucrative business. In 2002, there were five kidnappings in the northern part of the Malacca Strait. The next year, 2003, the number of incidents dropped to 4, but they rose again in 2004 to 14, as well as 8 unsuccessful attempts. Because kidnapping requires coercion to force victims off their ships, violence increased in the northern Malacca Strait as well. The brigands are almost always armed, often with automatic weapons and rocket-propelled grenades. Moreover, they are not reluctant to use them, routinely shooting at merchant ships' pilot houses to force them to stop.[86]

Not every attack is successful. On 8 August 2003, pirates attacked the MV *Dong Yih* in the Malacca Strait off Aceh. The pirate boats looked like oil-rig support craft so the *Dong Yih*'s crew ignored them at first. The crews of the two boats fired more than 200 rounds at the *Dong Yih* during an attack that lasted more than 2 hours. In the end, the *Dong Yih* did not slow, and the pirates were unable to board the vessel.[87]

The treatment of the crew of the oil tanker *Cherry 201* demonstrates the increased violence in the Malacca Strait. Pirates captured the tanker and crew on 5 January 2004. They released the captain so that he could transmit their demands. Initially, the pirates demanded more than $47,000, but the shipowners negotiated them down to a quarter of that amount. Unfortunately, when the shipping company tried to negotiate further, the pirates grew angry and killed four of the crewmembers. The rest of the hostages jumped overboard and escaped.[88]

Malaysian fishermen are the primary target of the pirates operating in the northern Malacca Strait.[89] Since the fishermen's state-of-the-art trawlers are usually manned by only four sailors and cost between $210,000 and $275,000, Malaysian fishing boats are lucrative targets that are relatively easy to take. During the 1990s, when Indonesian pirates hijacked fishing boats and held them for ransom, they typically received about $27,000. After 2001, more frequent maritime patrols in the strait made it more difficult for the brigands to escape with a hijacked vessel, so they began kidnapping the trawler captains instead. The amount of the ransom is normally about 10 percent of the value of the trawler.[90] Pirate depredations have clearly damaged the Malaysian fishing industry. Although most incidents are not reported to the IMB, on average, Indonesian pirates have taken one fishing vessel per month for the last 5 years. More important, the cost of ransom has risen from about $8,000 to $27,000. Compounding the problem, corrupt Indonesian officials often demand an additional payment of as much as $27,000 more to release the captured vessel.[91]

The peak years for piracy in Southeast Asia were 2003–2004. Almost 47 percent (see table 2) of all pirate attacks worldwide occurred in Southeast Asia in 2004. Reacting to that data in 2005, Lloyd's Joint War Council declared the Malacca Strait an area of enhanced risk. That decision, which took into account the activities of both the maritime criminals and Islamic militants at work in the region, enabled insurance companies to add a war surcharge of 0.10 percent of the total value of the cargo insured. The three states most affected by the decision, Indonesia, Malaysia, and Singapore, objected vigorously to the determination. The war risk judgment triggered further efforts to suppress piracy on the part of those nations and led to the revocation of the designation in mid-2006.[92]

It is important to avoid placing too much emphasis on statistics, however. According to the IMB, the number of maritime piracy incidents quadrupled from 107 attacks in 1991 to 445 in 2003.[93] But if we use 2005 as the end point, then the overall increase is less dramatic: 107 to 276, less than a threefold increase. From 2003 until 2008, on average, one-third of all acts of piracy were committed in Southeast Asia (see table 2). But even if we take a high year such as 2003, when 158 pirate attacks occurred, the number of incidents as a percentage of the overall regional traffic, which exceeds 50,000 commercial vessels each year, is miniscule—0.32 percent. With a probability of attack of less than one-third of 1 percent, there is little wonder why shipping companies or states such as Indonesia are reluctant to invest much money or resources into piracy prevention. Still, the impact of a pirate attack is significant to the victims, who are sometimes beaten, held hostage, and even killed.

One of the most significant barriers to effective actions against the pirates has been the reluctance of Malaysia, Indonesia, and Singapore to work together. They jealously guard their sovereignty, fearful that any weakness might lead to another nation claiming their territory. Still they have, from time to time, worked out agreements that have positively affected antipiracy operations in the region. In May 1992, Malaysia, Indonesia, and Singapore established a joint patrol area. Two months later, Singapore and Indonesia agreed to coordinate patrols and share information about activity in the Singapore Strait and Phillip Channel. Coordinated patrols have reduced piracy in the Singapore Strait to some degree, but the agreements remain hamstrung by the requirement to stay within each nations' own waters.[94] As long as maritime law enforcement forces are not allowed to pursue pirates into a neighbor's territorial waters, such initiatives will be largely ineffective.[95] Thus, antipiracy efforts in the region continue to founder on the shoal of sovereignty.

Unilateral operations can, of course, positively impact local conditions. For example, in June 1992, the Indonesian Navy conducted *Operasi Kikis Bajak* (Operation ENDING THE PIRATES) and intensely focused patrolling and intelligence-gathering efforts in the Riau Archipelago. Dozens of criminals were arrested and convicted. The operation produced a dramatic drop in pirate attacks that was sustained for several years. No attacks were reported in the Singapore Strait or Phillip Channel during the final third of 1992 and attacks were down by eight on an annual basis over the next 2 years.[96] Malaysia also took several unilateral actions in 2005 when the government began putting armed policemen on selected tugs and barges and it began offering escorts for ships carrying valuable cargoes through the Malacca Strait. Singapore also initiated a boarding and escort program in its waters.[97] But such operations must be sustained on a continuous basis or their effect will be short lived.

Incidents of piracy remained down for several years until a combination of events led to a resurgence. The 1997 Asian economic crisis followed by the fall of Suharto in 1998 and subsequent political instability led to an increase in piracy in the late 1990s. The number of attacks in Indonesian waters almost doubled in one year, rising to 115 incidents in 1999. Assaults on vessels underway jumped from 11 in 1997 to 49 in 1999. Even attacks in the Malacca Strait outside of Indonesian territorial waters grew from 3 in 1998 to 91 in 2000. The Indonesian Government initiated another round of arrests in early 2000 that, once again, suppressed piracy for a while.[98] Despite the Asian economic crisis, incidents of piracy in the waters surrounding Singapore and Malaysia were fairly low throughout the last decade of the 20th century. Both nations routinely committed more resources and attention to antipiracy operations than Indonesia. Moreover, when piracy surged in Malaysian waters in early 2000, the government stepped up antipiracy patrols.[99]

After another surge in 2003, Malaysia, Indonesia, and Singapore agreed to conduct joint maritime patrols (Operation MALSINDO) in the Malacca Strait. In July 2004, the three countries began conducting patrols in the 550-mile-long strait on a 24-hour basis. Soon thereafter, piracy in the Malacca Strait dropped from 38 attacks in 2004 to 12 in 2005 to 2 in 2008 (see table 3). Coordinating efforts between the three countries is, however, still difficult since vessels cannot cross over into one of the other state's territorial waters, and the ability of all three nations to sustain continuous patrols is limited.[100]

Hoping to leverage efforts to combat piracy and terrorism in the region, the United States proposed the Regional Maritime Security Initiative (RMSI) to improve security against piracy and other maritime threats through information sharing. Malaysia and Indonesia declined to participate in RMSI, however, after comments before Congress by Admiral Thomas B. Fargo, Commander of the United States Pacific Command, in March 2004 seemed to indicate that the United States intended to send Marines and Special Forces personnel in high-speed vessels to protect the Malacca Strait. Only Singapore willingly accepted that proposal. The United States remains a proponent of RMSI as a framework to synchronize

Table 3. Incidents of Piracy in the Malacca Strait

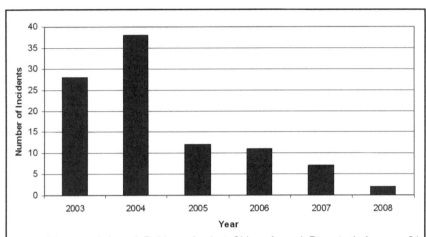

From: *Piracy and Armed Robbery Against Ships, Annual Report, 1 January–31 December 2008* (London: International Chamber of Commerce, International Maritime Bureau, January 2009), 5–6.

maritime operations. RMSI could be used to improve information sharing and thus situational awareness, facilitate better decisionmaking, boost nations' abilities to intercept potential threats, and promote international cooperation. At this time, RMSI is still in its formative stage, a vague concept of sharing information about piracy and other threats between a "coalition of the willing."[101]

In a further attempt to promote regional cooperation independent of the United States, Malaysia's deputy prime minister set forth some ideas about maritime security at a regional security conference in Singapore in June 2005. Mr. Najib Razak stated that maritime security in the region requires significant coordination and cooperation. If they could coordinate maritime air surveillance, link the coastal radar picture, and establish a radio tracking network to provide real-time information to law enforcement agencies using new technologies, Razak said, they could regain the initiative from the pirates. Razak argued that those actions were up to the regional states, which must retain primary responsibility for implementing all security measures. He also reiterated that the best way to suppress pirates is to eliminate their shore havens, cutting them off from their support systems. Although he emphasized cooperation and coordination, he also cautioned that any actions taken must not impinge on the sovereignty of the regional states. Thus, he undermined his own agenda since restricting the right of hot pursuit into adjacent territorial waters guaranteed that any such cooperation would be limited.[102]

Still suspicious of the US Regional Maritime Security Initiative, regional nations came up with several other alternatives. One such program is the Regional Cooperation Agreement on Combating Piracy and Armed Robbery Against Ships in Asia (ReCAAP). Growing slowly from four members, Singapore, Japan, Laos, and Cambodia, in 2005, it now includes 14 regional countries.[103] ReCAAP serves as a means of exchanging information, conducting research, and analyzing data about Asian piracy and armed robbery at sea.[104] All of the information flows from national sources, typically a member nation's coast guard or navy, into the Information Sharing Center in Singapore. The jury is still out on ReCAAP since Indonesia and Malaysia, the two nations most closely involved with the Southeast Asian piracy problem, have not ratified the ReCAAP agreement.[105] In addition, since part of the impetus for ReCAAP appears to be regional objections to a nongovernmental agency, the Piracy Reporting Center, serving as the piracy clearing house, it remains to be seen how objective and effective ReCAAP can be.

Another regional initiative is the Eyes in the Sky (EiS) program, a joint maritime air patrol operation over the Malacca Strait agreed to by Singapore, Malaysia, Indonesia, and Thailand.[106] Each nation contributes two aircraft to the scheme, which began in 2005. Unlike the other arrangements between these nations, this agreement does allow limited (3-mile) incursions into the airspace of the other signatories. The program has, however, received criticism as merely window dressing because eight flights per week cannot possibly provide effective coverage of the strait, and the countries lack sufficient surface vessels to investigate suspicious ships identified by the aircraft.[107]

Together, all of those actions have had a salubrious effect on piracy in the region. From a peak of 158 attacks in 2003 (see table 2), incidents of piracy in the region dropped to 47 in 2008. Indonesia, Malaysia, and Singapore deserve credit for what they have done and continue to do. Since they rejected the US RMSI overture, they had to come up with alternatives and they have done so.

Although much progress has been made in terms of cooperation, training, and the acquisition of patrol craft and surveillance equipment, much more needs to be done. Indonesia still does not have the resources it needs to unilaterally patrol its enormous territorial waters, thus making any effort to permanently suppress piracy problematic. Until Malaysia and

Indonesia either acquire more antipiracy resources or allow allied nations to assist with antipiracy operations in their waters, piracy will remain a threat to shipping in the region. Even though Indonesia has made some efforts to improve the economic well being of those living in areas prone to piracy, until the safe havens in the Riau Archipelago and along the eastern coast of Sumatra are permanently eliminated, piracy in Southeast Asia will continue to be a problem. But that is a domestic law enforcement problem that only Indonesia can solve.

Somali Piracy

Somalia, which has been described as a pirate's paradise, has all of the conditions necessary for piracy to thrive.[108] It has an excellent geographic location, there is considerable political turmoil, and there are numerous safe havens ashore. Together, those conditions created a place where today piracy flourishes.

Piracy along the coast of Somalia has been a problem for some time, but it exploded in 2008, surging from 44 attacks off the coast of Somalia and in the Red Sea in 2007 to 111 incidents in 2008 (table 4). One reason for the increase in piracy is that many Somalis discovered that piracy was a lucrative alternative to fishing, bringing them perhaps as much as 10 times more money than they earned from their once prosperous fishing industry.[109] Experts estimate that the Somalis garnered more than $150 million in ransom money during 2008.[110]

Somalia's geographic location makes it an ideal spot for piracy. Although it has more than 1,880 miles of coastline, it does not have thousands of small islands on which pirates can hide, waiting to pounce on victims like Indonesia.[111] What it does have is close proximity to the Gulf of Aden, through which some 20,000 ships, as well as tankers carrying 7 to 12 percent of the world's annual oil production, transit annually and the sealanes running from South Africa to the Persian Gulf.[112] This geographic

Table 4. Incidents of Piracy Off Somalia

Location	2003	2004	2005	2006	2007	2008	Totals
Gulf of Aden/ Red Sea	18	8	10	10	13	92	151
Somalia	3	2	35	10	31	19	100
Totals	21	10	45	20	44	111	251

From: *Piracy and Armed Robbery Against Ships, Annual Report, 1 January–31 December 2008* (London: International Chamber of Commerce, International Maritime Bureau, January 2009), 5–6.

position enables Somali-based pirates to dominate the Gulf of Aden and, so it seems, a large portion of the Indian Ocean as well (figure 14).

Somalia is also a country wracked by political turmoil. The country has not had a viable government since Mohamed Siad Barre was ousted from power in 1991. Since 1991, warlords, the Islamic Courts Union, and 14 transitional governments have tried to rule the country. None have succeeded and Somalia has another new leader after President Abdullahi Yusuf Ahmed resigned in December 2008. The current president is Sheik

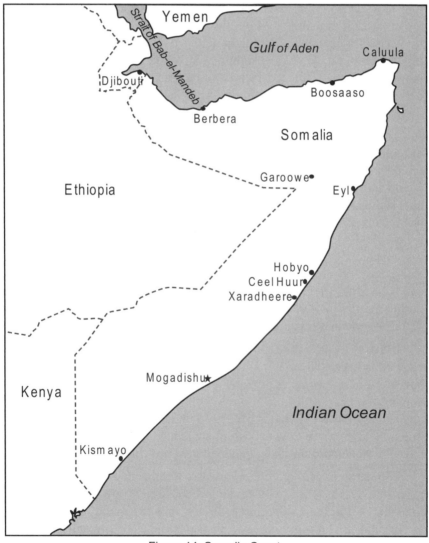

Figure 14. Somalia Coast.

Sharif Ahmed, a moderate Islamist and former leader of the Islamic Courts Union.[113]

The Transitional Federal Government was established in Kenya in August 2004 under President Abdullahi Yusuf Ahmed. During the summer of 2006, Islamic militias under the leadership of the Islamic Courts Union took control of Mogadishu. Their presence, in turn, precipitated a response by the United States and Ethiopia. In December 2006, Ethiopian troops intervened and drove the Islamist militia out of Mogadishu. The next month, President Yusuf entered Mogadishu for the first time. Despite his presence in the capital, little changed regarding governance of the country. Moreover, the presence of the hated Ethiopians gave rise to insurgency throughout the country.[114] As a result, some 10,000 people have died in fighting since late 2006. At least 1 million more have been displaced from their homes, and possibly as much as half of the country's population, which is about 7 million people, is on the verge of starvation.[115]

The food crisis in Somalia was made worse by both the political turmoil and piracy. Twenty aid workers were killed during the first half of 2008, causing some aid groups to suspend operations and others to pull out of Somalia completely. At the same time, after several aid ships were hijacked in 2005, aid groups stopped shipping food to the country unless the vessels had a military escort. When the Netherlands stopped escorting the World Food Program (WFP) ships in June 2008, all shipments by sea temporarily halted. Shipping food by ground transportation is just as dangerous and much more expensive. Militia groups frequently attack, and even hijack, the food convoys. Even worse, five drivers were killed during the first half of the year.[116] In the midst of such turmoil, it is not surprising to find piracy thriving.

In a country with little commerce, the money extorted by the pirates is a huge boon to coastal communities. Consequently, there are numerous safe havens along the coast of Somalia, providing vital support to the pirates. Among the most well-known ports are Eyl, Hobyo, and Xaradheere, all located in the break-away province of Puntland. The pirates operate with impunity from these towns, leading some analysts to conclude that they have the tacit approval of the Puntland government.[117]

The pirate havens are boom towns, with new houses, cars, and other consumer items. These contemporary buccaneers are heroes to many Somalis. According to one pirate leader, half the money received goes to the pirates who took the ship; 30 percent goes to investors who help finance the pirates' activities; and 20 percent goes to villagers who help guard the ship, serve as translators, or provide food and other supplies to the pirates. Like modern-day Robin Hoods, they also give money to the poor.[118]

In places like Garoowe and Eyl, everyone wants to be a pirate. A 12-year-old boy in Garoowe told a reporter, "When I finish high school, I will be a pirate man, I will work for my family and will get more money." If you cannot be a pirate, you can marry one. Thus, a young woman in Eyl promised, "I'll tie the knot with a pirate man because I'll get to live in a good house with good money."[119] With such enthusiastic support from the local populace, it will be difficult to eliminate piracy in Somalia.

Unlike the pirates of Southeast Asia, who commit the full range of piracy, including petty theft, low-level armed robbery, long-term ship seizures, hijackings, and ship theft, Somali pirates normally confine themselves to taking hostages and asking for ransoms. Ranging throughout the Gulf of Aden and far out into the Indian Ocean, this type of activity exploded in 2008, increasing from 177 hostages taken in 2007 to 815 in 2008 during 155 pirate attacks over the 2-year period (see table 5).[120] Despite the large number of incidents, deaths and injuries are rare: the pirates killed six crewmen and injured eight more although 14 crewmembers also went missing during that timeframe.[121]

Table 5. Types of Attacks Off Somali Waters

Type of Attack	2007		2008		Totals	
No. of Attacks	44		111		155	
Taken Hostage	177	86.3%	815	97.3%	992	95.1%
Kidnap/Ransom	20	9.8%	3	0.4%	23	2.2%
Threatened	0	0.0%	0	0.0%	-	0.0%
Assaulted	0	0.0%	0	0.0%	-	0.0%
Injured	6	2.9%	2	0.2%	8	0.8%
Killed	2	1.0%	4	0.5%	6	0.6%
Missing	0	0.0%	14	1.7%	14	1.3%
Totals	205	100.0%	838	100.0%	1,043	100.0%

From: *Piracy and Armed Robbery Against Ships, Annual Report, 1 January–31 December 2008* (London: International Chamber of Commerce, International Maritime Bureau, January 2009), 5–6.

Spokesmen for the pirates often claim that they are members of the Somali Coast Guard and are merely defending their territorial waters or exacting retribution for illegal fishing or dumping. In all likelihood, many of the original pirates probably were fishermen who turned to piracy after their sourced income was destroyed by illegal fishing. Somali fishermen maintain that foreign fishing vessels use illegal fishing equipment, steal their catches, cut their nets, and ram their fishing boats. Thus, they declare, any action they take is not piracy but justifiable retaliation. No doubt, the absence of an effective government in Mogadishu opened the door for illegal fishing in Somali waters by European and Asian fishing vessels. According to a UN estimate, more than 700 foreign fishing trawlers operated illegally in Somali waters in 2005. Analysts estimate that more than $300 million worth of fish are poached from Somali waters each year.[122] This is a crucial issue, for there is little chance that piracy emanating from Somalia will end unless illegal fishing is stopped and the fishing industry restored, thus giving Somalis some means of legitimately supporting themselves.

Somali pirates have become increasingly more sophisticated over the last few years. Initially, their tactics involved nothing more than launching a fishing boat from shore and attacking the first ship that happened by. Like the buccaneers in the Caribbean, they started out using small boats, but as they became more successful, they acquired bigger and faster vessels as well as more powerful weapons and more sophisticated navigational equipment. As the frequency of their attacks increased, merchant vessels moved farther and farther away from the shore. Many maritime security experts assumed that the pirates' small boats would be unable to operate 50, 100, or 200 miles from land because they were not sufficiently seaworthy and they lacked the fuel capacity to remain on station for very long. But the Somalis proved them wrong when they took the Saudi tanker *Sirius Star* some 420 nautical miles off the coast.[123] The Somalis adapted to the change in shipping patterns by capturing fishing trawlers and small freighters and using them as mother ships or afloat operating bases. Since they look like any other commercial vessel, mother ships help the pirates disguise their purpose and extend their range hundreds of miles out to sea. Now, the Somalis can hide in the shipping lanes, waiting for a likely target in relative comfort and security. Once they identify their quarry, the pirates swarm their victim in wolf pack-like style, using six or more high-powered speedboats. The Somalis are heavily armed to intimidate their quarry into giving up without resistance. To help them make that decision, they fire automatic weapons and rocket-propelled grenades (RPGs) at the pilot house to force the master to stop. If they can convince the merchant ship to slow or stop, they can board and take control of the ship in a matter of minutes.[124]

One of the earliest reported attacks in Somali waters exemplifies many of the techniques still used today. On 9 September 1994, a Somali dhow manned with 24 pirates accosted the MV *Bonsella* 3 miles north of Caluula in the Gulf of Aden. The pirates fired two mortar rounds at the *Bonsella* to force her to stop. When they came on board, the pirates claimed to be part of the Somali Coast Guard. They told the ship's master that they were going to use the *Bonsella* as a mother ship to apprehend trawlers fishing illegally without proper licenses. On the second day, they pursued two ships thought to be fishing vessels. Once the Somalis realized the ships were merchant vessels, they continued to pursue them. As with *Bonsella*, they fired mortar rounds to induce the ships to stop. In this case, neither vessel slowed down, and they both escaped. When asked why they continued to chase the merchant ships, the pirates indicated that they wanted to capture a ship faster than *Bonsella* so they could extend their patrol area. On 13 October, they made another failed attempt to capture another ship. Finally, on 14 October, after stealing all the cash on board, almost all of the ship's stores and equipment, and the entire cargo of aid supplies, the pirates set *Bonsella* free.[125]

Since Somali piracy is a kidnapping/ransom business, the pirates take reasonably good care of their hostages. In the port of Eyl, the pirates' main haven, several new restaurants have been opened to cater to the captives' culinary needs.[126] Shipping companies are more willing to meet the pirates' demands because they realize that the pirates do not intend to harm their crews, ships, or cargoes.[127] Moreover, there are few good options beyond paying the ransom. Attempting to take the vessel back by force might result in casualties among the crew, endanger the ship, or spark retaliatory violence by the Somalis. Allowing the ship to remain under their control is not a viable alternative since every lost day costs the shipping company as much as $25,000. Thus, it is in the best interests of both the victims and the perpetrators to pay the ransom and end the hostage situation.[128]

A good example of the dangers of trying to recapture hostages occurred recently when the French retook the yacht *Tanit*, which Somali pirates seized in the Gulf of Aden on 4 April 2009. Five French citizens were on board the ship, including the captain's 3-year-old son. A French naval vessel disabled the yacht by shooting holes in its sails to prevent it from making landfall in Somalia. With the boat adrift and ransom negotiations at a standstill, French commandos attacked on 9 April. During the gunfight, the yacht's skipper, Florent Lemaçon, was killed. His wife, son, and another couple survived. Two pirates were killed and three others captured.[129]

Claims of illegal entry into territorial waters or illegal fishing served as the justification for most pirate attacks in the 1990s. For example, Somali militia detained a Syrian ship towing a Bulgarian freighter in January 1998, claiming that the ships were in Somali waters illegally. They were released in February after the owners paid a $110,000 fine.[130] Later that year, Somali militiamen seized a Kenyan fishing vessel they claimed was illegally fishing off the coast near Eyl. The ship was fined $500,000 by a Somali court.[131]

Incidents of piracy in the Gulf of Aden and Somali waters were fairly infrequent until 2005. Only 23 incidents were reported in 2000. Assaults decreased further in 2001–2002 after Combined Task Force 150, a US-led Naval force, began patrolling the Indian Ocean, Northern Arabian Sea, and the Gulf of Aden in support of Operation ENDURING FREEDOM in 2001. Still, attacks did occur from time to time, so in August 2002, the IMB advised mariners to sail no closer than 50 miles off the coast of Somalia and to remain 100 miles offshore if possible because of several recent acts of piracy.[132] In early July 2002, Somali militiamen seized a Cypriot-owned ship off the coast of Puntland. The cargo ship *Aamir* was en route from the United Arab Emirates to Mogadishu when bad weather forced it to anchor off the northern coast of Somalia. While at anchor, Somali militiamen seized the ship.[133] The owners eventually paid $400,000 for the release of the ship. Later that month, Somali pirates seized a North Korean-owned ship and demanded $300,000 for her release.[134] By the end of 2002, the IMB warned that the likelihood of attack in Somali waters increased from a possibility to a certainty.[135] But instead of further increases, pirate attacks ebbed in 2003 and 2004, dropping to only 10 attacks in 2004.

The situation turned for the worse in 2005 when the Somalis carried out a number of high profile attacks that focused considerable attention to their activities. One of the most appalling incidents was the hijacking of the MV *Semlow*, which was carrying 850 tons of rice meant for Somali victims of the December 2004 Indian Ocean tsunami.[136] The ship was en route from Mombasa, Kenya, to Boosaaso, Somalia, when the pirates struck on 27 June 2005.[137] Captain Sellathurai Mahalingam recalled that the pirates came out of nowhere, fired 5 to 10 shots at the bridge, and then pulled alongside the ship in speedboats. Ten pirates armed with pistols, AK-47 rifles, and RPGs scrambled over the side of the ship and took control in less than 15 minutes. Mahalingam noted later that the pirates were very calm. *Semlow* was, they said, their 20th victim of the year. Once in control, they began ransacking the ship. They stole $8,500 from the ship's safe and personal items from the crew. Then, they directed Mahalingam to head for Ceel Huur.[138]

Once they arrived, they anchored off the coast within sight of land. Soon, life on board the ship fell into a routine. The pirates restricted the *Semlow*'s crew to the aft part of the ship. Although they were not mistreated, they ran short of food and had to ration water. Meanwhile, the pirates were relieved every 4 or 5 days. They spent their time cleaning their weapons, drilling on the main deck, and chewing khat, a native plant containing an amphetamine-like stimulant. The pirates also ate well. They brought goats, potatoes, tomatoes, and onions with them from the shore and freely used the World Food Program rice.[139]

Throughout the ordeal, the Somalis negotiated with both the Kenyan-based shipping company and the WFP, attempting to extort $500,000 in ransom. The director of the shipping company maintained that his was a poor company unable to pay the ransom. A group of UN, Kenyan, Sri Lankan, and Tanzanian officials flew to Somalia to discuss the situation with the transitional government and clan leaders.[140] When negotiations foundered, the WFP suspended aid shipments to the country.[141]

In late September, the pirates used the *Semlow* to strike another victim. An Egyptian cement carrier, MS *Ibn Batuta*, sailed near the *Semlow* on 23 September. The pirates used *Semlow* as a mother ship, steaming her close enough to the *Ibn Batuta* that they could approach her in their speedboats and capture her as well. After further negotiations, *Ibn Batuta* got underway for el Maan with *Semlow* under tow because *Semlow* had, by this time, run out of fuel. Along the way, the pirates abandoned both ships, leaving them free to continue on to el Maan, where *Semlow* offloaded the WFP rice.[142] Although the WFP did not pay any ransom, maintaining it would set a bad precedent, the pirates managed to extort $135,000 from the shipping company.[143]

By this time, a full-blown piracy crisis was brewing. On 8 October, 5 days after *Semlow* was released, Somali pirates captured the MV *Toregelow*, which was carrying food and fuel to *Semlow*.[144] They followed that up 4 days later by seizing another UN aid ship, MV *Miltzow*, on 12 October. They only held *Miltzow* for 2 days before releasing her without receiving any ransom.[145] Finally, on 19 October, Somali pirates captured MV *Pagonia*, a Ukrainian ship carrying iron ore. They demanded $700,000 for the release of this ship.[146]

Somali piracy gained even more notoriety when, early on the morning of 5 November 2005, pirates in two speedboats attacked the *Seabourn Spirit*, an American-owned luxury cruise ship. The ship, which carried 151 passengers and 161 crewmembers, was on a 16-day cruise from Alexandria, Egypt, to Singapore. When the pirates attacked at 0550, the captain woke the passengers, warned them of the danger, and directed them to muster in the dining room, which was in the center of the ship. At the same time, he activated the ship's LRAD defense system and sped up, leaving the pirates in his wake. The LRAD, a nonlethal weapon, emits a high-pitched tone that operators can direct at specific targets to drive them away. Still, the situation was rife with danger for the Somalis fired rifles and at least three RPG rounds, one of which struck the ship. No passengers were injured, but one crewmember suffered shrapnel wounds during the attack.[147]

Those attacks sparked a more determined response by the United States and other nations. On 21 January 2006, the USS *Winston Churchill* seized the dhow *Al Bisarat*, a Somali mother ship. Acting on a report from the Piracy Reporting Center, *Winston Churchill* located the suspected mother ship during the evening of 20 January. When the dhow refused to stop, *Winston Churchill* fired a warning shot over its bow, which quickly brought it to a halt. After boarding the dhow, sailors from the *Winston Churchill* discovered 10 pirates and an arms cache. The vessel's crew was apprehended and turned over to Kenya where they were sentenced to 7 years in jail.[148]

A couple of months later, on 18 March 2006, the USS *Gonzalez* and USS *Cape St. George* engaged a suspected mother ship with small-arms fire. The two US ships intercepted a suspicious-looking fishing dhow that was towing two smaller boats. As sailors from the *Gonzalez* prepared to board the dhow, they spotted men armed with RPG launchers. When the Somalis opened fire on the *Gonzalez*, striking her multiple times, both American ships responded. They destroyed the dhow, killed one pirate, and wounded five more. The Americans captured seven other pirates.[149]

In June 2006, the Islamic Courts Union took control of Mogadishu and much of the surrounding area. Believing that the pirates were in league with the warlords who opposed the Islamic Courts Union, Islamic militiamen shut down many of the pirate havens during the second half of the year. Thus, only 20 acts of piracy occurred in the vicinity of Somalia in 2006.[150] But attacks rebounded in 2007 after Ethiopian troops drove the Islamic Courts Union out of the country. Free to act with impunity, the pirates attacked 44 ships in 2007.

Once again, Somali pirates rashly hijacked a World Food Program ship. The MV *Rozen* was captured on 25 February 2007 and held for 40 days. The ship was captured off Puntland Province after delivering supplies to Berbera and Boosaaso, Somalia.[151]

The US Navy unsuccessfully engaged the pirates on two occasions in 2007. When brigands captured the Danish vessel *Danica White* on 2 June 2007, a US warship responded. The USS *Carter Hall* fired over the bow of the *Danica White* and shot flares at the ship in an attempt to prevent her from entering Somali waters. Although *Carter Hall* did not prevent the hijacking, it destroyed two pirate skiffs towed behind the merchant ship. *Carter Hall* broke off the engagement when the merchant ship entered Somali territorial waters.[152] The Japanese chemical tanker *Golden Nori* was hijacked on 28 October 2007 in the Gulf of Aden. The USS *Arleigh Burke* and USS *Porter* responded to the *Golden Nori*'s distress signal. The American ships tried to stop the attack by firing over the ship's bow, but the pirates refused to comply. Eventually, the Americans sank several small boats towed by the tanker, but they were unable to prevent the brigands from sailing the ship into Somali territorial waters.[153] In both cases, restrictive rules of engagement prevented the Navy from acting more forcefully to stop the pirates.

A third engagement turned out better. Somali pirates tried to hijack the North Korean cargo ship MV *Dai Hong* on 30 October 2007. The USS *James E. Williams* responded to the *Dai Hong*'s distress signal by sending its helicopter to investigate. When it arrived on station, the helicopter crew spoke to the pirates on the bridge-to-bridge radio and ordered them to put down their weapons. While the brigands were distracted by the helicopter, the ship's crew overpowered the Somalis. One pirate was killed and three were wounded during the melee. Three crewmen were also injured.[154]

The actions of the captain and crew of the cargo ship *Ibn Younos* demonstrate the importance of taking defensive actions. The Somalis failed to capture the ship during an attack on 14 May 2007. During that assault which lasted more than an hour, the pirates raked the ship's bridge with automatic weapons fire, and RPGs destroyed the crews' accommodation area. Still, the captain of the *Ibn Younos* refused to give in. Instead, he sped up and commenced a zigzag course to ward off the pirates.[155]

In 2008, Somali pirates had a banner year. They attacked 111 ships during the year and were successful 44 times. That effort brought in $30 million to $80 million in ransom payments.[156] Somali piracy was constantly in the news throughout much of the year. There were several dramatic attacks such as the MV *Faina* and the tanker *Sirius Star*.

There were also defeats such as when the French military captured several of the pirates who hijacked *Le Ponant*. The French luxury yacht *Le Ponant* was captured by Somali pirates on 4 April 2008. At the time, the pirates thought they had hit the jackpot. But for six of the pirates, it proved to be a false dream.[157] The drama began in early April when nine pirates, using two borrowed speedboats, captured a Yemeni trawler. They used the trawler as a mother ship, steaming through the Gulf of Aden in search of lucrative targets. They thought they found one on 4 April 2008 when they spotted the 850-ton, 3-mast yacht. Three pirates motored over to the yacht in one of the speedboats. When *Le Ponant*'s crew tried to resist by using fire hoses, the pirates began shooting at them. The other pirates abandoned the trawler and assisted with the assault. They soon had the unarmed crew under control and sailed the vessel to Garaad, where the locals assisted the pirates by standing guard and providing the pirates with other services. The pirates eventually settled on a $2 million ransom demand. For their assistance, each villager was promised $50, and each pirate was supposed to take home $11,000 to $20,000.[158]

Meanwhile, the French began mobilizing a force to strike back. The French frigate *Commandant Bouan* tracked the pirates to their lair. The frigate was soon joined by the aircraft carrier *Jeanne d'Arc*. When the pirates released the 30 crewmembers after receiving the ransom on 11 April, French commandos in helicopters struck back. They captured six of the nine pirates as they tried to escape from the area in cars.[159]

A few days after the pirates captured MV *Faina*, other Somali corsairs really did hit the jackpot when they captured the very large crude carrier *Sirius Star* on 15 November 2008. The tanker was loaded with about 2 million barrels of oil, which represented 25 percent of Saudi Arabia's daily production. The attack shocked most maritime experts because the ship was 450 miles east of Somalia en route to the United States via the Cape of Good Hope. Few people thought the pirates could operate that far from shore or take a vessel that big. But 10 pirates took control of the tanker in less than 20 minutes after forcing it to stop by shooting at the pilot house. They steamed the ship to Xaradheere, where they announced their ransom demand of $25 million. They eventually lowered their demands and released the ship on 9 January 2009 after receiving $3 million in ransom. Several of the brigands drowned as they headed for shore after splitting the money.[160]

In addition to these dramatic attacks, 2008 was also marked by more aggressive moves on the part of the multinational force tasked with suppressing piracy. A French frigate captured nine buccaneers in the Gulf of Aden in October.[161] In November, HMS *Cumberland* sank a suspected pirate ship that had attempted to capture a Danish cargo ship. The *Cumberland* spotted the dhow in the vicinity of the Dutch ship and tried to force it to stop. When it would not comply, *Cumberland* dispatched a boarding party in a rigid inflatable boat to force it to submit. Instead, the brigands opened fire on the British ship. During an exchange of gunfire, two pirates were killed, one was mortally wounded and five others were captured. One week later, they were transferred to Kenya, which agreed to prosecute those captured.[162] A short time later, the Indian Navy ship *Tabar* engaged a suspected mother ship and destroyed it as well. Only after a Cambodian sailor was rescued from the debris did the Indians learn that 15 other innocent fishermen died during the assault on the ship.[163] This incident underscores the difficulty of differentiating between legitimate fishermen and pirate vessels.

In early 2009, as the Somali pirates became increasingly more bold, coalition forces stepped up their level of aggressiveness to match the Somali's audacity. There is, however, much concern that the naval forces do not become too belligerent. Thus far, the pirates have behaved rationally, preserving the safety of the ships, cargo, and crews. If nations become more aggressive, it stands to reason that the pirates might change their attitude as well. That was certainly the case in the 18th and 19th centuries. The 18th-century pirates of the West Indies became progressively more brutal as Great Britain began executing them with greater regularity. By the 19th century, the policy of executing pirates was well established. Consequently, 19th-century pirates usually treated their captives much more harshly than their 16th-century counterparts did because they realized that it did not pay to leave survivors who might testify against them.

The situation off the coast of Somalia underscores the futility of trying to suppress piracy using only naval forces. Despite the presence of a powerful flotilla of ships—CTF 50—and the availability of sophisticated surveillance equipment, the coalition task force does not have the resources needed to guard more than 1 million square miles of ocean adjacent to Somali. The Somalis continue to operate with impunity. When American and French forces killed several pirates recently, the Somalis responded by taking four more ships almost immediately. They seemed to be sending a message that they know that there is little the coalition force can do to stop them. The best the naval antipiracy task force can do is to guard the primary sealanes and to encourage ship captains to only sail through those areas where the coalition naval force operates.

In the end, piracy emanating from Somalia can only be resolved ashore. That does not, however, mean merely attacking the shore havens. Such attacks would be transitory and of limited value. Somalia's piracy problem can only be solved by fixing Somalia. But Somalia remains in the midst of social and political chaos and there is no reason to believe that the current Transitional National Government will be able to accomplish any more than the previous 13 administrations. In light of the US experience in Somali in the early 1990s, it is understandable that American policymakers are reluctant to take on that task. But as in previous periods of piracy, resolution of this outbreak of piracy requires determined effort by the dominant naval power—the United States—acting both at sea and on land.

Notes

1. Nick Wadhams, "Somali Pirates' Unexpected Booty: Russian Tanks," *Time*, 26 September 2008, http://www.time.com/time/world/article/0,8599,1844914,00. html (accessed 1 April 2009).

2. Associated Press, "Ship Seized by Somali Pirates Carrying 33 Russian Tanks," *FoxNews.com*, 26 September 2008, http://www.foxnews.com/ story/0,2933,428582,00.html (accessed 2 April 2009).

3. Elizabeth A. Kennedy, "US Navy Watches Seized Ship With Sudan-Bound Tanks," *USA Today*, 29 September 2008, http://www.usatoday.com/news/ world/2008-09-28-1797517683_x.htm (accessed 23 March 2009).

4. Nick Wadhams, "Somali Pirates Hold Whip Hand in Standoff," *San Francisco Chronicle*," 26 October 2008, http://sfgate.com/cgi-bin/article.cgi?f=/ c/a/2008/10/26/MN6913NSJK.DTL (accessed 2 April 2009).

5. Wadhams, "Somali Pirates' Unexpected Booty: Russian Tanks."

6. Ibid.

7. US Naval Forces Central Command Public Affairs, "USS Howard Monitoring MV Faina," 25 September 2008, http://www.dvidshub. net/?script=news/news_show.php&id=24242 (accessed 27 March 2009).

8. Rear Admiral Kendall Card, Commander, Expeditionary Strike Group 3, telephone interview with James A. Wombwell, Combat Studies Institute, 1 April 2009.

9. "Ship Seized by Somali Pirates Carrying 33 Russian Tanks."

10. Bernard Momanyi, "Pay Up, Faina Pirates Demand," *Capital News*, 23 October 2008, http://www.capitalfm.co.ke/news/Local/Pay-up,-Faina-pirates-demand.html (accessed 1 April 2009).

11. Jeffrey Gettleman, "Hijacked Arms Ship Limps Into Port," *New York Times*, 13 February 2009, http://www.nytimes.com/2009/02/13/world/ africa/13pirate.html (accessed 2 April 2009).

12. Jeffrey Gettleman and Mohammed Ibrahim, "Somali Pirates Get Ransom and Leave Arms Freighter," *New York Times*, 6 February 2009, http://www. nytimes.com/2009/02/06/world/africa/06pirates.html?_r=1&pagewanted=print (accessed 1 April 2009).

13. David W. Munns, "Rise in Murders, Kidnappings at Sea Makes Piracy a Top Naval Priority Worldwide," *Sea Power*, October 2004, 11, http://www. military.com/NewContent/0,13190,NL_Piracy_102604-P1,00.html (accessed 11 April 2009).

14. Stefan Eklöf, *Pirates in Paradise: A Modern History of Southeast Asia's Maritime Marauders* (Copenhagen: NIAS Press), 2006, 2.

15. All data referenced came from the International Chamber of Commerce (ICC), International Maritime Bureau. See ICC, International Maritime Bureau, *Piracy and Armed Robbery Against Ships, Annual Report, 1 January–31 December 2008*, London: ICC, International Maritime Bureau, January 2009,

5–6, for 2003–2008 data; Martin N. Murphy, *Small Boats, Weak States, Dirty Money: Piracy and Maritime Terrorism in the Modern World* (London: Hurst & Co., 2008), 62, for 1995–2002 data.

16. Murphy, 68–69.

17. International Chamber of Commerce, Commercial Crimes Services, "International Maritime Bureau," no date, http://www.icc-ccs.org/index.php?option=com_content&view=article&id=27&Itemid=16 (accessed 5 April 2009).

18. G.O.W. Mueller and Freda Adler, *Outlaws of the Ocean: The Complete Book of Contemporary Crime on the High Seas* (New York: Hearst Marine Books, 1985), 141–143.

19. Eklöf, 91.

20. Ibid., 90–91.

21. Ibid., 93.

22. Ibid., 92.

23. Adam J. Young and Mark J. Valencia, "Conflation of Piracy and Terrorism in Southeast Asia: Rectitude and Utility," *Contemporary Southeast Asia*, 25 (2003), http://www.southchinasea.org/docs/Young%2BValencia,%20Conflation%20of%20Piracy%20and%20Terrorism.htm (accessed 25 November 2008).

24. ICC, International Maritime Bureau, *Piracy and Armed Robbery Against Ships, Annual Report, 1 January–31 December 2007* (London: ICC International Maritime Bureau, January 2008), 2.

25. Eklöf, 94.

26. *Piracy and Armed Robbery Against Ships, Annual Report, 1 January–31 December 2007*, 2.

27. Eklöf, 94.

28. *Piracy and Armed Robbery Against Ships, Annual Report, 1 January–31 December 2007*, 3.

29. Ibid.

30. Murphy, 14–16.

31. Dana R. Dillon, *The China Challenge: Standing Strong Against the Military, Economic, and Political Threats That Imperil America* (Lanham, MD: Rowman & Littlefield Publishers, 2007), 86.

32. Ibid., 85.

33. Ibid., 89.

34. Murphy, 8.

35. Young and Valencia; Rupert Herbert-Burns, "Compound Piracy at Sea in the Early Twenty-First Century: A Tactical to Operational-Level Perspective on Contemporary Multiphase Piratical Methodology," in *Violence at Sea: Piracy in the Age of Global Terrorism*, ed. Peter Lehr (New York: Routledge, 2007), 102–103.

36. Dillon, 88–89.

37. Young and Valencia; Eklöf, 46–47.

38. Young and Valencia.

39. Peter Chalk, *The Maritime Dimension of International Security: Terrorism, Piracy, and Challenges for the United States* (Santa Monica, CA: Rand Corporation, 2008), 10.

40. Ibid., 11–14.

41. Eklöf, 129–130; David Axe, "4 Fronts for Pirate-Navy Battles as Pirate Attacks Continue," *Popular Mechanics*, 29 September 2008, http://www.popularmechanics.com/technology/military_law/4285201.html?page=4 (accessed 20 January 2009).

42. Andrew Gray, "Armed Guards Would Deter Somali Pirates: US Navy," *The Manama Dialogue, IISS Regional Security Summit*, 13 December 2008, http://www.iiss.org/whats-new/iiss-in-the-press/press-coverage-2008/december-2008/armed-guards-would-deter-somali-piratesus-navy/ (accessed 21 April 2009).

43. Chris O'Brien, "Shippers Resist Calls to Arm Against Pirates," *Washington Times*, 21 April 2009, http://www.studentnewsdaily.com/daily-news-article/shippers-resist-calls-to-arm-against-pirates/ (accessed 21 April 2009). See also Associated Press, "Private Security Companies Hired To Protect Ships From Pirates," *St. Petersburg Times*, 28 October 2008, http://www.sptimes.ru/story/27485 (accessed 21 April 2009).

44. Kim Sengupta, "Blackwater Gunboats Will Protect Ships," *The Independent*, 19 November 2008, http://www.independent.co.uk/news/world/africa/blackwater-gunboats-will-protect-ships-1024582.html (accessed 21 April 2009).

45. Gregory Viscusi, "Mercenary Guards Jump Ship as Somali Pirates Remain Undeterred," *Asian Energy*, 18 December 2008, http://asianenergy.blogspot.com/2008/12/mercenary-guards-jump-ship-as-somali.html (accessed 21 April 2009); Catherine Z. Raymond, "Piracy in Southeast Asia: New Trends, Issues and Responses," *Harvard Asia Quarterly* 9, no. 4 (Fall 2005), http://www.asiaquarterly.com/content/view/30/1/ (accessed 21 April 2009).

46. Viscusi.

47. Raymond.

48. Murphy, 50.

49. Chalk, 16.

50. Alexandria Lewis, "Kidnap Insurance Costs Up Tenfold in Gulf of Aden," Aon Corporation Web site, 9 April 2009, http://aon.mediaroom.com/index.php?s=43&item=1526 (accessed 21 April 2009).

51. John W. Miller, "Piracy Spurs Threats to Shipping," *The Wall Street Journal*, 19 November 2009, http://www.studentnewsdaily.com/daily-news-article/piracy-spurs-threats-to-shipping-costs/ (accessed 21 April 2009).

52. Associated Press, "Piracy Drives Up Insurance Rates for Ships in Gulf," *Portland Press Herald*, 13 April 2009, http://pressherald.mainetoday.com/story.php?id=250548&ac=PHbiz&pg=1 (accessed 21 April 2009).

53. *Piracy and Armed Robbery Against Ships, Annual Report, 1 January–31 December 2007*, 5–6.

54. Graham Gerard Ong-Webb, "Southeast Asian Piracy: Research and Developments," in *Piracy, Maritime Terrorism and Securing the Malacca Straits*, ed. Graham Gerard Ong-Webb (Singapore: Institute of Southeast Asian Studies, 2006), xviii.

55. Dillon, 83.

56. In 1990, China's GDP was 1.854 trillion Yuan RMB. By 2000, it had grown to 8.946 trillion Yuan RMB. See "GDP Growth, 1952–2008," *Chinability*, 4 May 2008, http://www.chinability.com/GDP.htm (accessed 3 April 2009).

57. Munns, 14.

58. Vijay Sakhuja, "Sea Piracy in South Asia," in *Violence at Sea: Piracy in the Age of Global Terrorism*, ed. Peter Lehr (New York: Routledge, 2007), 23.

59. Murphy, 72.

60. Central Intelligence Agency, "Indonesia," *The 2008 World Fact Book* (Washington, DC: Office of Public Affairs, Central Intelligence Agency, 2008), https://www.cia.gov/library/publications/the-world-factbook/geos/id.html (accessed 23 February 2009).

61. Central Intelligence Agency, "Malaysia," *The 2008 World Fact Book* https://www.cia.gov/library/publications/the-world-factbook/geos/my.html (accessed 23 February 2009).

62. Sakhuja, 23.

63. Murphy, 73.

64. Eklöf, 133.

65. Raymond.

66. Murphy, 73–74.

67. Pranamita Baruah, "Japan's Response to Sea Piracy," *Institute for Defence Studies and Analyses*, 30 March 2009, http://www.idsa.in/publications/stratcomments/PranamitaBaruah300309.html (accessed 21 April 2009).

68. Dillon, 45–46.

69. Mueller and Adler, 151.

70. John Burnett, *Dangerous Waters: Modern Piracy and Terror on the High Seas* (New York: Dutton, 2002), 166–167.

71. Chalk, 16.

72. Eklöf, 48.

73. J.N. Mak, "Pirates, Renegades, and Fishermen: The Politics of 'Sustainable' Piracy in the Strait of Malacca," in *Violence at Sea: Piracy in the Age of Global Terrorism*, ed. Peter Lehr (New York: Routledge, 2007), 201–203.

74. Eklöf, 44.

75. Ibid., 133–135.

76. Ibid., 44.

77. Graham Gerard Ong-Webb, "Piracy in Maritime Asia: Current Trends," in *Violence at Sea: Piracy in the Age of Global Terrorism*, ed. Peter Lehr (New York: Routledge, 2007), figure 3.3, 50.

78. Ibid., figure 3.15, 60.

79. Eklöf, 69.

80. Ibid., 73–74.

81. Raymond.

82. Eklöf, 77–80; Munns, 14.

83. Eklöf, 80–82.

84. Herbert-Burns, 100; International Chamber of Commerce, Commercial Crime Services, "Violence Resumes in Malacca Straits," 15 March 2005, http://www.icc-ccs.org/index.php?option=com_content&view=article&id=80:violence-resumes-in-malacca-straits&catid=60:news&Itemid=51 (accessed 6 April 2009); Republic of the Philippines, "Filipino Seaman Abducted in Malacca Strait Freed," 21 March 2005, http://www.gov.ph/news/default.asp?i=7530 (accessed 6 April 2009).

85. Eklöf, 53.

86. Ibid.

87. Herbert-Burns, 105.

88. Eklöf, 53–54.

89. Mak, 203.

90. Ibid., 206–208.

91. Ibid., 213–214.

92. Chalk, 33 and note 9.

93. Ong-Webb, "Southeast Asian Piracy," xxvii.

94. Chris Rahman, "The International Politics of Combating Piracy in Southeast Asia," in *Violence at Sea: Piracy in the Age of Global Terrorism*, ed. Peter Lehr (New York: Routledge, 2007), 195.

95. Young and Valencia; Eklöf, 135–136.

96. Eklöf, 136–137.

97. Raymond.

98. Eklöf, 137–139.

99. Ibid., 140.

100. Rahman, 195.

101. Ibid., 194.

102. Ong-Webb, "Southeast Asian Piracy," xxix–xxx.

103. Ibid., xxxiv.

104. Members of ReCAAP are People's Republic of Bangladesh, Brunei Darussalam, the Kingdom of Cambodia, the People's Republic of China, the Republic of India, Japan, the Republic of Korea, the Lao People's Democratic Republic, the Union of Myanmar, the Republic of the Philippines, the Republic of Singapore, the Democratic Socialists Republic of Sri Lanka, the Kingdom of Thailand, and the Socialist Republic of Vietnam. See Regional Cooperation Agreement on Combating Piracy and Armed Robbery Against Ships in Asia (ReCAAP) Information Sharing Center, *Adding Value, Charting Trends: 2007 Annual Research Report*, Singapore, 2008, www.southchinasea.org/docs/Recaap_Trends.pdf (accessed 6 April 2009), 5.

105. Ong-Webb, "Southeast Asian Piracy," xxxv; Rahman, 191.

106. Ong-Webb, xxx.

107. Raymond.

108. Peter Lehr and Hendrick Lehmann, "Somalai—Pirates' New Paradise," in *Violence at Sea: Piracy in the Age of Global Terrorism*, ed. Peter Lehr (New York: Routledge, 2007), 2.

109. Axe.

110. Derek S. Reveron, "Think Again: Pirates," *Foreign Policy* (January 2009), http://www.foreignpolicy.com/story/cms.php?story_id=4626&page=0 (accessed 2 April 2009).

111. Central Intelligence Agency, "Somalia," *The World Fact Book*, 2008, https://www.cia.gov/library/publications/the-world-factbook/geos/so.html (accessed 4 April 2009).

112. Brian Wilson and James Kraska, "Anti-Piracy Patrols Presage Rising Naval Powers," *Yale Global*, 13 January 2009, http://yaleglobal.yale.edu/display. article?id=11808 (accessed 4 April 2009).

113. Abdi Guled, "Somali Pirates Move to Aid Comrades," *Mail & Guardian*, 11 April 2009, http://www.mg.co.za/article/2009-04-11-somali-pirates-move-to-aid-comrades (accessed 10 April 2009).

114. BBC, "Timeline: Somalia," BBC News Web site, 29 October 2008, http://news.bbc.co.uk/go/pr/fr/-/2/hi/africa/country_profiles/1072611.stm (accessed 7 November 2008).

115. Dana Hughes, "Somalia Piracy: On Land and Sea," ABC News Web site, 17 November 2008, http://blogs.abcnews.com/worldview/2008/11/somalia-chaos-a.html (accessed 21 November 2008); Rob Crilly, "Wanted: Countries to Stand Guard on Ships," *The Times*, 20 September 2008, http://www.timesonline. co.uk/tol/news/world/asia/article4791107.ece (accessed 13 November 2008).

116. Steve Bloomfield, "'Hidden Famine' in Horn of Africa Puts 14 Million at Risk," *The Independent*, 23 July 2008, http://www.independent.co.uk/news/ world/africa/hidden-famine-in-horn-of-africa-puts-14m-at-risk-874873.html (accessed 20 November 2008).

117. Mary Harper, "Life in Somalia's Pirate Town," BBC News Web site, 18 September 2008, http://news.bbc.co.uk/2/hi/africa/7623329.stm (accessed 6 November 2008).

118. Jay Bahadur, "I'm Not a Pirate, I'm the Saviour of the Sea," *The Times*, 16 April 2009, http://www.timesonline.co.uk/tol/news/world/africa/ article6100783.ece (accessed 21 April 2009).

119. Harper; Daniel Howden and Mohamed Guled, "Off the Coast of Somalia: We're Not Pirates. These Are Our Waters, Not Theirs," *The Independent*, 14 November 2008, http://www.independent.co.uk/news/world/africa/off-the-coast-of-somalia-were-not-pirates-these-are-our-waters-not-theirs-1017962.html (accessed 4 April 2009).

120. *Piracy and Armed Robbery Against Ships, Annual Report, 1 January–31 December 2007*, 13; *Piracy and Armed Robbery Against Ships, Annual Report, 1 January–31 December 2008*, 13–14.

121. Ibid.

122. Christopher Jasparro, "Somalia's Piracy Offers Lessons in Global Governance," *YaleGlobalOnline*, 6 April 2009, http://yaleglobal.yale.edu/ display.article?id=12210 (accessed 10 April 2009); Peter Lehr, "Dealing With Somali Pirates," *The Guardian*, 25 November 2008, http://www.china.org.cn/ international/opinion/2008-11/25/content_16820148.htm (accessed 10 April 2009).

123. Reveron.

124. Axe; Lehr.

125. Murphy, 101; National Geospatial-Intelligence Agency, *Anti-Shipping Activity Messages*, Single ASAM Ref. Number 1995–71, http://www.nga. mil/portal/site/maritime/index.jsp?epi-content=RAW&beanID=844643208& viewID=query_results&MSI_queryType=ASAM&MSI_generalFilterType=S pecificNumber&MSI_generalFilterValue=1995_71&MSI_additionalFilterTy pe1=None&MSI_additionalFilterType2=-999&MSI_additionalFilterValue1=- 999&MSI_additionalFilterValue2=-999&MSI_outputOptionType1=SortBy&M SI_outputOptionType2=-999&MSI_outputOptionValue1=Date_DESC&MSI_ outputOptionValue2=-999 (accessed 10 April 2009).

126. Jonathan Clayton, "Business Booms in Somalian Pirate Village Eyl," *The Australian*, 19 November 2008, http://www.theaustralian.news.com.au/ story/0,25197,24674415-32682,00.html (accessed 2 April 2009).

127. Reveron.

128. Alastair Dalton, "Two More Hijacked in Piracy Crisis," *The Scotsman*, 19 November 2008, http://www.scotsman.com/latestnews/Two-more-ships- hijacked-in.4706852.jp (accessed 2 April 2009).

129. John Lichfield and Daniel Howden, "French Sailor Killed in Gun Battle as Special Forces Storm Hijacked Yacht," *The Independent*, 11 April 2009, http:// www.independent.co.uk/news/world/africa/french-sailor-killed-in-gun-battle-as- special-forces-storm-hijacked-yacht-1667275.html (accessed 11 April 2009).

130. BBC, "Somali Faction Frees Foreign Ships," BBC News Web site, 13 February 1998, http://news.bbc.co.uk/2/hi/africa/56514.stm (accessed 7 November 2008).

131. BBC, "Ship's Crew Fined for Illegal Fishing Off Somali Waters," BBC News Web site, 24 December 1998, http://news.bbc.co.uk/2/hi/africa/242103.stm (accessed 7 November 2008).

132. BBC, "Somali Pirates Hold Greek Tanker, BBC News Web site, 12 August 2002, http://news.bbc.co.uk/2/hi/africa/2188900.stm (accessed 7 November 2008).

133. Hassan Barise, "Somali Gunmen Hijack Cargo Ship," BBC News Web site, 3 July 2002, http://news.bbc.co.uk/2/hi/africa/2090651.stm (accessed 7 November 2008).

134. "Somali Pirates Hold Greek Tanker.

135. BBC, "Pirate Warning for Somalia's Coastline," BBC News Web site, 30 January 2003, http://news.bbc.co.uk/2/hi/business/2709339.stm (accessed 7 November 2008).

136. BBC, "WFP Ultimatum Over Somali Ship," BBC News Web site, 12 July 2005, http://news.bbc.co.uk/2/hi/africa/4677155.stm (accessed 6 November 2008).

137. BBC, "Pirates Hijack Tsunami Aid Ship," BBC News Web site, 30 June 2005, http://news.bbc.co.uk/2/hi/africa/4636695.stm (accessed 6 November 2008).

138. Simon Robinson and Xan Rice, "In Peril on the Sea," *Time*, 7 November 2005, http://www.time.com/time/magazine/article/0,9171,1126762,00.html (accessed 1 April 2009).

139. Ibid.

140. Ibid.

141. BBC, "Somali Aid Suspended After Hijack," BBC News Web Site, 4 July 2005, http://news.bbc.co.uk/2/hi/africa/4649825.stm (accessed 6 November 2008).

142. Associated Press, "How Pirates Hijacked Us," *News24.com*, 6 October 2005, http://www.news24.com/News24/Africa/News/0,,2-11-1447_1812108,00.html (accessed 2 April 2009).

143. Robinson and Rice.

144. BBC, "Somali Shock at New Ship Hijack," BBC News Web site, 11 October 2005, http://news.bbc.co.uk/go/pr/fr/-/2/hi/africa/4330492.stm (accessed 6 November 2008).

145. BBC, "Somali Pirates Free Hijacked Ship," BBC News Web site, 14 October 2005, http://news.bbc.co.uk/2/hi/africa/4341196.stm (accessed 6 November 2008).

146. BBC, "Pirates Hijack Ship Off Somalia," BBC News Web site, 21 October 2005, http://news.bbc.co.uk/2/hi/africa/4363344.stm (accessed 6 November 2008).

147. Michael S. McDaniel, ed., "Pirate Cruise Ship Attack," *The Cargo Letter*, 5 November 2005, http://www.cargolaw.com/presentation_casualties.05.html#Seabourne-Spirit (accessed 5 April 2009).

148. Murphy, 104; Steven D. Smith, "US Navy Captures Pirate Vessel Off Somali Coast," *Armed Forces Press Service*, 24 January 2006, http://www.defenselink.mil/news/newsarticle.aspx?id=14539 (accessed 5 December 2008); BBC, "Jail Sentence for Somali Pirates," BBC News Web site, 1 November 2006, http://news.bbc.co.uk/2/hi/africa/6105262.stm (accessed 6 November 2008).

149. Murphy, 104; "Somali Pirates Open Fire on US Navy Ships," *Ports & Ships*, 20 March 2006, http://ports.co.za/navalnews/article_2006_03_20_3048.html (accessed 10 April 2009).

150. Murphy, 104–105.

151. "WFP Welcomes Release of Hijacked Ship, MV Rozen," *Shipping Times*, 8 April 2007, http://www.shippingtimes.co.uk/item399_rozen.htm (accessed 15 December 2008).

152. BBC, "Ransom Paid to Free Danish Ship," BBC News Web site, 23 August 2007, http://news.bbc.co.uk/go/pr/fr/-/2/hi/africa/6959729.stm (accessed 21 November 2008).

153. Andrew Scutro, "In Chasing Pirates, Navy Comes Full Circle," *Navy Times*, 4 November 2007, http://www.navytimes.com/news/2007/11/navy_pirates_071103w/ (accessed 10 April 2007).

154. BBC, "Pirates 'Overpowered' off Somalia," BBC News Web site, 31 October 2007, http://news.bbc.co.uk/go/pr/fr/-/2/hi/africa/7069026.stm (accessed 21 November 2008); Scutro.

155. "Pirates Attack Cargo Ship with Rocket Launchers," *Shipping Times*, 15 May 2007, http://www.shippingtimes.co.uk/item603_pirate_attack.htm (accessed 15 December 2008).

156. Todd Pitman, "Somali Pirates a Far Cry From Buccaneers of Old," 11 April 2009, http://news.yahoo.com/s/ap/20090411/ap_on_re_af/piracy_somalia_s_swashbucklers (accessed 11 April 2009).

157. Mike Lee, "Real-Life Pirates Can't Match 'Capt. Jack Sparrow,'" ABC News Web site, 2008, http://abcnews.go.com/International/story?id=4641039&page=1 (accessed 21 November 2008).

158. AFP, "Pirates Used 'Good Conduct Guide' in French Yacht Seige: Source," AFP News Web site, 17 April 2009, http://afp.google.com/article/ALeqM5ic4lMhcdvj6BV5HsRB-uabBjyUmA (accessed 21 November 2008).

159. BBC, "France Frees Sailors From Pirates," BBC News Web site, 16 September 2008, http://afp.google.com/article/ALeqM5ic4lMhcdvj6BV5HsRB-uabBjyUmA (accessed 21 November 2008).

160. "Pirates Took Just 16 Minutes to Steal Super-Tanker," *Indian Express.com*, 21 November 2008, http://www.indianexpress.com/news/pirates-took-just-16-minutes-to-steal-supertanker/388724/ (accessed 26 November 2008); "Somali Pirates Demand Tanker Ransom, Three Ships Seized," *Khaleej Times Online*, 19 November 2008, http://www.khaleejtimes.com/DisplayArticle08.asp?xfile=data/international/2008/November/international_November1334.xml&section=international (accessed 19 November 2008); CNN, "Pirates Take 'Super-Tanker' Toward Somalia," *CNN.com/world*, 19 November 2008, http://www.cnn.com/2008/WORLD/africa/11/17/kenya.tanker.pirates/index.html (accessed 19 November 2009).

161. "France 'Captures Somali Pirates.'"

162. Ministry of Defense, "Suspected Pirates Caught by the Royal Navy Handed Over to Kenya," *Defense News*, 18 November 2008, http://www.mod.uk/DefenceInternet/DefenceNews/MilitaryOperations/SuspectedPiratesCaughtByTheRoyalNavyHandedOverToKenya.htm (accessed 11 April 2009).

163. Daily Mail, "Somali Pirate 'Mother Ship' Sunk by Indian Navy Turns Out to be Thai Trawler," *Daily Mail*, 26 November 2008, http://www.dailymail.co.uk/news/worldnews/article-1089514/Somali-pirate-mother-ship-sunk-Indian-navy-turns-Thai-trawler.html (accessed 11 April 2009).

Chapter 6

Conclusion

> Piracy is a nontraditional security threat that cannot be solved through military solutions . . . piracy should be rooted out by attacking sources of their strength on land, disrupting their organizational structure, and isolating them from their sources of support. In particular, this means destroying their bases and hideouts; cutting off their sources of capital, technology, and recruitment; and crippling the middlemen and markets that allow them to dispose of their loot.*

By looking at piracy over both time and space, it is clear that naval operations alone will not eliminate the costly and criminal operations of pirates. The best approach is to remove one of the three pillars of piracy: geography, political instability, or safe havens. Since the first pillar, geography, is almost impossible to change, primary consideration must be given to the remaining pillars, both of which are land based.

Piracy in the West Indies flourished for hundreds of years because of the geography, political situation, and the availability of safe havens. During the 17th and 18th centuries, when Great Britain moved to eliminate piracy, British authorities had to change political conditions as well as eliminate the safe havens. It required removing corrupt officials who benefited from piracy and unauthorized privateering and making illegal trade with the pirates not worth it to the merchants of Jamaica and the American colonies. It took people like Woodes Rogers and Governor Alexander Spottswood of Virginia to eliminate the pirates' havens. With no one to purchase their plundered goods and no place for them to hide from the authorities, the pirates eventually withered away.

Piracy reemerged in the West Indies in the 19th century because of political instability caused by the Wars for Latin American Independence. Since the geography of the area remained conducive to piracy, once the political conditions in the area deteriorated and safe havens ashore became available, piracy resurfaced. As in the earlier era, the advent of privateering led to piracy. Spanish merchants and officials, resentful over American

---

*Graham Gerard Ong-Webb, "Piracy in Maritime Asia: Current Trends," in *Violence at Sea: Piracy in the Age of Global Terrorism*, Peter Lehr, ed. (New York: Routledge, 2007), 90.

sympathy for the rebels, tacitly supported the brigands, providing them with political support and safe havens. Commodore David Porter finally made inroads against the buccaneers when he ignored Spanish concerns about the sovereignty of their Cuban and Puerto Rican possessions and allowed his forces to pursue the pirates ashore. Even then, it was the Spanish decision to stop providing support to the pirates, more than actions of the American and British Navies, that led to the end of piracy in the Caribbean.

The Barbary pirates preyed on shipping in the Mediterranean and Atlantic for hundreds of years. Great powers such as Britain and France used them as an instrument of their national power, calculating that whatever the corsairs did to other nations' ships would benefit them. After the American Revolution, when the United States no longer enjoyed the protection of the Royal Navy, the Barbary corsairs became a threat to the United States. The American effort during the first Barbary War depended, at first, exclusively on naval power. Despite the presence of American naval forces off the coast of Tripoli for several years, the war threatened to drag on indefinitely until William Eaton introduced a land element. At that point, threatened from both sea and land, the Pasha of Tripoli accepted the American terms. But the treaty did not eliminate any of the three pillars of piracy, so when the threat of American retaliation dissipated during the years leading up to the War of 1812, Barbary corsairs began preying on American shipping again. Once the War of 1812 ended, the United States dispatched another squadron to the Mediterranean to deal with the pirates.

Much like the current situation off Somalia, the second Barbary War depended entirely on naval power. But this naval force was strong enough to force the Barbary corsairs to accept the terms of the treaty. There was also a key difference between the Barbary states and Somalia—piracy from the Barbary nations emanated from a few, easily indentified safe havens, making the American blockade much more effective than anything contemporary naval forces can do to Somalia. Still, piracy originating from the Barbary states did not really end until France invaded North Africa in the 1830s and took control of the Barbary kingdoms, thus permanently eliminating their safe havens.

Greek piracy in the 1830s was the direct result of the political turmoil caused by the Greek Revolution. Once the political situation in the Greek isles deteriorated, piracy surged in the region because the other two pillars were already in place. The geography of the Greek islands, sitting astride the shipping lanes to the Levant, favored pirates and the numerous islands provided untold havens for the pirates. The British, French, Austrians, and Americans all sought to use naval power to control the problem. Despite being the largest naval power in the world, not even the United Kingdom had enough resources to suppress Greek piracy by itself. Unable to effectively strike the pirate havens, Admiral Sir Edward Codrington eventually threatened the Greek Government with bleak consequences if it did not act to eradicate the shore havens used by the pirates.

Asian piracy in the 19th century also demonstrates the futility of trying to control pirates using only naval forces. When piracy in the Persian Gulf became a nuisance, the British dispatched two naval squadrons to chastise the pirates. While they burned dhows and bombarded towns, their actions were not sufficient enough to stop the Arab corsairs. Finally, a third expedition that included a substantial land element attacked and occupied the primary pirate base. This time, Arab leaders realized the permanence of the situation and submitted to the British. Likewise, the Southeast Asian pirates of Sumatra and Borneo remained active until their shore havens were damaged or destroyed. By this time, the British also had an important technological advantage—the steam-powered ship.

British and American actions against the Chinese pirates benefited greatly from the use of steam-powered vessels. They were highly effective against the sail-powered junks the pirates used. Still, British and American naval forces were never able to completely eliminate piracy in Chinese waters because they could not remove any of the three pillars. The Chinese Government was unable to take care of the pirates and was also unwilling to accept help from the British and Americans. Consequently, since the British and Americans could only take half measures, they were never able to finish off the pirates. But their steam-driven ships gave them such an advantage that they were able to greatly decrease the magnitude of the problem.

Modern antipiracy efforts face a situation similar to that faced by the British and Americans in China. Although they had the power to act, they could not do so without violating China's sovereignty. Similarly, the United States and its allies have the power to eliminate piracy but cannot use it to full advantage without violating the sovereignty of the nations plagued by piracy. Thus, in the case of the coalition forces off the coast of Somalia, they are forced to react to Somali depredation rather than take decisive action to eliminate it. In Southeast Asia, since the pirates operate in the waters of nations with viable governments, the United States has even less leeway. The best it can do is provide financial and technical support to those willing to accept such assistance.

Ultimately, piracy is a land-based problem. President Monroe made that clear in 1824 when he laid out the three alternatives: using hot pursuit ashore to capture or kill the pirates, conducting reprisals against those who help the corsairs, or blockading the pirate havens. President Monroe's conclusions are still valid today. If you eliminate the shore havens or modify the political conditions that make piracy possible, then piracy will die out. If those pillars remain in tact, then no amount of naval patrols are going to fully suppress piracy.

Because of the actions of Somali corsairs, piracy is frequently in the news these days. The situation in Somalia is a difficult one. The political turmoil that has embroiled the country since the early 1990s makes piracy possible. There are several potential solutions to the current situation, none of which will be easy. Since it is unlikely that the United States, remembering the events of the early 1990s, will intervene in Somalia, then we must look to President Monroe's three alternatives. The United States and other naval powers, acting under the auspices of the United Nations, could pursue the pirates ashore and kill or capture the perpetrators. Much like the British treatment of the Arab pirates, the Somalis will have to be taught that piracy is too dangerous to continue. The French have tried this course of action with some degree of success. The United States could also conduct reprisals against those who help the corsairs. American forces know where their bases are and should be able to identify those who have benefited from piracy. Once again, the objective would be to teach the Somalis that piracy is too dangerous to continue. This course of action would, of course, require considerable political fortitude since there is a likelihood that innocent Somalis would be injured or killed during such reprisals. Finally, we could impose a blockade on the primary pirate ports. It would not be difficult to establish a blockade of the primary ports and check all outgoing vessels. But blockades are long-term measures and are expensive to maintain. Moreover, since Somali piracy is relatively unsophisticated, the pirates could easily shift their operations to another port and continue as before. The best answer, of course, is to facilitate the establishment of a stable government in Somalia, which could police its shores and eliminate piracy. However, that is, most likely, years away.

In the end, if the world wants to suppress piracy off the coast of Somalia, it can be done. But President Monroe's policy will have to be aggressively employed. We will have to pursue the pirates ashore, conduct reprisals against those who assist the pirates, and blockade the major pirate havens, thus preventing them from using the support infrastructure that has evolved over the last several years. These measures would require a level of international cooperation and resolve that is probably unobtainable, since there would also be considerable potential for civilian casualties. Instead, we will probably maintain the status quo, keeping a task force in the region to keep a lid on Somali activities without actually suppressing their actions or solving the root causes. There is little reason to expect more than that because the costs of both defensive measures and aggressive actions outweigh the benefits. While the Somali pirates have had some sensational successes, the money they have extorted is only a small fraction of overall world trade. With little financial justification for further defensive measures, the shipping industry seems willing to risk captures by pirates because the odds are in their favor and insurance ameliorates their losses. Further, if merchant captains and their crews are willing to continue risking capture, then it is likely that nations will not risk their reputations and resources trying to permanently suppress something that is more of a nuisance than a true threat to their national interests.

Bibliography

United States Government Publications

Central Intelligence Agency. *The CIA World Fact Book*. Washington, DC: Central Intelligence Agency, Office of Public Affairs, 2008. https://www.cia.gov/library/publications/the-world-factbook/ (accessed 23 February 2009).

Department of the Navy. *Dictionary of American Naval Fighting Ships*. Washington, DC: Naval Historical Center. http://www.history.navy.mil/danfs/index.html.

National Geospatial-Intelligence Agency. *Anti-Shipping Activity Messages, Single ASAM Ref. Number 1995–71*. http://www.nga.mil/portal/site/maritime/index.jsp?epi-content=RAW&beanID=844643208&viewID=query_results&MSI_queryType=ASAM&MSI_generalFilterType=SpecificNumber&MSI_generalFilterValue=1995_71&MSI_additionalFilterType1=None&MSI_additionalFilterType2=-999&MSI_additionalFilterValue1=-999&MSI_additionalFilterValue2=-999&MSI_outputOptionType1=SortBy&MSI_outputOptionType2=-999&MSI_outputOptionValue1=Date_DESC&MSI_outputOptionValue2=-999 (accessed 10 April 2009).

US Congress. *On the Expediency of Sending Two Additional Sloops-of-War to the Mediterranean Sea, for the Suppression of Piracy by the Greeks*. 20th Cong., 1st sess., no. 361, 11 March 1828. http://www.ibiblio.org/pha/USN/1828/18280311Piracy.html (accessed 18 February 2009).

Interview

Card, Rear Admiral Kendall, Commander, Expeditionary Strike Group 3. Telephone interview by James A. Wombwell, Combat Studies Institute, Fort Leavenworth, KS. 1 April 2009.

Books

Allen, Gardner W. *Our Navy and the West Indian Pirates*. Salem, MA: Essex Institute, 1929.

Anderson, R.C. *Naval Wars in the Levant, 1559–1853*. Princeton, NJ: Princeton University Press, 1952.

Boot, Max. *The Savage Wars of Peace: Small Wars and the Rise of American Power*. New York: Basic Books, 2002.

Bradlee, Francis B.C. *Piracy in the West Indies and Its Suppression*. Salem, MA: The Essex Institute, 1923.

Burgess, Douglas R. Jr., *The Pirates' Pact: The Secret Alliances Between History's Most Notorious Buccaneers and Colonial America*. Chicago: McGraw-Hill, 2008.

Burnett, John. *Dangerous Waters: Modern Piracy and Terror on the High Seas*. New York: Dutton, 2002.

Chalk, Peter. *The Maritime Dimension of International Security: Terrorism, Piracy, and Challenges for the United States*. Santa Monica, CA: Rand Corporation, 2008.

Clowes, William L. *The Royal Navy: A History From the Earliest Times to the Present*. Vol. III. London: Sampson Low, Marston and Company, 1898.

———. *The Royal Navy: A History From the Earliest Times to the Present*. Vol. VI. London: Sampson Low, Marston and Co., 1901.

Cordingly, David, consulting ed. *Pirates: Terror on the High Seas From the Caribbean to the South China Sea*. Atlanta, GA: Turner Publishing, 1996.

Cordingly, David. *Under the Black Flag: The Romance and the Reality of Life Among the Pirates*. New York: Random House, 1995.

Dakin, Douglas. *The Greek Struggle for Independence, 1821–1833*. Berkeley: University of California Press, 1973.

Davies, C.E. "Britain, Trade and Piracy: The British Expeditions Against Ras Al-Khaima of 1809–10 and 1819–20." In *Global Interests in the Arab Gulf*. Edited by Charles E. Davies. New York: St. Martin's Press, 1992.

Dillon, Dana R. *The China Challenge: Standing Strong Against the Military, Economic, and Political Threats That Imperil America*. Lanham, MD: Rowman & Littlefield Publishers, 2007.

Dupuy R. Ernest, and William H. Baumer. *The Little Wars of the United States*. New York: Hawthorn Books, 1968.

Earle, Peter. *The Pirate Wars*. New York: Thomas Dunne Books, 2005.

Eklöf, Stefan. *Pirates in Paradise: A Modern History of Southeast Asia's Maritime Marauders*. Copenhagen: NIAS Press, 2006.

Ellms, Charles. *The Pirates Own Book: Authentic Narratives of the Most Celebrated Sea Robbers*. Philadelphia, PA: Thomas, Cowperthwait, & Co., 1837.

Field, James A. *America and the Mediterranean World, 1776–1882*. Princeton, NJ: Princeton University Press, 1969.

Fox, Grace E. *British Admirals and Chinese Pirates, 1832–1869*. London: Kegan Paul, Trench, Trubner & Co., 1940.

Fremont-Barnes, Gregory. *The Wars of the Barbary Pirates; to the Shores of Tripoli: The Rise of the US Navy and Marines*. Oxford: Osprey Publishing, 2006.

Gordon, Thomas. *History of the Greek Revolution*. Vol. II. Edinburgh: William Blackwood, 1832.

Gosse, Philip. *The History of Piracy*. New York: Tudor Publishing Company, 1932.

———. *The Pirates' Who's Who: Giving Particulars of the Lives and Deaths of the Pirates and Buccaneers*. Boston: Charles E. Lauriat & Co., 1924.

Haring, C.H. *The Buccaneers of the West Indies in the XVII Century*. New York: E.P. Dutton & Co., 1910.

Herbert-Burns, Rupert. "Compound Piracy at Sea in the Early Twenty-First Century: A Tactical to Operational-Level Perspective on Contemporary

Multiphase Piratical Methodology." In *Violence at Sea: Piracy in the Age of Global Terrorism*. Edited by Peter Lehr. New York: Routledge, 2007.

Hoppe, E.O. *Pirates, Buccaneers, and Gentlemen Adventurers*. South Brunswick, NJ: A.S. Barnes & Co., 1972.

Johnson, Captain Charles. *The History of the Lives and Actions of the Most Famous Highwaymen, Street-Robbers, etc. to Which Is Added, a Genuine Account of the Voyages and Plunders of the Most Noted Pirates*. London: Longman, Hurst, Rees, Orme & Brown, 1813.

Johnson, Robert E. *Far China Station: The US Navy in Asian Waters, 1800–1898*. Annapolis, MD: US Naval Institute Press, 1979.

Jones, C.G. Pitcairn, ed. *Piracy in the Levant, 1827–28: Selected From the Papers of Admiral Sir Edward Codrington, KCB*. London: Navy Records Society, 1934.

Kelly, J.B. *Britain and the Persian Gulf, 1795–1880*. Oxford: Clarendon Press, 1968.

Knox, Dudley W. *A History of the United States Navy*. New York: G.P. Putnam's Sons, 1936.

Konstam, Angus. *Blackbeard: America's Most Notorious Pirate*. Hoboken, NJ: Wiley, 2006.

Lambert, Frank. *The Barbary Wars: American Independence in the Atlantic World*. New York: Hill and Wang, 2005.

Lane, Kris E. *Pillaging the Empire: Piracy in the Americas, 1500–1750*. Armonk, NY: M.E. Sharpe, 1998.

Lehr, Peter, ed. *Violence at Sea: Piracy in the Age of Global Terrorism*. New York: Routledge, 2007.

Lehr, Peter, and Hendrick Lehmann. "Somalia—Pirates' New Paradise." In *Violence at Sea: Piracy in the Age of Global Terrorism*. Edited by Peter Lehr. New York: Routledge, 2007.

Lewis, Brenda. *The Pirate Code: From Honorable Thieves to Modern-Day Villains*. Guilford, CT: Lyons Press, 2008.

Long, David F. *Gold Braid and Foreign Relations: Diplomatic Activities of United States Naval Officers, 1798–1883*. Annapolis, MD: United States Naval Institute Press, 1988.

Lowe, Peter. *Britain in the Far East: A Survey From 1819 to the Present*. London: Longman, 1981.

MacIntyre, Donald. *Sea Power in the Pacific: A History From the Sixteenth Century to the Present Day*. New York: Russell and Co., 1972.

Maclay, Edgar S. *A History of the United States Navy From 1775 to 1894*. Vol. II. New York: D. Appleton and Company, 1894.

Mak, J.N. "Pirates, Renegades, and Fishermen: The Politics of 'Sustainable' Piracy in the Strait of Malacca." In *Violence at Sea: Piracy in the Age of Global Terrorism*. Edited by Peter Lehr. New York: Routledge, 2007.

Marrin, Albert. *The Sea Rovers: Pirates, Privateers, and Buccaneers*. New York: Atheneum, 1984.

Mueller G.O.W., and Freda Adler., *Outlaws of the Ocean: The Complete Book of Contemporary Crime on the High Seas*. New York: Hearst Marine Books, 1985.

Murphy, Martin N. *Small Boats, Weak States, Dirty Money: Piracy and Maritime Terrorism in the Modern World*. London: Hurst & Co., 2008.

Murray, Dian H. *Pirates of the South China Coast, 1790–1810*. Stanford, CA: Stanford University Press, 1987.

Ong-Webb, Graham Gerard. "Piracy in Maritime Asia: Current Trends." In *Violence at Sea: Piracy in the Age of Global Terrorism*. Edited by Peter Lehr. New York: Routledge, 2007.

———. "Southeast Asian Piracy: Research and Developments." In *Piracy, Maritime Terrorism and Securing the Malacca Straits*. Edited by Graham Gerard Ong-Webb. Singapore: Institute of Southeast Asian Studies, 2006.

Ong-Webb, Graham Gerard, ed. *Piracy, Maritime Terrorism and Securing the Malacca Straits*. Singapore: Institute of Southeast Asian Studies, 2006.

Onley, James. *The Arabian Frontier of the British Raj: Merchants, Rulers, and the British in the 19th Century Gulf*. Oxford: Oxford University Press, 2007.

Paullin, Charles O. *American Voyages to the Orient, 1690–1865: An Account of Merchant and Naval Activities in China, Japan, and the Various Pacific Islands*. Annapolis, MD: United States Naval Institute Press, 1971.

Phillips, W. Alison. *Modern Europe, 1815–1899, Period VIII*. 2nd ed. London: Rivingtons, 1902.

———. *The War of Greek Independence, 1821–1833*. New York: Charles Schribner's Sons, 1897.

Rahman, Chris. "The International Politics of Combating Piracy in Southeast Asia." In *Violence at Sea: Piracy in the Age of Global Terrorism*. Edited by Peter Lehr. New York: Routledge, 2007.

Rankin, Hugh F. *The Golden Age of Piracy*. New York: Holt, Rinehart & Winston, 1969.

Rogozinski, Jan. *A Brief History of the Caribbean: From the Arawak and the Carib to the Present*. New York: Facts on File, 1992.

———. *Pirates! Brigands, Buccaneers, and Privateers in Fact, Fiction, and Legend*. New York: De Capo Press, 1996.

Sakhuja, Vijay. "Sea Piracy in South Asia." In *Violence at Sea: Piracy in the Age of Global Terrorism*. Edited by Peter Lehr. New York: Routledge, 2007.

Sherry, Frank. *Raiders and Rebels: The Golden Age of Piracy*. New York: Hearst Marine Books, 1986.

St. John, Captain H.C., RN. *Notes and Sketches From the Wild Coasts of Nipon, With Chapters on Cruising After Pirates in Chinese Waters*. Edinburgh: David Douglas, 1880.

Tarling, Nicholas. *Imperial Britain in South-East Asia*. London: Oxford University Press, 1975.

Turnbull, C.M. "Country Traders." In *Southeast Asia: A Historical Encyclopedia From Angkor Wat to East Timor*. Edited by Ooi Keat Gin. Santa Barbara, CA: ABC-CLIO, 2004.

Ward, Ralph T. *Pirates in History*. Baltimore, MD: York Press, 1974.

Watts, David. *The West Indies: Patterns of Development, Culture and Environmental Change Since 1492*. New York: Cambridge University Press, 1987.

Wheeler, Richard. *In Pirate Waters*. New York: Thomas Y. Crowell Company, 1969.

Woodward, Colin. *The Republic of Pirates: Being the True and Surprising Story of the Caribbean Pirates and the Man Who Brought Them Down*. Orlando, FL: Harcourt, 2007.

Reports

Piracy and Armed Robbery Against Ships, Annual Report, 1 January–31 December 2007. London: International Chamber of Commerce, International Maritime Bureau, January 2008.

Piracy and Armed Robbery Against Ships, Annual Report, 1 January–31 December 2008. London: International Chamber of Commerce, International Maritime Bureau, January 2009.

Regional Cooperation Agreement on Combating Piracy and Armed Robbery Against Ships in Asia (ReCAAP) Information Sharing Center. *Adding Value, Charting Trends: 2007 Annual Research Report*. ReCAAP, Singapore, 2008. www.southchinasea.org/docs/Recaap_Trends.pdf (accessed 6 April 2009).

Articles

AFP. "Pirates Used 'Good Conduct Guide' in French Yacht Seige: Source." AFP Web site, 17 April 2009. http://afp.google.com/article/ALeqM5ic4lMhcdvj6BV5HsRB-uabBjyUmA (accessed 21 November 2008).

Associated Press. "How Pirates Hijacked Us." *News24.com*, 6 October 2005. http://www.news24.com/News24/Africa/News/0,,2-11-1447_1812108,00.html (accessed 2 April 2009).

———. "Piracy Drives Up Insurance Rates for Ships in Gulf." *Portland Press Herald*, 13 April 2009. http://pressherald.mainetoday.com/story.php?id=250548&ac=PHbiz&pg=1 (accessed 21 April 2009).

———. "Private Security Companies Hired To Protect Ships From Pirates." *The St. Petersburg Times*, 28 October 2008. http://www.sptimes.ru/story/27485 (accessed 21 April 2009).

———. "Ship Seized by Somali Pirates Carrying 33 Russian Tanks." *FoxNews.com*, 26 September 2008. http://www.foxnews.com/story/0,2933,428582,00.html (accessed 2 April 2009).

Axe, David. "4 Fronts for Pirate-Navy Battles as Pirate Attacks Continue." *Popular Mechanics*, 29 September 2008. http:// www.popularmechanics.com/technology/military_law/4285201. html?page=4 (accessed 20 January 2009).

Bahadur, Jay. "I'm Not a Pirate, I'm the Saviour of the Sea." *The Times*, 16 April 2009. http://www.timesonline.co.uk/tol/news/world/africa/ article6100783.ece (accessed 21 April 2009).

Barise, Hassan. "Somali Gunmen Hijack Cargo Ship." BBC News Web site, 3 July 2002. http://news.bbc.co.uk/2/hi/africa/2090651.stm (accessed 7 November 2008).

Baruah, Pranamita. "Japan's Response to Sea Piracy." *Institute for Defence Studies and Analyses*, 30 March 2009. http://www.idsa.in/publications/ stratcomments/PranamitaBaruah300309.html (accessed 21 April 2009).

BBC. "France 'Captures Somali Pirates.'" BBC News Web site, 23 October 2008. http://news.bbc.co.uk/2/hi/africa/7686806.stm (accessed 21 November 2008).

———."France Frees Sailors From Pirates." BBC News Web site, 16 September 2008. http://afp.google.com/article/ALeqM5ic4lMhcdvj6BV5HsRB-uabBjyUmA (accessed 21 November 2008).

———. "Jail Sentence for Somali Pirates." BBC News Web site, 1 November 2006. http://news.bbc.co.uk/2/hi/africa/6105262.stm (accessed 6 November 2008).

———. "Pirate Warning for Somalia's Coastline." BBC News Web site, 30 January 2003. http://news.bbc.co.uk/2/hi/business/2709339.stm (accessed 7 November 2008).

———. "Pirates Hijack Ship Off Somalia." BBC News Web site, 21 October 2005. http://news.bbc.co.uk/2/hi/africa/4363344.stm (accessed 6 November 2008).

———. "Pirates Hijack Tsunami Aid Ship." BBC News Web site, 30 June 2005. http://news.bbc.co.uk/2/hi/africa/4636695.stm (accessed 6 November 2008).

———. "Pirates 'Overpowered' Off Somalia." BBC News Web site, 31 October 2007. http://news.bbc.co.uk/go/pr/fr/-/2/hi/africa/7069026.stm (accessed 21 November 2008).

———. "Ransom Paid To Free Danish Ship." BBC News Web site, 23 August 2007. http://news.bbc.co.uk/go/pr/fr/-/2/hi/africa/6959729.stm (accessed 21 November 2008).

———. "Ship's Crew Fined for Illegal Fishing Off Somali Waters." BBC News Web site, 24 December 1998. http://news.bbc.co.uk/2/hi/africa/242103. stm (accessed 7 November 2008).

———. "Somali Aid Suspended After Hijack." BBC News Web site, 4 July 2005. http://news.bbc.co.uk/2/hi/africa/4649825.stm (accessed 6 November 2008).

———. "Somali Faction Frees Foreign Ships." BBC News Web site, 13 February 1998. http://news.bbc.co.uk/2/hi/africa/56514.stm (accessed 7 November 2008).

———. "Somali Pirates Free Hijacked Ship." BBC News Web site, 14 October 2005. http://news.bbc.co.uk/2/hi/africa/4341196.stm (accessed 6 November 2008).

———. "Somali Pirates Hold Greek Tanker." BBC News Web site, 12 August 2002. http://news.bbc.co.uk/2/hi/africa/2188900.stm (accessed 7 November 2008).

———. "Somali Shock at New Ship Hijack." BBC News Web site, 11 October 2005. http://news.bbc.co.uk/go/pr/fr/-/2/hi/africa/4330492.stm (accessed 6 November 2008).

———. "Timeline: Somalia." BBC News Web site, 29 October 2008. http://news.bbc.co.uk/go/pr/fr/-/2/hi/africa/country_profiles/1072611.stm (accessed 7 November 2008).

———. "WFP Ultimatum Over Somali Ship." BBC News Web site, 12 July 2005. http://news.bbc.co.uk/2/hi/africa/4677155.stm (accessed 6 November 2008).

Bloomfield, Steve. "'Hidden Famine' in Horn of Africa Puts 14 Million at Risk." *The Independent*, 23 July 2008. http://www.independent.co.uk/news/world/africa/hidden-famine-in-horn-of-africa-puts-14m-at-risk-874873.html (accessed 20 November 2008).

Clayton, Jonathan. "Business Booms in Somalian Pirate Village Eyl." *The Australian*, 19 November 2008. http://www.theaustralian.news.com.au/story/0,25197,24674415-32682,00.html (accessed 2 April 2009).

CNN. "Pirates Take 'Super-tanker' Toward Somalia." *CNN.com/world*, 19 November 2008. http://www.cnn.com/2008/WORLD/africa/11/17/kenya.tanker.pirates/index.html (accessed 19 November 2009).

"Commander E.W. Vansittart to Rear Admiral Sir J. Stirling." Letter dated 2 September 1855, in *Allen's Indian Mail and Register of Intelligence for British and Foreign India, China, and All Parts of the East*. Vol. XIV, January–December 1856. London: Wm. H. Allen and Co., 1856.

"Commodore John R. Goldsborough, USN." *A Naval Encyclopedia*. Philadelphia, PA: L.R. Hamersly and Co., 1881.

Crilly, Rob. "Wanted: Countries to Stand Guard on Ships." *The Times*, 20 September 2008. http://www.timesonline.co.uk/tol/news/world/asia/article4791107.ece (accessed 13 November 2008).

Dalton, Alastair. "Two More Hijacked in Piracy Crisis." *The Scotsman*, 19 November 2008. http://www.scotsman.com/latestnews/Two-more-ships-hijacked-in.4706852.jp (accessed 2 April 2009).

Fowler, Robin. "Pirates of the Mediterranean: Pillaging and Plundering in Ancient Times," *Suite101.com*, 21 May 2007. http://ancient-culture.suite101.com/article.cfm/pirates_of_the_mediterranean (accessed 29 January 2009).

Gettleman, Jeffrey. "Hijacked Arms Ship Limps into Port." *New York Times*, 13 February 2009. http://www.nytimes.com/2009/02/13/world/africa/13pirate.html (accessed 2 April 2009).

Gettleman, Jeffrey, and Mohammed Ibrahim. "Somali Pirates Get Ransom and Leave Arms Freighter." *New York Times*, 6 February 2009. http://www.nytimes.com/2009/02/06/world/africa/06pirates.html?_r=1&pagewanted=print (accessed 1 April 2009).

"GDP Growth, 1952–2008." *Chinability*, 4 May 2008. http://www.chinability.com/GDP.htm (accessed 3 April 2009).

Gray, Andrew. "Armed Guards Would Deter Somali Pirates: US Navy." *The Manama Dialogue*, International Institute for Strategic Studies Regional Security Summit, 13 December 2008. http://www.iiss.org/whats-new/iiss-in-the-press/press-coverage-2008/december-2008/armed-guards-would-deter-somali-piratesus-navy/ (accessed 21 April 2009).

Guled, Abdi. "Somali Pirates Move to Aid Comrades." *Mail & Guardian*, 11 April 2009. http://www.mg.co.za/article/2009-04-11-somali-pirates-move-to-aid-comrades (accessed 10 April 2009).

Harper, Mary. "Life in Somalia's Pirate Town." BBC News Web site, 18 September 2008. http://news.bbc.co.uk/2/hi/africa/7623329.stm (accessed 6 November 2008).

"HMS Caroline." *Michael Phillips' Ships of the Old Navy*. http://www.ageofnelson.org/MichaelPhillips/info.php?ref=0460 (accessed 15 January 2009).

"HMS Liverpool." *Michael Phillips' Ships of the Old Navy*. http://www.ageofnelson.org/MichaelPhillips/info.php?ref=1348 (accessed 14 January 2009)

Howden, Daniel, and Mohamed Guled. "Off the Coast of Somalia: We're Not Pirates. These Are Our Waters, Not Theirs." *The Independent*, 14 November 2008. http://www.independent.co.uk/news/world/africa/off-the-coast-of-somalia-were-not-pirates-these-are-our-waters-not-theirs-1017962.html (accessed 4 April 2009).

Hughes, Dana. "Somalia Piracy: On Land and Sea." ABC News Web site, 17 November 2008. http://blogs.abcnews.com/worldview/2008/11/somalia-chaos-a.html (accessed 21 November 2008).

International Chamber of Commerce, Commercial Crimes Services. "International Maritime Bureau." No date. http://www.icc-ccs.org/index.php?option=com_content&view=article&id=27&Itemid=16 (accessed 5 April 2009).

———. "Violence Resumes in Malacca Straits." 15 March 2005. http://www.icc-ccs.org/index.php?option=com_content&view=article&id=80:violence-resumes-in-malacca-straits&catid=60:news&Itemid=51 (accessed 6 April 2009).

Jasparro, Christopher. "Somalia's Piracy Offers Lessons in Global Governance." *Yale Global Online*, 6 April 2009. http://yaleglobal.yale.edu/display.article?id=12210 (accessed 10 April 2009).

Kennedy, Elizabeth A. "US Navy Watches Seized Ship With Sudan-Bound Tanks." *USA Today*, 29 September 2008. http://www.usatoday.com/news/world/2008-09-28-1797517683_x.htm (accessed 23 March 2009).

Lee, Mike. "Real-Life Pirates Can't Match 'Capt. Jack Sparrow.'" ABC News Web site, 2008. http://abcnews.go.com/International/story?id=4641039&page=1 (accessed 21 November 2008).

Lehr, Peter. "Dealing With Somali Pirates." *The Guardian*, 25 November 2008. http://www.china.org.cn/international/opinion/2008-11/25/content_16820148.htm (accessed 10 April 2009).

Lewis, Alexandria. "Kidnap Insurance Costs Up Tenfold in Gulf of Aden." Aon Corporation Web site, 9 April 2009. http://aon.mediaroom.com/index. php?s=43&item=1526 (accessed 21 April 2009).

Lichfield, John, and Daniel Howden. "French Sailor Killed in Gun Battle as Special Forces Storm Hijacked Yacht." *The Independent*, 11 April 2009. http://www.independent.co.uk/news/world/africa/french-sailor-killed-in-gun-battle-as-special-forces-storm-hijacked-yacht-1667275.html (accessed 11 April 2009).

McDaniel, Michael S., ed. "Pirate Cruise Ship Attack." *The Cargo Letter*, 5 November 2005. http://www.cargolaw.com/presentation_casualties.05. html#Seabourne-Spirit (accessed 5 April 2009).

Middle East Research and Information Project. "Neo-Piracy in Oman and the Gulf: The Origins of British Imperialism in the Gulf," *MERIP Reports* no. 36 (April 1975).

Miller, John W. "Piracy Spurs Threats to Shipping." *The Wall Street Journal*, 19 November 2009. http://www.studentnewsdaily.com/daily-news-article/piracy-spurs-threats-to-shipping-costs/ (accessed 21 April 2009).

Ministry of Defense. "Suspected Pirates Caught by the Royal Navy Handed Over to Kenya." *Defense News*, 18 November 2008. http://www. mod.uk/DefenceInternet/DefenceNews/MilitaryOperations/SuspectedPiratesCaughtByTheRoyalNavyHandedOverToKenya.htm (accessed 11 April 2009).

Momanyi, Bernard. "Pay Up, Faina Pirates Demand." *Capital News*, 23 October 2008. http://www.capitalfm.co.ke/news/Local/Pay-up,-Faina-pirates-demand.html (accessed 1 April 2009).

Munns, David W. "Rise in Murders, Kidnappings at Sea Makes Piracy a Top Naval Priority Worldwide." *Sea Power*, October 2004. http://www.military. com/NewContent/0,13190,NL_Piracy_102604-P1,00.html (accessed 11 April 2009).

O'Brien, Chris. "Shippers Resist Calls to Arm Against Pirates." *Washington Times*, 21 April 2009. http://www.studentnewsdaily.com/daily-news-article/shippers-resist-calls-to-arm-against-pirates/ (accessed 21 April 2009).

Parry, Richard L. "Indonesian Waters Become Centre of World Piracy Boom." *The Independent*, 25 January 2000. http://www.independent.co.uk/news/world/asia/indonesian-waters-become-centre-of-world-piracy-boom-727302.html (accessed 20 November 2008).

Phillips, Michael. "Ships of the Old Navy," 2007. http://www.ageofnelson.org/ MichaelPhillips/index.html (accessed 15 January 2009).

"Pirates Attack Cargo Ship With Rocket Launchers." *Shipping Times*, 15 May 2007. http://www.shippingtimes.co.uk/item603_pirate_attack.htm (accessed 15 December 2008).

"Pirates Took Just 16 Minutes to Steal Super-Tanker." *Indian Express.com*, 21 November 2008. http://www.indianexpress.com/news/pirates-took-just-16-minutes-to-steal-supertanker/388724/ (accessed 26 November 2008).

Pitman, Todd. "Somali Pirates a Far Cry From Buccaneers of Old." 11 April 2009. http://news.yahoo.com/s/ap/20090411/ap_on_re_af/piracy_somalia_s_ swashbucklers (accessed 11 April 2009).

Raymond, Catherine Z. "Piracy in Southeast Asia: New Trends, Issues and Responses." *Harvard Asia Quarterly* 9, no. 4 (Fall 2005). http://www. asiaquarterly.com/content/view/30/1/ (accessed 21 April 2009).

Reid, Anthony. "An 'Age of Commerce' in Southeast Asian History." *Modern Asian Studies* 24, no. 1 (February 1990).

Republic of the Philippines. "Filipino Seaman Abducted in Malacca Strait Freed." *Gov.Ph News*, 21 March 2005. http://www.gov.ph/news/default. asp?i=7530 (accessed 6 April 2009).

Reveron, Derek S. "Think Again: Pirates." *Foreign Policy* (January 2009). http://www.foreignpolicy.com/story/cms.php?story_id=4626&page=0 (accessed 2 April 2009).

Risso, Patricia. "Cross-Cultural Perceptions of Piracy: Maritime Violence in the Western Indian Ocean and Persian Gulf Region During a Long Eighteenth Century." *Journal of World History* 12, no. 2 (Fall 2001).

Robinson, Simon, and Xan Rice. "In Peril on the Sea." *Time*, 7 November 2005. http://www.time.com/time/magazine/article/0,9171,1126762,00.html (accessed 1 April 2009).

Scutro, Andrew. "In Chasing Pirates, Navy Comes Full Circle." *Navy Times*, 4 November 2007. http://www.navytimes.com/news/2007/11/navy_ pirates_071103w/ (accessed 10 April 2007).

Sengupta, Kim. "Blackwater Gunboats Will Protect Ships." *The Independent*, 19 November 2008. http://www.independent.co.uk/news/world/ africa/blackwater-gunboats-will-protect-ships-1024582.html (accessed 21 April 2009).

Smith, Steven D. "US Navy Captures Pirate Vessel Off Somali Coast." Armed Forces Press Service, 24 January 2006. http://www.defenselink.mil/ news/newsarticle.aspx?id=14539 (accessed 5 December 2008).

"Somali Pirate 'Mother Ship' Sunk by Indian Navy Turns Out to be Thai Trawler." *Daily Mail*, 26 November 2008. http://www.dailymail.co.uk/news/ worldnews/article-1089514/Somali-pirate-mother-ship-sunk-Indian-navy-turns-Thai-trawler.html (accessed 11 April 2009).

"Somali Pirates Demand Tanker Ransom, Three Ships Seized." *Khaleej Times Online*, 19 November 2008. http://www.khaleejtimes.com/DisplayArticle08.asp?xfile=data/international/2008/November/international_November1334.xml&section=international (accessed 19 November 2008).

"Somali Pirates Open Fire on US Navy Ships." *Ports & Ships*, 20 March 2006. http://ports.co.za/navalnews/article_2006_03_20_3048.html (accessed 10 April 2009).

Swartz, Peter M. "US-Greek Naval Relations Begin: Antipiracy Operations in the Aegean Sea." Alexandria, VA: Center for Naval Analysis, Center for Strategic Studies, June 2003.

Sweet, L.E. "Pirates or Polities? Arab Societies of the Persian or Arabian Gulf, 18th Century." *Ethnohistory* 11, no. 3 (Summer 1964).

US Naval Forces Central Command Public Affairs. "USS Howard Monitoring MV Faina." 25 September 2008. http://www.dvidshub.net/?script=news/news_show.php&id=24242 (accessed 27 March 2009).

Viscusi, Gregory. "Mercenary Guards Jump Ship as Somali Pirates Remain Undeterred." *Asian Energy*, 18 December 2008. http://asianenergy.blogspot.com/2008/12/mercenary-guards-jump-ship-as-somali.html (accessed 21 April 2009).

Wadhams, Nick. "Somali Pirates Hold Whip Hand in Standoff." *San Francisco Chronicle*, 26 October 2008. http://sfgate.com/cgi-bin/article.cgi?f=/c/a/2008/10/26/MN6913NSJK.DTL (accessed 2 April 2009).

———. "Somali Pirates' Unexpected Booty: Russian Tanks." *Time*, 26 September 2008. http://www.time.com/time/world/article/0,8599,1844914,00.html (accessed 1 April 2009).

"WFP Welcomes Release of Hijacked Ship, MV Rozen." *Shipping Times*, 8 April 2007. http://www.shippingtimes.co.uk/item399_rozen.htm (accessed 15 December 2008).

Wilson, Brian, and James Kraska. "Anti-Piracy Patrols Presage Rising Naval Powers." *Yale Global*, 13 January 2009. http://yaleglobal.yale.edu/display.article?id=11808 (accessed 4 April 2009).

Wright, H.R.C. "The Anglo-Dutch Dispute in the East, 1814–1824." *The Economic History Review* 3, no. 2 (1950).

Young Adam J., and Mark J. Valencia. "Conflation of Piracy and Terrorism in Southeast Asia: Rectitude and Utility." *Contemporary Southeast Asia* 25 (2003). http://www.southchinasea.org/docs/Young%2BValencia,%20Conflation%20of%20Piracy%20and%20Terrorism.htm (accessed 25 November 2008).

Appendix A

United Nations Convention on the Law of the Sea of 10 December 1982

PART VII

HIGH SEAS

SECTION 1: GENERAL PROVISIONS

Article 100

Duty to cooperate in the repression of piracy

All States shall cooperate to the fullest possible extent in the repression of piracy on the high seas or in any other place outside the jurisdiction of any State.

Article 101

Definition of piracy

Piracy consists of any of the following acts:

(a) any illegal acts of violence or detention, or any act of depredation, committed for private ends by the crew or the passengers of a private ship or a private aircraft, and directed:

    (i) on the high seas, against another ship or aircraft, or against persons or property on board such ship or aircraft;

    (ii) against a ship, aircraft, persons or property in a place outside the jurisdiction of any State;

(b) any act of voluntary participation in the operation of a ship or of an aircraft with knowledge of facts making it a pirate ship or aircraft;

(c) any act of inciting or of intentionally facilitating an act described in subparagraph (a) or (b).

Article 102

Piracy by a warship, government ship or government aircraft whose crew has mutinied

The acts of piracy, as defined in article 101, committed by a warship, government ship or government aircraft whose crew has mutinied and taken control of the ship or aircraft are assimilated to acts committed by a private ship or aircraft.

Article 103
Definition of a pirate ship or aircraft

A ship or aircraft is considered a pirate ship or aircraft if it is intended by the persons in dominant control to be used for the purpose of committing one of the acts referred to in article 101. The same applies if the ship or aircraft has been used to commit any such act, so long as it remains under the control of the persons guilty of that act.

Article 104
Retention or loss of the nationality of a pirate ship or aircraft

A ship or aircraft may retain its nationality although it has become a pirate ship or aircraft. The retention or loss of nationality is determined by the law of the State from which such nationality was derived.

Article 105
Seizure of a pirate ship or aircraft

On the high seas, or in any other place outside the jurisdiction of any State, every State may seize a pirate ship or aircraft, or a ship or aircraft taken by piracy and under the control of pirates, and arrest the persons and seize the property on board. The courts of the State which carried out the seizure may decide upon the penalties to be imposed, and may also determine the action to be taken with regard to the ships, aircraft or property, subject to the rights of third parties acting in good faith.

Article 106
Liability for seizure without adequate grounds

Where the seizure of a ship or aircraft on suspicion of piracy has been effected without adequate grounds, the State making the seizure shall be liable to the State the nationality of which is possessed by the ship or aircraft for any loss or damage caused by the seizure.

Article 107
Ships and aircraft which are entitled to seize on account of piracy

A seizure on account of piracy may be carried out only by warships or military aircraft, or other ships or aircraft clearly marked and identifiable as being on government service and authorized to that effect.

*   *   *   *   *   *   *

Article 110
Right of visit

1. Except where acts of interference derive from powers conferred by treaty, a warship which encounters on the high seas a foreign ship, other

than a ship entitled to complete immunity in accordance with articles 95 and 96, is not justified in boarding it unless there is reasonable ground for suspecting that:

(a) the ship is engaged in piracy;

(b) the ship is engaged in the slave trade;

(c) the ship is engaged in unauthorized broadcasting and the flag State of the warship has jurisdiction under article 109;

(d) the ship is without nationality; or

(e) though flying a foreign flag or refusing to show its flag, the ship is, in reality, of the same nationality as the warship.

2.   In the cases provided for in paragraph 1, the warship may proceed to verify the ship's right to fly its flag. To this end, it may send a boat under the command of an officer to the suspected ship. If suspicion remains after the documents have been checked, it may proceed to a further examination on board the ship, which must be carried out with all possible consideration.

3.   If the suspicions prove to be unfounded, and provided that the ship boarded has not committed any act justifying them, it shall be compensated for any loss or damage that may have been sustained.

4.   These provisions apply *mutatis mutandis* to military aircraft.

5.   These provisions also apply to any other duly authorized ships or aircraft clearly marked and identifiable as being on government service.

Article 111
Right of hot pursuit

1.   The hot pursuit of a foreign ship may be undertaken when the competent authorities of the coastal State have good reason to believe that the ship has violated the laws and regulations of that State. Such pursuit must be commenced when the foreign ship or one of its boats is within the internal waters, the archipelagic waters, the territorial sea or the contiguous zone of the pursuing State, and may only be continued outside the territorial sea or the contiguous zone if the pursuit has not been interrupted. It is not necessary that, at the time when the foreign ship within the territorial sea or the contiguous zone receives the order to stop, the ship giving the order should likewise be within the territorial sea or the contiguous zone. If the foreign ship is within a contiguous zone, as defined in article 33, the pursuit may only be undertaken if there has been a violation of the rights for the protection of which the zone was established.

2.   The right of hot pursuit shall apply *mutatis mutandis* to violations in the exclusive economic zone or on the continental shelf, including safety zones around continental shelf installations, of the laws and regulations

of the coastal State applicable in accordance with this Convention to the exclusive economic zone or the continental shelf, including such safety zones.

3. The right of hot pursuit ceases as soon as the ship pursued enters the territorial sea of its own State or of a third State.

4. Hot pursuit is not deemed to have begun unless the pursuing ship has satisfied itself by such practicable means as may be available that the ship pursued or one of its boats or other craft working as a team and using the ship pursued as a mother ship is within the limits of the territorial sea, or, as the case may be, within the contiguous zone or the exclusive economic zone or above the continental shelf. The pursuit may only be commenced after a visual or auditory signal to stop has been given at a distance which enables it to be seen or heard by the foreign ship.

5. The right of hot pursuit may be exercised only by warships or military aircraft, or other ships or aircraft clearly marked and identifiable as being on government service and authorized to that effect.

6. Where hot pursuit is effected by an aircraft:

    (a) the provisions of paragraphs 1 to 4 shall apply *mutatis mutandis*;

    (b) the aircraft giving the order to stop must itself actively pursue the ship until a ship or another aircraft of the coastal State, summoned by the aircraft, arrives to take over the pursuit, unless the aircraft is itself able to arrest the ship. It does not suffice to justify an arrest outside the territorial sea that the ship was merely sighted by the aircraft as an offender or suspected offender, if it was not both ordered to stop and pursued by the aircraft itself or other aircraft or ships which continue the pursuit without interruption.

7. The release of a ship arrested within the jurisdiction of a State and escorted to a port of that State for the purposes of an inquiry before the competent authorities may not be claimed solely on the ground that the ship, in the course of its voyage, was escorted across a portion of the exclusive economic zone or the high seas, if the circumstances rendered this necessary.

8. Where a ship has been stopped or arrested outside the territorial sea in circumstances which do not justify the exercise of the right of hot pursuit, it shall be compensated for any loss or damage that may have been thereby sustained.

Appendix B

Types of Ships and Boats

Sailing Warship Rates

By the 18th century, naval vessels were organized into six rates. The first through fourth rates were considered ships-of-the-line. The fifth and sixth rates, which were not large enough to sail in the line of battle, were known as frigates. All other smaller vessels were deemed nonrated ships.

First Rate—With three continuous gundecks, these were the largest ships in any fleet. They carried 60 to 80 guns in the 17th century, but the number of guns increased to more than 100 by the 18th century.

Second Rate—Older three-deck ships were consigned to second-rate status during much of the 17th century. By the 1680s, this category became an identifiable class carrying 80 to 100 guns.

Third Rate—These two-deck ships, which were the most common ship-of-the-line, carried 64 to 80 guns.

Fourth Rate—This was the smallest rate considered a ship-of-the-line. These vessels only carried 30 to 40 guns in the first half of the 17th century. By the end of the century, the rate was standardized to encompass ships carrying 50 to 60 guns.

Fifth Rate—This rate includes all large frigates. By the 18th century, these vessels carried 30 to 44 guns.

Sixth Rate—This rate was the smallest vessel in the Royal Navy commanded by a captain. During the 16th century, these vessels could carry as few as 16 guns, but by the end of the century, sixth-rate frigates carried 20 to 28 guns.

Types of Ships

Barge—A long (32-foot), lightweight boat rowed by 10 to 20 oars. It was normally used to transport senior officers and admirals.

Bark or barque—A sailing vessel with three or more masts, two or more of which were square rigged. The mizzenmast, or aftermast, was always rigged with fore and aft sails. (Example: USCG *Eagle*)

Boat—Essential auxiliary vessel for every sailing ship. Since many ships anchored out instead of laying up alongside a pier, small boats were used to transport personnel and cargo from ship to shore. They were also used to tow the sailing ship, conduct rescue missions, and carry out patrols in shallow waters. Small boats came in many shapes and sizes and performed various functions.

Bomb vessel—Special craft designed to carry heavy mortars. The hulls of these vessels were strengthened to accommodate the additional weight of the mortars and they did not have a foremast. These vessels were sometimes called bomb ketches although they were typically ship rigged by the 1760s.

Brig—A two-mast square-rigged ship with a fore-and-aft gaff-and-boom main sail. Brigs were standard cargo ships. (Example: USS *Somers*, 1842)

Brigantine—A two-mast ship similar to a brig except that the aftermast is fore-and-aft rigged. Many brigantines also had sweeps to propel them when there was no wind.

Caravel—A small (250-ton average) three-mast sailing vessel used well into the 17th century. It was either square-sail or lateen-sail rigged. (Example: Columbus' vessels the *Nina* and *Pinta*)

Carrack (or Nao)—The largest European sailing vessel of the 15th century at more than 1,000 tons. Carracks were characterized by very high bows and sterns that seriously hindered their sailing capabilities. (Example: Columbus' vessel the *Santa Maria*)

Corvette—A French term for small three-mast square-rigged vessels. Corvettes, which displaced 400 to 600 tons, were sometimes designated "sloops of war."

Cutter—Fast-sailing boats that were usually sailed rather than rowed. When rowed, they were double-banked, meaning two oarsmen sat beside one another, and were thus broader in the beam than other types of boats.

Dhow—A lateen-rigged sailing vessel used by Arabs in the Persian Gulf and Indian Ocean. Lateen rigging is distinguished by a triangular sail hung from a yard secured to the mast at a 45-degree angle.

Dinghy—A name given to a warship's smallest boat. Dinghies were used to ferry personnel or cargo. Although they could be rigged for sails, they were more typically propelled by oars.

Dory—A short (15- to 20-foot), shallow-draft, oar-powered boat characterized by high sides and a sharp bow. Dories typically held two to four people.

East Indiaman—A large, heavily armed merchant vessel used for trade between Europe, India, and the East Indies. English East Indiamen were chartered by the East India Company and designed to carry both passengers and cargo. Since they sailed far from England, they were well armed for protection against pirates, privateers, and foreign naval vessels.

Felucca—A small, fast lateen-rigged vessel used primarily in the Mediterranean.

Fireship—A vessel used as a floating incendiary device. Fireships were designed to allow the crewmembers to ignite the ship at the last moment, thus giving them an opportunity to survive the attack.

Fluyt—A large-capacity three-mast, square-rigged Dutch merchant ship. This design, which was adopted by many nations, was popular because of its substantial cargo-carrying capability and the small crew needed to operate the vessel. Since fluyts were lightly armed, they had difficulty fending off pirates and privateers. The British called them flyboats. (Example: Blackbeard's ship *Queen Anne's Revenge*)

Frigate—A fast, seaworthy warship that was too small to be included in the line of battle but large enough to conduct independent operations. Unlike ships-of-the-line, frigates only had one gun deck although guns were also mounted on the quarterdeck and forecastle. (Example: USS *Constitution*)

Full-Rigged Ship—A square-rigged ship of three or more masts. This description distinguishes ships from other vessels.

Galleon—A large 16th-century square-rigged three- or four-mast square-rigged, multideck warship. Although large galleons were generally lightly armed, the ship's design was obsolete by the mid-17th century. Spanish treasure ships, however, retained the designation "galleon" regardless of their actual design. (Example: Magellan's ship the *Golden Hind*)

Galliot—A small Dutch coastal vessel that used a square sail with a standing gaff on the mainmast and a lateen sail on the mizzenmast.

Gig—A light, narrow boat that was typically better under oars than sail.

Gunboat—A large boat equipped with one or more guns. A ship's boat was sometimes converted into a gunboat by arming it with a small gun. Over time, nations built specifically designed gunboats that were larger and more seaworthy.

Hoy—A small coastal vessel, normally sloop rigged, used to transport passengers and cargo. Hoys were also used as dockyard work boats.

Jollyboat—A name applied to a ship's smallest boat, usually a cutter. Jollyboats were typically all-purpose boats used for light duties.

Junk—A Chinese sailing vessel characterized by a high, overhanging stern, projected bow, and square sails reinforced by bamboo battens. The sails can be spread or closed like venetian blinds with the pull of one line.

Ketch—A two-mast ship with the tallest mast (mainmast) forward of the second. The shorter aftermast (mizzenmast) was placed forward of the rudder. Although some ketches were ship rigged, most were fore-and-aft rigged. (Example: The ketch *Intrepid* was used by Stephen Decatur to destroy the *Philadelphia*.)

Launch—A large, flat-bottom boat that replaced the longboat by the 1780s because of its larger capacity. It was not as capable under sail as a longboat so it was normally rowed.

Lighter—A large barge that was originally used to lighten ships by offloading equipment and cargo while in port. The name later applied to any vessel working around dockyards and anchorages.

Longboat—The largest boat carried by a ship. Despite the name, longboats were often shorter than other boats but their rugged construction meant they were capable of operating in rough seas and handling heavy cargos. Like cutters, they were designed for sailing but could also be rowed by 8 to 10 double-banked oarsmen. Because of their size and weight, longboats were difficult to stow onboard ship.

Lorcha—A sailing vessel with a Western-style hull and junk rigging.

Lugger—A coastal craft with two or three masts rigged with lugsails. Since luggers were fast vessels that performed well in coastal tidewaters, they were often used by smugglers and privateers.

Mystiko—The Greek version of the xebec.

Pink—A small, three-mast, square-rigged sailing vessel with a narrow overhanging stern.

Pinnace—A long (up to 35 feet), light boat used as a tender to guide vessels into port or carry messages between larger ships. At first, pinnaces were smaller versions of the longboat and operated under sail or oars. Later, they became more narrow and lighter and evolved into a rowed craft used by junior officers.

Polacre—A Mediterranean trading vessel with three lateen-rigged masts although they later acquired square sails set on a single mast as well.

Proa—A multihull vessel of two unequal parallel hulls, similar to an outrigger canoe, used by many Southeast Asian islanders.

Schooner—A vessel rigged with fore-and-aft sails on two or more masts. Later versions, called topsail schooner, had square topsails on the foremast. (Example: schooner USS *Enterprise*, 1799; topsail schooner USS *Porpoise*, 1820)

Ship-of-the-Line—A warship powerful enough to sail in the line of battle during a naval engagement. Ships in the first through fourth rates were called ships-of-the-line. (Example: USS *Independence*, 1815)

Skiff—A small light flat-bottom boat that was usually rowed rather than sailed. Skiffs had pointed bows and flat sterns.

Sloop—A single-mast ship with fore-and-aft rigged sails typically displacing less than 25 tons.

Sloop-of-war—A term applied to smaller vessels, below the sixth rate, commanded by a master and commander. The designation "sloop-of-war" was, in effect, a seventh rate and included brigs, corvettes, snows, and other types of ships. (Example: USS *Wasp*, 1806; USS *Constellation*, 1855)

Snow—A large two-mast sailing ship similar to a brig. The primary difference between a snow and a brig was that a brig hoisted its fore-and-aft gaff-and-boom sail from the mainmast while a snow hoisted its gaff-and-boom sail from an auxiliary (trysail) mast.

Xebec—A fast, lateen-rigged sailing vessel used in the Mediterranean. Xebecs had a shallow draft and a low freeboard that afforded them excellent maneuverability in restricted waters and light winds, but those same characteristics caused them to be poor vessels in the open ocean or in rough weather. They could also be rowed when necessary.

Sources

"Boat Types." *Wikipedia.org*, http://en.wikipedia.org/wiki/Category:Boat_types (accessed 14 May 2009).

Gardiner, Robert. *The Line of Battle: The Sailing Warship, 1650–1840*. London: Conway Maritime Press, 1992.

Moore, Ryan. "An In-Depth Analysis of the Xebec." Xebec, Inc., 2004. http://www.geocities.com/xebecinc/info2.html (accessed 14 May 2009).

Ossian, Robert. "Complete List of Sailing Vessels." *Rob Ossian's Pirate Cove*. http://www.thepirateking.com/ships/ship_types.htm (accessed 14 May 2009).

"Sailing Ship." *Wikipedia.org*. http://en.wikipedia.org/wiki/Sailing_ship (accessed 14 May 2009).

"Sailing Ship Rigs." *Maritime Museum of the Atlantic*. http://museum.gov.ns.ca/mma/AtoZ/rigs.html (accessed 14 May 2009).

"Ship Types and Rates in the Age of Sail." *The Art of Age of Sail*. http://www.ageofsail.net/aoshipty.asp (accessed 14 May 2009).

"The "Stockholm Brig" Tre Kronor." *Nordic Underwater Archaeology*. http://www.abc.se/~pa/uwa/ (accessed 14 May 2005).

"Types of Sailing Ships." *Cadwalader Family of Criccieth*. http://freespace.virgin.net/r.cadwalader/maritime/types.htm#top (accessed 14 May 2009).

About the Author

Mr. James Wombwell joined the Combat Studies Institute in October 2007. A retired captain in the Naval Reserve, his last assignment was at the Naval Historical Center in Washington, DC, where he served as a Navy historian documenting current naval operations. While at the Naval Historical Center, he deployed to the Supreme Headquarters Allied Powers Europe, Mons, Belgium; US Naval Forces Central Command, Bahrain; and the Naval Special Warfare Command, San Diego, California. A Surface Warfare Officer, he served on the USS *Fiske* (DD-842) and USS *Texas* (CGN-39) and taught at the Surface Warfare Officers' School in Newport, Rhode Island, while on Active Duty. Mr. Wombwell earned a B.A. from Vanderbilt University and an M.A. from the University of Memphis. He has taught history at the University of Memphis and University of Kansas. The Combat Studies Institute Press recently published Mr. Wombwell's Occasional Paper 29, *Army Support During the Hurricane Katrina Disaster.*

GPO U.S. GOVERNMENT PRINTING OFFICE: 2010—652-819